D1242307

Blacks in Colonial Veracruz

BLACKS IN COLONIAL VERACRUZ

RACE, ETHNICITY, AND REGIONAL DEVELOPMENT

Patrick J. Carroll

UNIVERSITY OF TEXAS PRESS, AUSTIN

*For
Donna,
Amy,
Jenny,
Patrick,
and Katie*

Second edition, 2001

Requests for permission to reproduce material from this work should
be sent to Permissions, University of Texas Press, Box 7819, Austin,
Texas 78713-7819.

☺ The paper used in this publication meets the minimum requirements
of American National Standard for Information Sciences—Permanence
of Paper for Printed Library Materials, ANSI Z39.48-1984.

Library of Congress Cataloging-in-Publication Data
Carroll, Patrick James.
  Blacks in colonial Veracruz : race, ethnicity, and regional development /
Patrick J. Carroll.—2nd ed.
    p.   cm.
  Includes bibliographical references and index.
  ISBN 978-0-292-71233-1
  1. Blacks—Mexico—Veracruz (State)—History. 2. Veracruz
(Mexico : State)—Economic conditions.   3. Veracruz (Mexico :
State)—Social conditions.   4. Veracruz (Mexico : State)—Race
relations. I. Title.
F1371.C298   2001
972'.6200496—dc21   2001027194

Contents

Figures

Acknowledgments

NUMEROUS PEOPLE and organizations have contributed to this study in many ways. Nettie Lee Benson gave the most. She provided guidance and encouragement from its inception. Adriana Naveda Chávez-Hita provided nearly as much as did Miss Benson. Adriana shared ideas and data and helped with the field research in Jalapa and Córdoba. I am deeply grateful to both these individuals.

Over the years a number of scholars have read all or parts of various drafts of the study, offered suggestions and encouragement, and/ or supported grant requests. John Tutino, Franklin Knight, Marvin Bernstein, Jonathan Brown, David Quinlan, Linda Arnold, Richard Tansey, David Sweet, Susan Deans-Smith, Frederick Bowser, William Taylor, James Lockhart, Mark Szuchman, Brian Hamnett, Harley Browning, Stanley Ross, Joe Frantz, Robert Wooster, Leonardo Carrillo, Eliot Chenaux, Richard Graham, Thomas Philpott, Standish Meacham, Timothy Anna, Carl Degler, and William Glade all provided one or more of these types of assistance. Frederick Cervantes, Ross Purdy, Louie Miller, and Charles McKenzie helped with the statistical analysis.

Shannon Davies and Barbara Spielman, members of the University of Texas Press editorial staff, made helpful suggestions. Sarah Buttrey copyedited the manuscript, Karen Crowther did the overall book design, and Donna Senf Carroll painted the jacket illustration. I wish to sincerely thank all these individuals for converting my manuscript into a book.

Takako Sudo de García and Bernardo García Martínez facilitated my work in countless ways. Josefina Vázquez, Ricardo Corso, Padre Ernesto Sánchez, Fernando Winfield-Capitaine, Ernesto de la Torre Villar, the late Rubio Mané, Andrea Sánchez, Miguel Angel de Hesa, and Aurelio de los Reyes all aided my research in one way or another. Carlos and Suzanna Carraza y Pardo introduced me to both sugar culture and the warmth of their friendship. Laura Paniagua de Murillo gave us a home and a family in Veracruz. Personnel of the Archivo General de la Nación, the Biblioteca Nacional, and the Museo de Antropológia e Historia (especially Antonio Pompa y Pompa) provided competent and cooperative service. In Jalapa the staffs of the Biblioteca Central and the Centro de Estudios Históricos of the Universidad Veracruzana gave extraordinary support, as did archivists at the Archivo del Ayuntamiento de Jalapa and the Archivo Municipal de Córdoba.

I wish to thank Laura Gutiérrez-Witt, Jane Garner, Carmen Sacromani, and Wanda Turnley of the Nettie Lee Benson Latin American Collection at the University of Texas at Austin for going far beyond normal service in aiding my investigations.

The largest source of funding for the work came from Corpus Christi State University Organized University and College Faculty Research Grants. A joint Institute of Latin American Studies–Rockefeller Foundation summer grant helped a great deal. The Pan-American Round Table of Corpus Christi also provided critical financial support for microfilming notarial and parish records for Córdoba and Jalapa, Veracruz.

Finally, I want to acknowledge the support and sacrifices of my family. They gave up as much as I to complete this work.

Introduction

IN THE first introduction to this book, written in 1990, I wrote:

> Afro-Veracruzanos represent a largely forgotten people who have re-
> ceived less attention than other groups that contributed to the emer-
> gence of colonial New Spain. This study attempts to add to the handful
> of post–World War II works that include, among others, the ground-
> breaking investigations of Gonzalo Aguirre Beltrán,[1] the overview of
> Colin Palmer,[2] the comparative perspective of Gerald Cardoso,[3] and
> the regional Veracruz inquiries of Adriana Naveda Chávez-Hita and
> Gilberto Bermúdez Gorrochotegui.[4]

Because of increasing attention devoted to Afro-Mexicans over the
last decade, the above statements are no longer true. Since 1990 not
only has the number of studies on blacks in colonial Mexico prolif-
erated, but the level of their sophistication has increased as well. In
my mind, this monograph has one central point in common with
these newer works. Their overarching goal is to place Afro-Mexicans
in some type of broader context. The exact nature of that context and
the strategies to accomplish this may vary from scholar to scholar,
but the goal of each is to determine what Afro-Mexicans had in common with and what set them apart from other groups in this complex organic colonial setting. Brief mention of but a few of these new
investigations and their findings will illustrate this point.

Most of the new studies, like this one, took a regional approach to
the Afro-Mexican experience, and, I suspect, for many of the same
reasons explained below. Matthew Restall has begun publication of
a variety of inquiries on the black experience in Yucatán. Therein
he focuses on evolving views of nationality and identity that Afro-
Yucatecos, Indians, and Spaniards held of themselves and each other.
He then analyzes the impact of these perceptions of "alterity" on
the everyday lives of members of each group both within their sub-
communities and within the regional society as a whole. Restall is
joined in his Afro-Yucatecan inquiry by Francisco Fernández Repetto

and Genny Negroe Sierra.[5] Norma Angélica Castillo Palma and Francisco González Hermosillo Adams study the black experience in the Puebla region. Their work focuses on the intersection of such social constructs as race, ethnicity, class, and gender with the aim of gauging their effects on the lives of individuals and groups within a broader societal context.[6] Juan Manuel de la Serna examines black slave labor within the *obraje* industry of colonial Querétaro. Assuming a broad structuralist perspective on this theme, he sheds light on the interplay of economic and demographic forces in dictating the viability or inviability of black slave labor in a proto-industrial setting.[7] Brígedo Redondo has also published a monograph on blacks in the southern state of Campeche.[8] And María Luisa Herrera Casasús has written a short ethnographic study of black slaves in the Huasteca region that included parts of many of the mid- and northeastern states of the Republic. It too endeavors to place this group within a broader regional setting.[9]

Researchers at the Universidad Veracruzana continue to do groundbreaking work on the theme. Former Aguirre Beltrán student Fernando Winfield Capitaine has remained active in the field for thirty years now. His anthropological and structural line of inquiry on the topic continues to inform us all. Adriana Naveda Chávez-Hita has also added new contributions to Afro-Veracruzano studies. She is currently completing a doctoral thesis dealing with the intersections of race, ethnicity, class, and gender within a rapidly changing eighteenth-century Córdoba, Veracruz, urban environment. This study, *Annales* in approach, will provide an urban dimension to the rural experience of Afro-Córdobans which she has already given us in her *Esclavos negros en las haciendas azucareras de Córdoba, Veracruz, 1690–1830.*[10]

Two scholars have produced important works that do not focus principally on Afro-Veracruzanos, but do shed light on their lives. Gilberto Bermúdez Gorrochotegui's recent book on seventeenth-century Xalapa devotes a good deal of attention to Afro-Veracruzanos and their interaction with other groups.[11] His exhaustive research and fine interpretive analysis provide added insights into the history of this important provincial capital and adds to our understanding of the context in which Afro-Xalapans lived during this period. Susan Deans-Smith's work complements my own on black Veracruzanos in three ways. First, she provides a much fuller description of eighteenth-century economic development in Orizaba than I do. Second, whereas I provide a bottom-up approach, she provides a top-down perspective into economic development in the districts of Córdoba and Orizaba. And, finally, her much more in-depth discussion of the late colonial competition between tobacco and sugar culture (especially in her fourth chapter) has obvious implications for understanding Córdoba's unusually persistent adherence to slave labor in the late eighteenth century.[12]

Not surprisingly, a number of important new works on Afro-Mexicanos and related fields have focused on central Mexico. Brígida von Mentz' monumental study of labor ranks among the best. Well researched and well conceived, it explores themes of race, ethnicity, labor, gender, and power in some depth. It adds significantly to our understanding of blacks within the core of Mexico's colonial society. R. Douglas Cope's fine investigation offers a thoughtful alternative to ethnographic approaches for integrating the black experience into that of colonial Mexico City as a whole. He argues that a more "plebeian" based set of cultural- and class-derived distinctions superseded racial differentiation in determining social status by the end of the seventeenth century in Mexico City. Cope suggests that recognition of this development is prerequisite to understanding late colonial blacks' and other groups' "fit" into the capital's overall late colonial social order. Juan Pedro Viqueira Albán makes a similar argument in his remarkable study of folk culture and behavior in Mexico City during the Bourbon period.[13]

Impressive new studies on special themes such as the family, gender, and colonial institutions that deal with black Mexicans in the main or in part have also appeared in the last decade. Ben Vinson's work on the *pardo* militia stands out among this genre of new investigations. Using an accommodationist rather than an assimilative interpretive[14] approach, his findings highlight black community formation and agency in the process of Afro-Mexicans' integration into colonial Mexican society. He has a manuscript currently under publication consideration with a major university press which promises to make a major contribution to the field. Herman Bennett is another fine young scholar who applies an accommodationist approach to the study of Afro-Mexicans. His work on family, identity, and black community relations with other groups is very promising. From this perspective he mirrors the work of scholars who have treated these themes in other spatial and temporal contexts. María Elena Cortés de Jacome's study of the black family also deserves mention.[15]

Finally, new works on gender have contributed to our knowledge of Afro-Mexican life vis à vis the lives of their white and Indian counterparts. Some of Solange Alberro's and Susan Kellog's inquiries illustrate this body of literature. Steve Stern's insightful study of gendered negotiations in eighteenth-century Mexico, although broader in focus, also tells us a good deal about Afro- and plebeian women's agency in struggles with men for power within their homes and their communities.[16] And all of these works inform us about some of the consequences of the interplay of such social constructs as gender, race, ethnicity, and class in the lives of colonial women.

The above list of new scholars who entered or continued in the field of Afro-Mexican studies is not by any means exhaustive. Yet it suffices to illustrate the rapid growth of this line of inquiry. I would estimate that more scholarly publications have appeared on Afro-Mexican studies or on related themes in the decade since the first printing of *Blacks in Colonial Veracruz* than in all the previous decades of the twentieth century combined. If this rate of growth in the field continues much longer, future investigators will no longer be able to refer to Afro-Mexicans as a "forgotten people." The last ten years have witnessed enormous strides in filling this void in Mexican history. I feel privileged to include this second edition of my work among such a valuable corpus of studies that are beginning to allocate Afro-Mexicans their rightful historical place in the evolution of the Mexican nation.

Blacks in Colonial Veracruz employs an *Annales* approach to the study of Afro-Mexicans and their "fit" within evolving Mexican society. This holistic perspective on historical development offers two distinct advantages in this endeavor. It invites comparisons and contrasts with other groups, however defined, and thereby places Afro-Mexicans within, instead of apart from, Mexican society. Such a perspective, in my judgment, more closely approximates the actual black Mexican experience. It also provides a subaltern view of broader themes such as economic, social, and, to a lesser degree in this case study, political development. I shall say more about this advantage a bit later.

For many of the early years (1521–1640), blacks outnumbered whites in New Spain. And, contrary to popular notions about their distribution, Afro-Mexicans were not confined to coastal lowland regions. Blacks were present in virtually every setting within the viceroyalty. African slaves played a critical role in the economic take-off of the colony between 1550 and 1630. Despite restrictive legislation, blacks were the most socially outgoing of any of the racial groups in the emerging society. As a result, they contributed much more heavily to the racial and ethnic integration of the colonial community than their slave status would have implied.[17] Politically, Afro-Mexicans had limited and primarily indirect influence over the developing order. Their greatest early impact was in the form of slave revolt. At times this danger caused royal and local officials alike to alter their administrative policies. During the independence and immediate post-independence period, however, Mexican-black political input became more direct and powerful. Racially mixed descendants of African slaves maintained a high profile in the

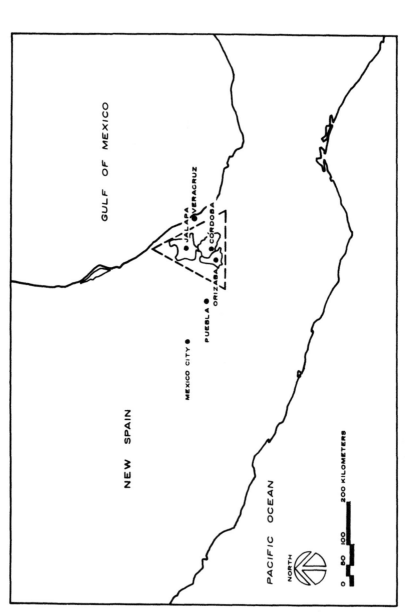

Map 1. Mexico and the central Veracruz triangle

ranks of revolutionary forces. They also made their presence felt in politics during the first federal period of the new nation (1824–1830).

The second dimension of this work goes beyond a description of what happened to blacks in Mexico. Although this is a very important question, it leads to an even broader one. Relatively speaking, how did the Afro-Mexican experience compare to the experiences of other groups in colonial New Spain? To answer this query it is necessary to place blacks and their descendants in Mexican society, and consequently an unusual perspective on the development of New Spain surfaces. Afro-Mexicans, both slave and free, were working class individuals. This subaltern view of societal formation is extremely difficult to tap from a historiographical perspective. Poor working folk leave a scant paper trail. Researchers have found it difficult to reconstruct the past from their vantage point. Black slaves, and to a lesser degree free black racial hybrids, remain somewhat of an exception to this rule. Bondpersons, as extremely valuable property, were listed more frequently in records than free laborers who toiled and socially interacted with them. White racism and consequent attempts to discriminate against and subordinate slaves and free persons of African descent also heightened the likelihood of their appearance in written records, including laws as well as notarial, parish, criminal, and census records. With this relatively heavy subaltern representation in these types of historical records, and with the objective to place Afro-Veracruzanos in context within New Spain's developing broader colonial community, we are able to provide a bottom-up view of overall development, one that yields fresh insights into the changing profile of the overall society and the dynamics shaping it. The study's temporal breadth, stretching from 1570 to 1830, enhances our understanding of these phenomena.

Unfortunately, the complexity of placing Afro-Mexicans within the colonial society dictated some compromises. The most important methodological accommodation was to limit the investigation to a regional focus. Probing such questions at the viceregal/national level would have been far beyond the resources of one researcher. I selected central Veracruz as my region of focus because it is a lightly researched zone of colonial development, and records necessary to support my research design were accessible. Since that time a number of regionally based inquiries have provided critical conceptual, methodological, and comparative contributions that have greatly facilitated my task. Adriana Naveda Chávez-Hita's and Gerald Cardoso's works on Veracruz, Cheryl Martin's book on rural Morelos, Nancy Fariss' study of Yucatan, and John Chance's investigations on Oaxaca have been most helpful because of their comparable chronological scopes stretching throughout the colonial period.[18] Added to these monographs are a number of more chronologically limited but equally insightful works by such scholars as William Taylor, David Brading, Peter Bakewell, Eric Van Young, and Brian Hamnett.[19]

When possible I compared my findings in central Veracruz both for blacks and for the broader regional society with the findings of the above-mentioned scholars. This placed the events in central Veracruz within better context. In the end a historical tapestry emerged by interweaving threads from the local physical setting and racially and ethnically pluralistic populations that constantly changed in size, age, gender, and health. The tension of the weave was always changing as a result of the introduction of new technology that is not only physical but organizational and social in character. Steel, draft animals, the arch, and gunpowder had obvious impacts. The influence of foreign concepts involving whole economic and political systems was less obvious. Religion, imperialism, racism, and persistent ethnocentrism proved even more subtle forces of change. The mesh of those fibers was heavily overlaid at times with the gilded threads of European imperial pressures that were most prominent in the early (1550–1630) and the late colonial years (1720–1820).

The sculptured fabric of the society that the intertwining strands of physical environments, populations, technologies, and imperial forces wove was three-dimensional in character. Multi-ethnic Afro-Mexicans, whites, and Indians were caught up in these threads and together formed an evolving economic structure for the ongoing material well-being, and sometimes ill-being, of the broader regional society. The mix of forces outlined social relationships. These relationships in turn gave rise to informal beliefs and practices that helped order this extremely complex setting.[20] Finally, the interplay of these various pressures created an equally changing polity that was a blend of local, viceregal, and international colors which provided a more formal structure to Veracruz' cultural tapestry through laws, agencies, and institutions.

Beyond the foregoing structural context, this work supplies a human dimension. It is, after all, a history, a record of human events. The collective lives of Afro-Mexicans, of Indians, of persons of mixed race, as well as of whites produced the color and light that illuminates this structural fabric of regional life. Therefore my study ultimately becomes the story of people's lives, their trials, and their accomplishments. We should remember such past experiences because our present and future rest upon them.

Blacks in Colonial Veracruz

1

The Human and Material Consequences of Indian and European Contact

MEXICO REPRESENTS an environmental mosaic with many and varied pieces to the national whole. It is a setting where tropical rain forests stand in the shadow of snow-capped mountains, where deserts border lush green croplands, where plateaus ring jagged peaks. Understandably, geographers have had great difficulty in classifying the country into climate zones. Some have divided it into as few as three regions, others as many as thirteen, but all agree that, regardless of the number of settings one sees, little physical continuity exists.[1] Indeed, tremendous topographical and consequent climatic variance within small spatial areas marks the land. The present state of Veracruz on the eastern coast of the country illustrates this. Tropical rain forests cover much of the region's southeastern sector. Coastal savannah dominates the northeast. The middle and northwestern districts have hills and even mountains raising the area to an elevated "veranda" that runs north and south along the upper half of the state and links the low-lying coast with the highland interior. Citlaltéptl, the pre-Colombian Indian term for Mount Orizaba, dominates the landscape of this transitional environmental zone. At 5,747 meters, it stands as the second highest peak in all of North America. At the base of this majestic snow-capped giant lie the steamy semitropical vegetation of the district of Córdoba, the more mixed temperate and semitropical lands of the district of Jalapa to the north, and the cool arid plains of Perote to the northwest.[2] An eighteenth-century trip from the port of Veracruz to the plateau of Perote took four days of travel by horse or mule. This journey represented the first leg of the most-traveled route in all colonial Mexico, the path between the port of Veracruz and Mexico City. Along it flowed the wealth of the East and West Indies.[3] Humans and beasts trekked over approximately fifty kilometers of flat, hot coastal savannah, ten kilometers of ascent onto a transi-

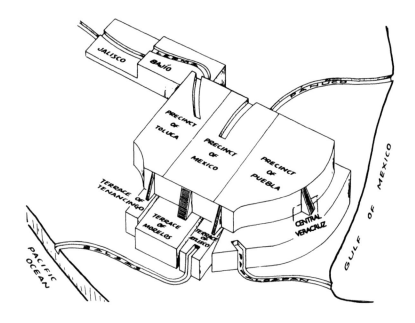

Figure 1. A schematic diagram of Mexico (adapted from Eric Wolf, *Sons of the Shaking Earth*, 7).

tional elevated shelf occupied by the provinces of Córdoba, Jalapa, and Orizaba and that stretched for another fifteen kilometers, and then the final climb of the remaining ten to fifteen kilometers up to the central plateau. The three principal settlements along the route, the port of Veracruz, Jalapa, and Perote, offer a pretty good indication of the different lifestyles that resulted from the varying climate along the way.

Despite the fact that the city of Veracruz remained the most important port of the richest possession within the Spanish colonial empire, it never had a population of more than ten thousand.[4] Oppressive heat, clouds of disease-bearing mosquitos, and often polluted drinking water made the site and its environs an extremely unpleasant and unsafe human habitat. The port and its environs served as a zone that most people and goods passed through on their way to someplace else. It existed to handle Atlantic commerce and represented one of the most tangible products of European influence on the post-1521 central Veracruz landscape.

Jalapa, the locale of main focus for this study, rests at about fifteen hundred meters above sea level on the side of Macuilteptl, one of the mountains that dot the region. The dividing line for the yellow-fever zone fell just a few kilometers to the east. An arid, wind-swept plain stretches beyond the district's western boundary running south from Jalapa to beyond the province of Orizaba. Perote represented the principal settlement in this westernmost of central Veracruz zones. Here, daytime temperatures drop to ten to eleven degrees centigrade, quite a contrast with the balmy climate of Jalapa and even more of a change from the steamy heat of the coast.[5]

In the space of just ninety kilometers on an east-west axis lie four distinct climatic settings, three of them represented in a twenty-five–kilometer stretch that makes up the province of Jalapa. Table 1 more precisely documents Jalapa's physical contrasts. Such environmental variation in a relatively small spatial area commonly occurs in Mexico. As one student of Mesoamerica has stated, any generalization about the topography of the country "is likely to breakdown locally, yielding not one but many Mexicos."[6] As a result of such environmental diversity, extreme cultural differences followed. Jalapa illustrates this point.

Environment and Ethnicity in Jalapa

In Jalapa, as in other parts of Mexico, environmental unevenness encouraged ethnic plurality (Map 2). Immediately prior to European

Table 1. *Environmental Zones of the Province of Jalapa by Altitude, Temperature, and Rainfall*

	Humid Tropical Zone	Humid Temperate Zone	Humid Alpine Zone
Altitude	0–799 m	800–1599 m	1600–2400 m
Mean annual temperature	21–23°C	15–20°C	11–14°C
Mean annual rain	500–1900 mm	500–1800 mm	1801–2200 mm

Source: William T. Saunders, "The Anthropogeography of Central Veracruz," in *Huastecos, Totonocos, y sus vecinos*, edited by Ignacio Bernal and Eusebio Davalos Hurtado, 30–78; Alfonso Contreras Arias, *Mapa de las provincias climatológicas de la República Mexicana*, 46–50; *La República Mexicana, Veracruz*, 36–63; *Boletín de Geografía de Veracruz*, 65–117; *Compendio estadístico del Estado de Veracruz*, 50–52, 59–60.

arrival, several ethnic groups resided in segregated zones of the area. Teochichimecs dominated the central temperate plain and parts of the northwestern alpine highlands. Nahua-speaking peoples maintained an ethnic enclave in the southern corner of the western highlands. Totonocs occupied the uplands just to the north of them. Toltec-descended peoples dominated the semitropical southeastern lowlands.[7]

Aztecs, or Mexica, pushed into and conquered the area during the second half of the fifteenth century. They modified the local economies through an elaborate tribute system that demanded greater levels of surplus production of certain items such as *purga de Jalapa*, a medicinal herb that grew naturally in the area. Politically, the region's multiple cultural groups pledged themselves to military alliances with their conquerors. Previous invaders had settled in the region and altered their lifestyles to fit local environmental and demographic pressures. The Aztec presence signified something new. Their garrison towns maintained "outside" influence in the area. Aztecs introduced a measure of dependency on forces from beyond the borders of central Veracruz into the dynamics of local development.[8] From that point onward change in the region resulted from a combination of competing foreign and local pressures. Yet Jalapa's ethnic diversity remained intact. Aztecs did not push for cultural conformity.[9]

In 1519, Jalapa fell to a new invader. These conquerors differed from the Aztecs. They came from unknown lands across the sea in ships that flew on large white wings. They had lighter skin, facial hair, and spoke in a strange tongue. The garments of many proved

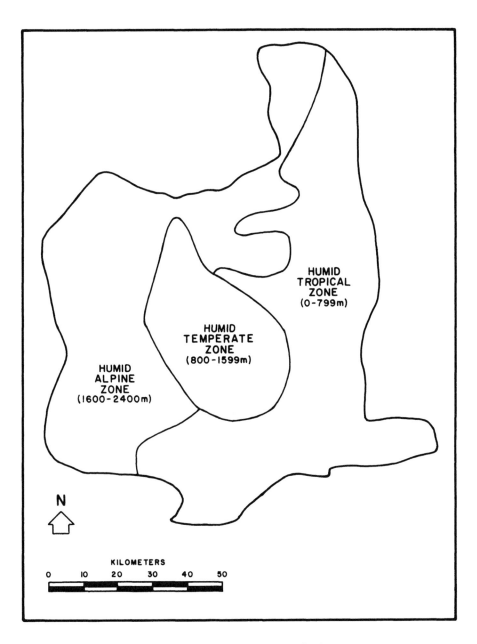

Map 2. Environmental zones of the province of Jalapa, ca. 1600

impenetrable to obsidian-edged arrows, lances, and war clubs. Some appeared half beast and half human, walking on four legs and with two heads. They wielded awesome weapons, large and small sticks that harnessed the roar of thunder and the flash and destructiveness of lightning. They seemed more god-like than human, and they asked far more of their vanquished than mortal Aztecs did. These new conquerors demanded material, military, and social tribute.

The Arrival of Europeans

Miguel Zaragoza was probably the first European to set foot in the district of Jalapa. The Francisco de Grijalva expedition abandoned him on the coast of Veracruz in 1518. Other Spaniards soon followed, and the level of the indigenous culture they found impressed them. Narratives of Cortés and his followers, as well as those of others, contain many references to the marvels of central Veracruz. Cempoala, the first coastal city of consequence that the Spaniards encountered, had about 40,000 residents; Xicochimalco, the largest city in the Jalapa region, had over 120,000.[10] In comparison, London had 50,000 inhabitants.[11] Due to their sophisticated level of organization, central Veracruz cities served as commercial, political, and social centers.[12] This gave Spaniards ready-made bases of power: by establishing Iberian urban centers that juridically and economically controlled and served surrounding hinterlands, Spaniards employed an urban-hinterland relationship that native peoples could identify with from their pre-Columbian past. Spaniards' prior Old World experience also shaped colonial development in Veracruz.

The end of the fifteenth century represented a watershed in Spanish history. At that time the nation had come together while the last Moorish stronghold on the peninsula fell. To the veterans of holy wars against Moslem invaders, the New World offered additional opportunities to conquer more infidels for Christ and their homeland and to turn a personal profit as well. American Indians represented just so many more pagans that the Spanish would subdue, convert, and put to work—the spoils of just wars.[13] Iberians that came to central Veracruz displayed the racial and cultural arrogance of conquerors rather than the respect of awed observers. These newcomers exercised extreme cultural bias (ethnocentrism) and even racism in their treatment of Indian subjects. They tried to remake Mexico into "New Spain," as the Jalapa experience illustrates. But the conquerors fell short of their goal.

European attempts to acculturate native peoples met formidable obstacles. Indian cultural roots ran deep. Physical barriers also impeded acculturation. The latter tremendously hampered Spanish efforts to impose their customs and beliefs on native peoples. The horse, the wheel, steel, and even gunpowder could not neutralize the rugged terrain of central Veracruz areas such as Jalapa, Orizaba, and Córdoba. Many Indian communities remained relatively isolated from Spanish cultural and administrative centers because of hills and mountains that made travel difficult in good weather and impossible in the rainy season. Limited and irregular contact with agents of Spanish cultural transformation caused pockets of indigenous lifestyle to persist in the region's hinterlands throughout the colonial period. Thus, the introduction of Spanish culture further complicated the region's social climate.

The Demographic Impact of European Contact

Several factors magnified Spaniards' impact in central Veracruz beyond the force of their numbers. Some have argued that Europeans primarily owed their victory to the superiority of their technology. Others have pointed to divisiveness in pre-Columbian societies as the key to whites' success. But nearly all agree that the dramatic demographic decline that Indians suffered had something to do with the collapse of resistance to Spanish domination.

When Cortés landed on the coast of Mexico in 1519, he brought with him an unwanted ally. It emerged a few months later when Pánfilo de Narváez led a second expeditionary force onto the coast to seize Cortés for insubordination to the Spanish governor of the island of Cuba, a partner in the Cortés expedition. As one of the chroniclers of the period noted, "Narváez brought with him a Negro who was in smallpox; an unfortunate importation for this country, for the disease spread with inconceivable rapidity, and the *naturales* [a Spanish term for the Indians] died by the thousands."[14] Estimates of the general population decline that followed range anywhere from 75 to 96 percent over a ninety-year period. Military confrontation probably only accounted for a small fraction of these deaths. The introduction of Old World diseases into a New World disease environment proved the primary cause. Some of these sicknesses threatened the lives of non-Indians as well. Smallpox, typhoid, yellow fever, dysentery, and possibly bubonic plague carried off members of all racial and ethnic groups in central Veracruz and the rest of Mexico. But other afflictions discriminated against natives. Mild types of influenza, measles, mumps, and chickenpox debilitated most non-Indians but killed most Indians.

This scourge did not spare central Veracruz. The pattern of decline experienced by the populations in and around Jalapa illustrates this point. Disease first began to ravage the area in the 1540s. It exacted a very heavy toll on the inhabitants for the next three to four generations. Constantino Bravo de Lagunas, the highest-ranking crown appointment in the region for many of these years, reported to the viceroy in 1580. He spoke of diseases and their devastating effect on the town of Jalapa: "Today this town has about 639 tributaries: in Moctezuma's [sic] time [the Aztec emperor at Cortés' arrival] before the arrival of the conquistadors, they say there were over 30,000."[15] Bravo attributed the high death rate to natives' unfamiliarity with European sicknesses. To the natives all the new diseases appeared the same; they used one term to describe the lot. *Cocolistli* had wiped out the area's indigenous population, bewildering and frightening them. Bravo observed that no part of the province escaped. Indeed, the capital was not even the hardest hit. Outlying Indian pueblos suffered even higher death rates. There, Spanish influence remained weak, and natives relied on their own remedies to combat the strange new maladies.[16] The result proved a demographic nightmare. Jalapa lost an estimated 80 percent of its population during this period. Two major epidemics struck. The first lasted from 1546 to 1550 and the second raged from 1576 to 1577. In both instances the victims displayed similar symptoms. They began with severe headaches. Next, fever set in, followed by delirium and convulsions. Nose bleeds proved the final symptom. All this usually transpired over an eight- or nine-day period. Very few Indians survived the ordeal. On both occasions the epidemics broke out in native pueblos. Even when the epidemics spread to areas of Spanish settlement such as the capital and outlying plantations, whites seldom fell victim because they had built a greater resistance to Old World maladies.[17]

Decline of the Indian population threatened the colonial order in many ways. They had to serve as vassals of the crown, they supported the colonial economy, and their souls needed Christian salvation. From the Indian point of view, disease not only threatened lives but also threatened Indian culture. The conquest had seriously undermined faith in pre-Columbian beliefs; many Indians associated the old ways with defeat. Imagine the added psychological burden of such virulent disease patterns in the immediate postconquest period. An apocalyptic scenario emerged, reflected in numerous passages in native sixteenth century writings. Those that clung to the old ways seemed to perish with them.

As Europeans' numbers grew in locales such as Jalapa, their need for land increased. This held true especially in and around urban enclaves they had carved out. In response to this need, newcomers began to encroach upon *capulli* acreage (a local sociopolitical unit based on extended kinship ties). When the town of Jalapa expanded to the fringes of *capulli* holdings, it incorporated these settlements as *barrios*. As the urban site grew, it engulfed the *capullis/barrios* as well, and the latters' physical and cultural integrity broke down.[18] By the late colonial period this process was well under way. By 1773 the town had expanded to meet several Indian *capulli* communities, forcing them into *barrio* status (Map 3). Under these changing conditions, racial distinctions remained somewhat clear, at least between Indians and non-Indians. But identifying ethnic characteristics began to decrease as more and more Indians from the physically and culturally disintegrating *capulli* began to relocate in the town or in other *capulli*. Parish registries generally document these movements. Baptismal records for 1641–1646, the earliest period for which reliable data appears, reveal that the neighboring *capulli* communities already had weakened under the influence of Spanish presence on their borders. Of the over eight hundred Indian adults participating in these ceremonies, nearly three hundred lived outside the *capulli* of their origin.[19] Unfortunately, similar data does not exist for earlier or later years. Thus, to document fully the cycle from *capulli* to *barrio* to full urban integration remains impossible.[20]

Under the weight of these constantly growing Spanish pressures many, but not all, *capulli* began to break down physically and culturally. Only those communal kinship groupings more removed from Spanish settlement continued to persist as both territorial and ethnic units. Villagers' ongoing legal battles with Spanish estate owners over land and water rights attest to this persistence. Outsiders penetrated these communities but in small numbers. Moreover, few of these newcomers were Spaniards. The majority of the inhabitants of rural Indian communities had not adopted Spanish as their principal language even by the end of the colonial period. Toward the close of the sixteenth century, Bravo Lagunas echoed a lament of future Spanish administrators: the outlying Indians refused to learn Castilian. In his mind, and those of many of his successors, the only possible explanation was a native incapacity to learn a more sophisticated tongue. To Bravo Lagunas, the Indians had the mentality of European eight-year-olds.[21] A more likely ex-

Map 3. Hispanic and Indian settlement of the town of Jalapa, 1773

planation for the natives' failure to adopt the lingua franca of the colonial order lies in both their physical isolation from Spaniards, in remote *capulli*, and the natural impulse of groups to preserve their traditions and beliefs even in culturally pluralistic settings.[22]

The Changing Patterns of Land Tenure

Europeans got most of the land in central Veracruz by default as the Indian population went into its dramatic sixteenth-century decline creating vast stretches of *tierras baldías*, or vacant lands. Spaniards acquired these tracts from the crown and from shrinking Indian *capullis*. The peaceful nature of exchange had important sociopolitical implications. It greatly enhanced Iberians' political control of the area as wealth generated by newly acquired territories induced them to import more human and material resources from Europe to reinforce their position in Mexico. Also, the peaceful acquisition of this important economic resource helped offset the more adversarial nature of social contact between Indians and non-Indians. As a consequence of their new lands, Europeans and their descendents established permanent ties to the area. In Jalapa, as in other parts of the viceroyalty, large commercial agricultural estates sprang up and bound new European owners to central Veracruz.[23] Sugar plantations, livestock ranches, and haciendas produced staple crops, such as corn, beans, and wheat, for local and regional markets. Although very few records have survived documenting the beginnings of this shift in land tenure from Indians to Spaniards, by conservative estimate around 10 percent of the arable territory in the province changed hands in this way between 1520 and 1540. These estimates are based on the formation of a number of European estates within the area during the period.[24] Once disease broke out in the 1540s, many Indian holdings became vacant. Some of them reverted to the crown as *tierras baldías*, others local Spaniards bought from village and *capulli* members. Table 2 illustrates the magnitude of land transfer during this period of extreme demographic stress on the Indian population. It lists documented first sales of land from natives to Europeans on a decade by decade basis beginning in 1543 and ending in 1602.

The table reveals that while Old World diseases ravaged the indigenous population, Spaniards bought at least 16 percent of all the cultivable land in the province. This amount, when added to the 10 percent already in the hands of Europeans before 1540, meant that by the end of the sixteenth century Spaniards owned over one quarter of Jalapa's arable acreage. Given that this total has its base

Table 2. *Jalapa Indian Lands Sold to Spaniards by Decade,*
1543–1602

Years	Hectares Sold
1543–1552	845.0
1553–1562	2,622.7
1563–1572	16,679.4
1573–1582	18,428.0
1583–1592	23,116.6
1593–1602	414.6
Total 59 years	62,106.3 hectares out of 269,639 total hectares in the province

Source: AGN, Hospital de Jesús, Legajo 247, expendiente 8; AGN, Mercedes, vol. 2, leaves 177v–178; AGN, Mercedes, vol. 13, leaf 59v; "Almolonga," bound volume, leaves 2–3, 139–140; ANJ, vol. 1578–1594, leaf 220; ANJ, vol. 1594–1600, leaves 56, 115–115v; Fernando Sandoval, *La Industria del azúcar en Nueva España*, 49, 126–127; Constantino Bravo de Lagunas, *Relación de Xalapa, 1580,* 10–11; Francisco del Paso y Troncoso, ed., *Papeles de Nueva España,* vol. 5, 100–101; Manuel Rivera, *Historia antiqua y moderna de Jalapa,* 5, vol. 1, 70–71; Gilberto Bermúdez Gorrochotegui, "Jalapa en el siglo XVI," 2 vols. (master's thesis, Universidad Veracruzana, 1977), vol. 1, 80–101; Peter Gerhard, *A Guide to the Historical Geography of New Spain,* 376.

in surviving documents of land sales, it probably falls far short of the total land transfer that actually took place. In all likelihood, Spaniards controlled between 40 and 50 percent of the district's agricultural lands by the close of the sixteenth century. This transfer of land represented the genesis of the great estate in the region, and herein lay the origins of the agrarian disputes that plagued central Veracruz from the middle of the nineteenth century onward.

Map 4 locates holdings of Jalapa's Spanish residents around the beginning of the seventeenth century. But the lands in Table 2 and their locations on Map 4 do not wholly reflect Spanish material gains of the period. By European agricultural standards about half of the province was useless. It proved either too rocky, too cold, or too mountainous.

Generally, Iberians claimed land in the flatter areas, ranging from 900 to 1500 meters in elevation. At these heights the climates ranged from warm and wet to temperate and wet, the best conditions for commercial agriculture. They became the centers of European settlement in the region. Indians retained mountaintop, hillside, and isolated valley lands. If these considerations are taken into

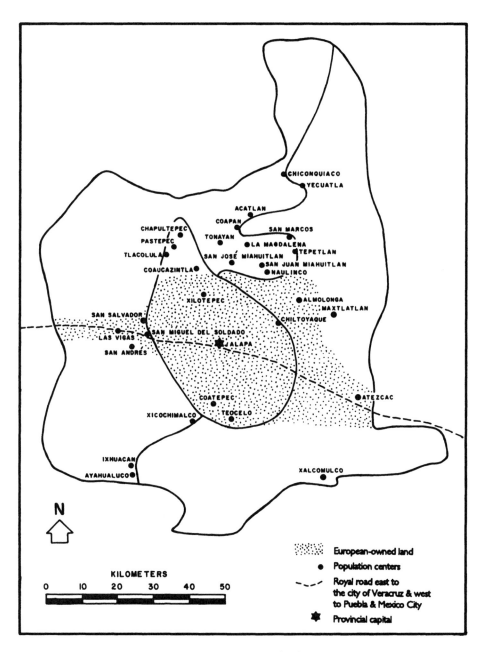

Map 4. Spanish lands in the province of Jalapa, ca. 1600

account, the full impact of the sixteenth-century land transfer becomes more clear. Spaniards had not just gained 25 to 50 percent of the arable acreage in the district, they had acquired the majority of the prime arable land in the region. The fact that only about twenty Spanish families lived in the area during this period magnifies the socioeconomic consequences of this land transfer. Miguel Pimentel, the chief magistrate of the port of Veracruz, headed one of Jalapa's new landed families. He established his estate early in 1543. Rodrigo de Albornoz founded a second plantation in the same year. In the 1590s ten more estates came into existence as a result of Spanish acquisition of Indian lands.[25] With the indigenous population shrinking at alarming rates, Iberians literally inherited the natives' part of the earth by simply surviving.

New Systems of Labor

Central Veracruz' colonial economic development mirrored that of other provinces in the most heavily populated sections of New Spain. Each area contributed to the imperial economic order in a way that best suited the marriage of imperial needs and local resources. In the case of seventeenth-century Córdoba, commercial sugar agriculture flourished. In the districts of Jalapa and Veracruz, economic development proved more diversified. Like Córdoba, Jalapa and the city of Veracruz established sugar agriculture. Due to their location along the strategic royal road between Mexico City and the coast, they also became heavily involved in imperial commerce. The importance of the city of Veracruz in this trade is well known. It handled goods from throughout the Spanish empire, and this activity strongly influenced local economic growth. Commerce supplied the lifeblood of the local population; sugar agriculture ran a close second in importance. The Jalapa case illustrates a slightly different pattern. In all but half of the eighteenth century, commerce, although important, took a back seat to sugar in the economic growth of this province.

Inhabitants of the mountainous northern and western towns of Tlacolula and Naulinco traded in the lumber they had manufactured before the Aztec conquest. People of the temperate lands around Xilotepec exported balsam. The Nahua town of Xicochimalco, located in the provincial lowlands, traded forest-gathered products such as the medicinal herb *purga*, a widely used cathartic, and sasparilla, purportedly good for stomach disorders and for high fevers. Xalcomulco, located on the banks of a river separating the provinces of Jalapa, Córdoba, and Orizaba, marketed freshwater fish.[26]

One new item that the European market craved was sugar. Hernán Cortés had a sugar-cane plantation in operation in southern Veracruz as early as 1529.[27] Once Spaniards discovered that central Veracruz and other parts of Mexico offered ideal climate and soil conditions for the crop, they strongly encouraged its cultivation. In order to support this highly labor-intensive agriculture, colonists attempted to utilize native workers in two ways. The first and least successful strategy attempted to redirect independent Indian labor. Spaniards tried to convince Indian villagers to switch to sugar production on communal lands and sell the crop to Europeans, but this strategy posed several problems.[28] Indians did not share Spaniards' enthusiasm for sugar agriculture, and Iberians could do little, short of force, to effect the desired production change. Moreover, sugar agriculture required not only great labor outlays but also great capital investments as well. Technology proved expensive, and sugar production demanded more technology than native staple-crop production of items such as beans, peppers, and corn. Indian society was not nearly as specie oriented as Spanish society. Barter fueled the indigenous economy. Money necessary to purchase refining machinery and irrigational works existed in short supply within indigenous communities. Tradition, like any other form of inertia, may also have proven a powerful force in inhibiting the introduction of a new production system within most local Indian settings. Indians had the natural tendency to ignore Spanish inducements to convert to sugar agriculture. Instead, natives generally continued to commit their human and material resources to the production of the same items they had produced for hundreds of years before the arrival of the Europeans. On the other hand, the refusal to grow sugar may have represented what William Taylor termed a "passive resistance" to Spanish pressures to alter corporate Indian village life. Such activity as growing sugar fit the European peasant mold. Assessing the persistence of indigenous village life in eighteenth-century Oaxaca, Taylor concluded, "The fierce corporate identity on many landholding villages was inevitably inconsistent with the peasant condition within the imperial system."[29] And the early Veracruz sugar industry was tied to imperial commerce. Eric Van Young points to a second weakness in the European plan to "de-peasantize" Indians. As a result of population depletion during this period, scarcity involved labor not land. Spaniards had little natural leverage to compel Indians to alter their labor habits and voluntarily integrate into sugar culture. As he put it, "Inducements . . . had to be very strong," and indeed they were.[30]

Outright Indian bondage represented one of the earliest Spanish strategies to involve natives in commercial sugar cultivation. Spaniards simply enslaved them through capture in "just wars." In order to do this, Europeans created an elaborate set of legal procedures to determine the "justness" of conflict and then regularly applied these steps when confrontations with Indians arose. They used this strategy in situations ranging from their initial conquest of natives to subduing later rebelliousness to transgressions against Christianity. In Iberians' minds such actions justified war and generated prisoners that could work for their conquerors.

But slavery as a means to provide the necessary labor for sugar culture in Veracruz proved short-lived. In 1542 the crown decided to abolish this institution on the grounds that it was too harsh and contributed to high Indian mortality rates. Legal Indian slavery no longer existed in central Veracruz by the mid-sixteenth century.

A somewhat milder form of forced Indian labor developed in the *encomienda*, a labor grant to a Spanish individual for meritorious service. The government gave this grant for a specified period of time that could not exceed the lifetime of the recipient. The grant required indigenous villages to supply the *encomendero* with a fixed number of workers for certain days during the year. The time usually coincided with planting and harvesting cycles. In return, the *encomendero* promised to defend the village, to instruct villagers in Christianity and other ways of European civilized life, and to make his laborers into *gente de razon* (people of reason), as contemporary Spaniards often put it. The crown tried to limit these grants because of their exploitative potential. The king also feared that wealth generated by this inalienable labor would give colonists too much independence and that they might come to challenge royal authority. Despite crown reservations, local officials gave out *encomiendas*. Indian labor represented a logical complement to land awards. Without workers to make them productive, lands proved useless. Central Veracruz officials and colonists recognized this fact and *encomiendas* continued over royal opposition until the early seventeenth century.[31]

The first recorded *encomienda* given in the Jalapa region went to Miguel Zaragosa in 1527. He received labor tribute from the residents of Coatepec and Chiltoyaque, both located in the central portion of the province. Shortly afterwards, Pedro Maldonado, one of the men who had served under Cortés in the initial conquest of Mexico, received a second *encomienda* for laborers from the towns of Almolonga, Maxtlatlan, and Xalcomulco on the eastern edge of the district. The viceroyalty awarded other grants to Martín de Mafra, Lucas Gallego, Bartholome Ramón, and Melchor de Arvello.

In a rare case of intergenerational transfer the crown passed Lucas Gallego's grant on to his son Martín and later to his grandson Miguel Arias. Royal officials issued at least ten *encomienda* grants in this one region during the first hundred years of contact.[32] Undoubtedly more existed. In all probability Spaniards exploited every one of the easily accessible Indian population centers as a source for commercial agricultural labor.

Despite the conversion from slave to *encomienda* labor, the alarming loss of Indian life continued. Again, many blamed oppressive labor demands. As a result, the *encomienda* as a system of forced labor went the way of the Indian slavery system.

A yet milder system of coerced labor replaced the *encomienda*: the *repartamiento*. The *repartamiento* put greater restrictions on Spanish colonists in their dealings with Indians. Under this system, Indians owed tribute labor to the crown, which in turn sublet it to colonists. This gave Spanish officials more control over the use of indigenous populations and presumably eliminated some of the abuses of the *encomienda* system. The new system did not endure much longer than its predecessor. In 1635 the crown abolished it also.[33] By this time colonists had invented more subtle and indirect means for the integration of Indians into the colonial labor force. Many colonists induced natives living in and around Spanish settlements to come into Hispanic towns and work as wage laborers.[34] The specie orientation of wage labor posed an initial problem because the concept of specie usage was not strong in pre-Columbian Mexican culture. Spaniards solved the dilemma by creating through taxation an Indian need for money. The crown early on imposed a variable head tax on the indigenous population. Full tributaries, healthy adult males, paid the highest rates. Women, children, and the aged paid a portion of the adult male tax. The church levied a second tax. The church's *diezmos* amounted to one tenth of the value of an individual's yearly production payable in specie.[35] Both of these demands created the need for Indians to accumulate some capital. This need forced them to more fully integrate into the developing colonial labor force.

How effectively indirect European mechanisms for Indian integration in the colonial economy operated is extremely difficult to gauge. Brian Hamnett suggests they proved moderately successful in Oaxaca.[36]

One way Indians could earn tax money in the greater Jalapa area was to work in the growing commercial sector of the Province of Veracruz. Merchants in the port of Veracruz maintained houses in the provincial capital as early as the last quarter of the sixteenth century. Merchants from the interior cities of Mexico City and Puebla waited in Jalapa for their consignments of goods rather than in the port.[37] Indians also earned wages working in the storage industry that came with Jalapa's position as a way station for international trade. Finally, money inevitably flowed into the region from profits made by local Spanish entrepreneurs who constantly dabbled in interregional commerce. Natives could work for these local merchant planters. In 1581, Spanish overseas shippers adopted the *flota* (convoy) system to protect their cargoes from corsairs such as Sir Francis Drake and Henry Hawkins of England who had begun to prey upon the rich trade that existed between important ports such as Veracruz and Cádiz. *Flotas* secured the commercial growth of Jalapa for the next two centuries. The first convoy arrived in 1581, the second two years later. Others followed in 1584, 1585, 1586, 1587, 1595, 1596, and 1599. Spaniards pressed natives into service in connection with this trade as muleteers, porters, blacksmiths' helpers, stable hands, domestic servants, and construction workers.[38]

Growing urban-based commerce insured the dominance of European culture in the provincial capital. However, the rural setting proved another matter. There, Spaniards managed to establish commercial estates that they economically linked to the capital but that existed as no more than Hispanic islands in an indigenous cultural sea.

Conclusion

Spanish efforts to build a new economic culture achieved varying levels of success. Iberian attempts to set up parallel political structures between the Hispanic and indigenous societies at the community level provided mixed ends in the Hispanization of *naturales*. Villages did begin to function within the Spanish imperial political system but only with a large degree of physical separation of both peoples. In the final analysis, Spaniards did not culturally overwhelm the area, but they did manage to Hispanicize enough natives to lay a cornerstone for the foundation of the ethnically and racially hybrid creole society. But this new order depended upon the expansion of regional economies like Jalapa's, and a crucial link in the new order came under great stress. At the very time Iberians needed them most, natives were dying. If naturales' high death rates made them an undependable source of labor, if royal legislation in an attempt to preserve this valuable resource had placed restrictions on their use, and if Indians through their isolation found means to avoid integrating into the colonial work force, then who would fill the labor need? Who would perform the myriad of menial tasks necessary to build the new society, make it function, and allow it to prosper? Europeans certainly would not![39]

When Spaniards began to seek an additional pool of workers, Africans presented a tried and proven choice. African slaves had performed well on the Iberian peninsula before the discovery of the Americas, and there was no reason to think that they would not make good workers in the new lands. Africa lay closer to the Western Hemisphere than Europe and other parts of the Old World, and Iberian traders had already established a traffic in slave labor on the continent's west coast. This trade merely expanded to meet the heightened demands presented by the Spanish and Portuguese American empires.[40]

Spaniards brought African slaves with them along every step of the way in their colonization of Latin America. African slaves aided in the taking of the Caribbean, and when disease depopulated the islands and mainland coastal areas, Africans took their place as the backbone of the basin's colonial labor force. African slaves also contributed to Spanish conquests in Mesoamerica, Andean America, and northern South America. In the face of the extraordinary decline in the native populations of these regions, forced African immigrants, rather than willing European adventurers, relieved the labor stress that resulted at a critical juncture in the early establishment of the colonial economy. Blacks' presence lightened the workload for debilitated native populations helping to facilitate Indians' recovery in the seventeenth century.[41]

Colonists substituted African labor for Indian labor in many of Mexico's most demanding and unhealthy work settings. They used them to work in commercial agriculture in Oaxaca, Puebla, Michoacán, and Nueva Galicia. They utilized blacks further in the mining areas of Zacatecas, Guanajuato, and Durango. They employed Africans on large livestock-raising estates that supplied mining areas with meat and hides.[42]

The tasks of these coerced laborers proved as multiple and complex as the settings they arrived in. In major cities, such as Mexico, Puebla, Valladolid, and Antequera they built roads, bridges, and buildings. On their backs they transported goods and people within and between these population centers. They worked in the *obrajes*, or small sweatshop factories, that sprang up. They hawked wares in the streets, cut and sold firewood, tended gardens and livestock, and of course kept house and waited on their masters.[43] Sugar production represented a prime example of a commercial agricultural environment that came to utilize African slave labor. Central Veracruz provided a regional variant of the overall Caribbean black experience in sugar culture. Central Veracruz lay on the mainland and encompassed highland as well as lowland areas. The region lay in the heartland of New Spain's sugar industry until nearly the end of the seventeenth century. During this time Mexico became a strong market for slaves. As many as two thousand Africans annually arrived at the port of Veracruz between 1580 and 1620. In this setting blacks integrated into variegated labor systems instead of a single slave-dominated system. African slaves represented a critical supplement rather than an alternative to other types of labor.

Bravo Lagunas, head of Jalapa's town council, mentions Africans' presence in the 1570s. By the turn of the century, Don Carlos Samano implemented a mixed Indian-African labor force on his sugar *ingenio* (large estate with a water-powered mill) of Almolonga five leagues to the north of the district capital. African slaves also worked alongside Indians in the town of Jalapa at the turn of the sixteenth century.[44] Here, as elsewhere in colonial mainland Spanish America, blacks did exactly what Spaniards had hoped they would do—fill the places left by dying Indians in the colonial labor force.

Spanish contact in 1519 enormously increased the influence of outside factors in shaping the development of societies in central Veracruz. For the next century these foreign influences seriously challenged local pressures for primacy in molding demographic, technological, economic, social, and political growth in the region. Africans represented a part of this imposed outside influence. The consequences of shifts in the weighting of outside/ local influences in the area's formative dynamic as well as Afro-Veracruzanos' role in these changes provide the central topics of the next three chapters.

2

The Hows, Whens, Whos, and Whys of the Afro-Veracruz Slave Trade

CATASTROPHIC POPULATION decline raised fears that mainland Indians would go the way of Caribbean island natives. Some group had to lighten the Mexican Indian labor load for humanitarian, for moral, and for very real economic reasons. New Spain's economy demanded a supplementary work force to augment thinning ranks of Indian tributaries.[1] Africans filled this role. The solution, however, did not come spontaneously. It evolved out of a series of events that took place in three settings. In the Western Hemisphere, of which New Spain existed as an important and precedent-setting part, the juxtaposition of growing regional economies and shrinking population created a market for controllable imported labor. With demand in place, the Spanish had to find a supply.

The African Cog

Africans proved ideally suited to American labor needs because of their adaptability, their availability, and their prior use as slaves elsewhere. Most New World bondspersons came from areas within two hundred miles of the West African coast, an area dominated by nations, empires, and kingdoms that in territory and population size rivaled European countries of the time. Smaller bands of people who often acted as trading intermediaries between larger groups also inhabited the zone.[2] Culturally, the subjects of these nations generally adhered to compatible values and beliefs with those emerging in colonial America. Africans and Euro-Americans accepted concepts of private property, surplus production, profit incentive, and complex labor systems. Many African societies even had a form of specie that supplemented barter exchange. Finally, the rank and file of slaves subsisted at the bottom of the West African labor scale.[3] Bondage within the African context, however, was not as debased a position as the one that evolved in the Americas. Pre-European socioeconomic climates in the principal sixteenth- and seventeenth-century African centers of the slave trade illustrate this point.

Active commercial ties formed among various Central African peoples like those occupying the Bights of Benin and Biafara. In these areas slaves became one of the items commonly exchanged. Individuals entered slavery in a variety of ways. Slavery came as a punishment for criminal, social, and economic offenses, serving as a means for controlling undesirables. Enslavement also aided in population redistribution. Families, villages, and nations traded away children, wives, and other dependents in times of population and environmental stress caused by drought, crop failure, flood, and other natural disasters. Kidnapping exemplified yet a third means of enslavement. Those who engaged in this type of activity did so for motives such as profit, revenge, and rivalry.[4]

In the Central African Congo and Luanda regions, cultural mechanisms existed that paved the way for the development of the Atlantic slave trade. This proved significant since the regions eventually produced the greatest proportion of the millions of captives shipped to the Americas between 1500 and 1870. Most of these bondspersons embarked at ports on the Congo and Angola coasts, an area that stretched from Cape López to Cape Frio.

For the most part slave traders drew their victims from African nation-states whose social systems stood organized around extended matrilineal kinship networks in which two underlying values provided social cohesion. Africans directed individual concern and allegiance toward the kin group and away from nonkin individuals. This made the population somewhat insensitive to the fate of troublemakers and outsiders. Selling nonkin persons into slavery became common practice long before Europeans arrived on the scene. A kinsperson who did not place the interest of the clan above personal interest ran the risk of removal. Sale to strangers developed as a convenient way of achieving this end. These practices created a variety of dependent statuses within communities that did not offer nearly as much personal or group security as clans did. They gave rise to new social ranks that Joseph Miller refers to as "pawns" and "slaves."[5] Just prior to the arrival of Iberian traders, the incidence of human sales escalated, largely as a result of political instability. Since an important measure of power and prestige in Congo and Angola societies related to the size of the clan, the quasi-lineage members—pawns or slaves—were readily purchased by ascending power groups from rival descending power groups. They may not have represented true kin, but their presence enlarged and empowered the clan. Thus slaves existed as a trade item before Europeans' arrival in West Africa.

Portuguese made first contact with West and Central Africa. They came to exchange their goods for indigenous products—gold, ivory, elephant hides, spices, and sometimes slaves. Thus, outsiders did not introduce slavery to Africa but bought into an internal African commerce in humans, creating a partnership. West Africans intensified their efforts to acquire slaves in response to rising European demand for them. Sometimes Africans secured slaves for barter through legitimate trade. This mechanism contributed peoples including those from the Bights of Biafara and Benin, as well as from the Luanda regions.[6]

Under certain conditions procurement did not present a problem. Political instability led to the enslavement of blacks. This proved the case in the Cape Verde region during the middle decades of the sixteenth century as Berbesi, Mandinga, Banol, and Wolofs (Gelofes, or Jolofs) fought in wars that racked the Wolof empire.[7] In the Bight of Biafara area, Bran entered into territorial struggles with invading Akan groups, thereby creating prisoner populations that the clashing rivals easily converted into marketable slaves.

In some instances European slave traders instigated or expanded African conflict. Within the Bight of Benin and Central African zones, as in the Congo and Luanda territories, African and Portuguese cooperation gave way to more one-sided relationships in favor of Europeans. Armed with greater power, Iberians occupied a better position from which to respond to growing labor demands in American markets. Portuguese traders exploited their advantage. They resorted to increasingly more direct and violent means of slave procurement. Conditions that facilitated this action partially involved the changing nature of African-European relations in the Congo and Luanda regions to the south.

Congo kings did not always use the wealth and power they derived from the Portuguese trade to change markedly their own societies. In other words, they did not duplicate European technology in such areas as firearm manufacture, nor did they foster the growth of new industries that would produce trade items that the Europeans imported to Africa (sometimes referred to as "import substituting industrialization," in present literature).[8] Outsiders continued to control production of these items. Instead, African power factions enhanced their positions among themselves by acquisition and redistribution of European trade items. Without control of means to produce these valuable exchange commodities, native rulers' relationships with European traders shifted from mutual cooperation to

African dependency.[9] This change provided European traders with the leverage needed to create a more efficient climate for obtaining slaves: military conflict. From about 1560 to 1668 Portuguese merchants and officials used their increasing power to promote wars of succession among rival members of ruling African kin groups. The tactic proved most successful in Luanda, the source of Angolan slaves. This land's tragic history involved not only increasing African dependency on European trade but also another critical ingredient for the escalation of the slave trade, direct European involvement in African wars.

In 1580 Spain's Philip II inherited the Portuguese throne, and from that time until 1640 Spain ruled both Iberian states. The time coincided with the period of severest demographic decline in much of Ibero-America, including Mexico. As a result the Spanish crown pressured Portuguese slavers to increase the African supply of bondspeople. Lisbon officials answered the call. First, they stepped up the level of conflict in the Congo region. They then began to push southward into Luanda. There they seized control of a contraband slave trade that São Tomen traders had developed after their displacement from the Congo commerce in the mid-sixteenth century. This set the stage for an even higher level of warfare than had previously existed in the Congo. São Tomens and their native Mbundu allies met the challenge. They entered into a constant struggle with Spanish-prodded Portuguese traders for the next forty-odd years. Fighting peaked during the period 1612–1622, a time known as the Angolan wars. In the end Portugal triumphed for Spain, breaking São Tomé's commercial ties with the area and replacing them with colonial Portuguese-Spanish rule. Europeans had gained an added measure of control over the production of African slaves through conquest.[10] Victorious Iberians annexed Mbundu territory and placed it under their rule. The unhappy Mbundu losers paid a heavy price for defeat. They forfeited their freedom and swelled the ranks of slaves bound for Latin America. Through this process of European and African interaction between about 1580 and 1620, the machinery came into position for the massive diaspora of Africans all over the Americas. Luanda, the source of Angolan slaves, would contribute an estimated 40 percent of all uprooted Africans involved in the Atlantic diaspora. The international slave trade needed one more gear to make it a powerful machine that could pull the New and Old Worlds together. This final part existed in the form of the European state and its bureaucratic marketing apparatus, in Mexico's case, imperial Spain.

Europe's Contribution

Europeans did not initially make contact with the sub-Saharan regions of West Africa in order to establish a slave trade. In 1415, the Portuguese captured the Moroccan port city of Cueta. This provided the Iberians with their first staging base for commercial penetration southward on the continent. They sought commodities in high demand in European markets, primarily gold and ivory. As a sideline to this trade they invariably took a few captives for sale on the Iberian Peninsula. This dimension of trade grew in direct proportion to commerce in the other two materials of exchange.[11] Traffic in Africans represented an important part of this trade and led to the introduction of a large African slave population into Spain and Portugal. By 1565 West Africans comprised an estimated 7 percent of the port city of Seville's population.[12] This proved a critical development in light of the later ties between that city and Spanish America. European priorities did not change from commodities to people, however, until the 1480s, more than half a century after Europeans established Ibero-African trade linkages. The shift emanated from growing labor demands in the broader Iberian economy. The foundation of sugar culture on the Atlantic islands off the coast of north central Africa represented a first step in that direction.

The Portuguese began planting sugar on the island of São Tome at virtually the same time that they opened their trade with the Congo-Angola region, around 1480. Labor demands increased sharply. São Tome planters by-passed traditional Portuguese commercial networks and ventured onto the African mainland to procure their own slaves. They quickly grasped the significance of Congo kings' dependence on them, and a symbiotic relationship developed. The monarchs sold São Tomens large numbers of their nonclan dependents. In return, the planters provided the rulers with muskets, powder, and other trade items that strengthened the kings' power against rivals. By 1500 the Congo became the major source of slave labor for São Tome. A decade later the island had two thousand slaves. The African and European cogs of the slave trade began to mesh. Soon the engine accelerated.

Concurrently (about the turn of the sixteenth century), the American market for slaves began to develop. Caribbean Indian populations started dying off at an alarming rate. Moved by the crisis, Spanish officials searched for an alternative labor force. The West African slave trade, developing at the same time, provided a logical solution to colonists' immediate labor needs. In 1503 the first shipment of Africans arrived on the island of Hispaniola. At the outset the trading network proved clumsy and indirect. Spain insisted that traders acculturate the slaves before their arrival in the Americas. In order to satisfy this prerequisite, São Tomens first had to ship their bondspeople to more established trading centers at Elmina, Madeira, the islands off Cape Verde, and Portugal itself. From there they took them to a Spanish port, commonly Seville, by that time a center for the Spanish-African slave trade. After this series of Iberian stops, the slaves presumably had acquired enough European cultural traits for traders to ship them to the Indies.[13]

By 1540 Caribbean Indians had become all but extinct. As a result the African slave trade proved more enduring an adjustment than most had anticipated. It spread and became a vital part of the New World experience. Mexico played an important role in solidifying this precedent. From the beginning African slaves acted as partners with their Iberian masters in the conquest of New Spain. They participated in virtually every major Spanish thrust into the colony, just as they had in other parts of the Americas.[14] At first it appeared as if Afro-Mexicans' role in the postconquest period would be a relatively minor one. After all, Anahuac teemed with native inhabitants, 25.2 million of them in 1518.[15] But the sad course of events that had taken place on the nearby islands seemed to repeat itself in Mexico; natives died in great numbers. Because of conditions in Mexico, the demand for African slaves increased dramatically after 1580. From that date until about 1620 New Spain's demand for slaves nearly equalled that of all other American areas combined.[16] To meet this growing need, Iberians streamlined the trading network in Africa and in Europe.

The mutually beneficial relationship between São Tomen slavers and Congo kings proved too restrictive an arrangement to meet the exploding demand side of the Atlantic slave trade. No matter how hard African rulers tried, they could not keep pace with the Mexican-driven American need for slaves. Africans' store of peacefully acquired nonlineage bondspeople fell woefully short of the combined São Tomen, Iberian, and American labor requirements. At the same time, Congo kings' material power grew rapidly from the profits and commodities they procured through the commerce. Seeking more tractable trading partners, European traders began to bypass them and deal directly with less powerful but equally ambitious interior rulers. This created an African climate of competition in which local power depended increasingly on commercial ties with European slavers. As trade linkages became more diffused, so did power. Inevitably, conflict ensued, helping to solve one problem. Violent means proved more productive than peaceful means for procuring African slaves. This, in turn, introduced a new level of instability to the African continent. Entrance of rival European slave traders onto the scene elevated the level of unrest. By the middle of the sixteenth century other nations began to challenge Portuguese influence on the west coast of Africa. French, English, and Dutch traders engaged in concerted efforts to enter into the lucrative commerce. Now rival African groups could obtain materials of war from a variety of competing suppliers. And each of the outsiders seemed only too happy to oblige them in return for the promise of enslaved prisoners delivered to the coast and sold at low prices. Warfare became endemic. Empires rose and fell, first the Congo kings in the 1560s, followed by the Songhia monarchs who ruled the interior of upper West Africa, then the Wolofs of the Senegambia region just to the east, the Yorubas of Nigeria, and finally the Dohemays of the Bight of Benin district. Periodic African wars provided a constant flow of thousands of prisoners for sale at a rapidly increasing number of coastal trading forts. Europeans had broadened their influence in Africa. The African supply side nearly matched the American demand side of the slave trade. Europeans had to make one more adjustment before the trade could flourish. Spain had to ease trade barriers to Spanish America. That happened in 1518. Charles I initiated two policy changes. He allowed direct importation of slaves from Africa to the New World, and he initiated the *asiento*, a royal license for an importation monopoly to a specific American colony. These changes dramatically revised the actual slave trading network. Direct introduction of un-hispanicized Africans, or *bozales*, as opposed to *ladinos*, Hispanicized Africans, represented a marked deviation from the cautious immigration policies of Charles' parents, Ferdinand and Isabella. These policy changes underscored the critical labor shortage on the Caribbean islands. Four years later Charles retreated a bit from his liberal stance. A revolt broke out on Hispaniola, led by disgruntled *ladinos* and *bozales* from the Wolof empire in West Africa. The king banned all Africans from Spanish America for a short time. But demographic exigencies in the Caribbean persuaded him to reconsider. By 1520 the trade restarted.[17] The Spanish administrative structure had evolved.

But Spain was not in a position to deliver unlimited numbers of Africans to the Americas. Portuguese merchants controlled West African trade, and Spain and Portugal viewed each other as rivals. As a result, Spain refused to grant *asientos* to the only group that could consistently secure African slaves in large numbers. As already noted, that problem disappeared in 1580 when Philip II of

Spain inherited the Portuguese crown. With the union of both countries the way stood clear for the full meshing of all the cogs of the sixteenth-century slave-trade machine.

Spain awarded Portuguese merchants six monopolies between 1595 and 1640. This more or less covered the period of most critical Mexican need for African slave labor, the years from 1580 to 1630, when native population decline proved greatest.[18]

Heavy importation of Africans into Mexico did not solely depend on New World conditions. Related conditions also existed in Europe and Africa. All three environments contributed to occurrence of the diaspora. The timing of ideal conditions on the three continents involved—namely, the periods of greatest Mexican demographic stress, African political instability, and union of the Spanish and Portuguese crowns—correlated to further support this conclusion. The first created high demand for imported labor; the second increased the rate of African enslavement; and the third facilitated a marketing network to link Mexican labor markets with African labor pools. Further, by dating changes in the flow of Africans into Mexico and Jalapa, one can chronologically match origins of Mexican slaves with centers of slave procurement in West Africa, in effect examining Mexico and Jalapa's involvement in the early sixteenth- and seventeenth-century supply, demand, and delivery dimensions of the Atlantic slave trade.

Mexican Trade

Gonzalo Aguirre Beltrán estimates that Mexico annually received an average of two thousand African slaves during the period 1580–1650.[19] Colin Palmer concludes that New Spain purchased nearly half of all Africans shipped to the New World between 1595 and 1622.[20] The volume of the trade immediately before this period remains difficult to gauge. Very little evidence exists for the sixteenth century traffic in slaves. What evidence exists suggests that the early trade involved relatively small numbers of Africans compared to the totals found in records dated a half century later. This is not surprising. In these first years New Spain's colonial economy, still in its infancy, offered little capital. Moreover, Spaniards did not yet fully realize the implications of Mexico's demographic stress. They would need time to react. Finally, the 1590–1620 expansion of European power into Luanda had not taken place. In the absence of these optimum conditions for Mexico's participation in the slave trade, patterns derived from limited sixteenth-century evidence appears reliable.

Until the 1590s the vast majority of slaves came from West Africa. Cape and Biafaran bondspeople filled early needs. The Capes and Biafarans existed as products of an expanding native African trade in slaves on the lower West African coast into which Europeans merely tapped. But soon the Mexican demand grew beyond these early regions' ability to supply slaves. Late sixteenth- and first-quarter seventeenth-century political strife provided even larger caches of captives from areas such as the Wolof empire, which not only enslaved its own people but those of subject groups as well, nations such as the Berbesi, Mandinga, Banol, and Bran. These later sources of labor offered a new climate of procurement.[21]

Central African states did not develop the capacity to produce large numbers of slaves until at least the end of the decade of the 1560s, and possibly even as late as the 1590s. Consequently, individuals from these regions did not regularly appear in the early sixteenth-century sample. East African slaves also proved rare. Europeans maintained light presence on this side of Africa because of its distance from American slave markets such as Mexico.

Existing evidence indicates a post-1560 rise in the Mexican slave trade. Patterns in the seventeenth century markedly differed from those of the sixteenth century. Mid-sixteenth-century trade figures indicate that West Africa provided 90 percent of all slaves entering Mexico during this period.[22] Central Africa represented a weak secondary source, making up less than 5 percent of the total cases. Later evidence suggests that in the following century a reversal in these two areas' level of involvement in the trade took place. West Africa's share of the sample dropped from 92 percent to 13 percent, while Central Africa's percentage rose from 4 percent to 80 percent.[23] These shifts coincide with European incursions southward down the African continent. Changing origins of Mexican slaves from about 1560 to 1650 seem to reflect geographic movement in the African center of slave production. A more in-depth parochial view of the operation of the slave trade adds weight to this conclusion.

Central Veracruz and the Atlantic Slave Trade

Patterns in the volume of the Jalapa trade chronologically parallel related events on both sides of the Atlantic, indicating that this particular Mexican province remained very sensitive to alternating conditions in the Atlantic trade.

With the union of the Iberian crowns from 1580 to 1640 and the awarding of the first of several Portuguese *asientos* beginning in 1595, marketing machinery became more efficient, making it better able to service the expanded supply and demand sides of the commerce. As Table 3 indicates, at the very time that Jalapa experienced its heaviest participation in the Atlantic slave trade Central Africa eclipsed West Africa as the major source of bond servants. This coincides with my findings for Mexico as a whole. Assuming that these concurring patterns are representative, the Jalapa case takes on added significance since it more precisely dates these trends.

The peak period of Jalapa's purchase of African slaves falls between 1597 and 1610.[24] Between 1578 and 1597, just before the peak sales period, and between 1611 and 1670, just after it, planters purchased an average of two to three *bozales* yearly. From 1670 onward the trade virtually ceased. Masters bought ten more Africans in the last thirty years of the century. No new *bozales* entered the district until a century later, toward the end of the colonial period. Of the 478 Africans sold in Jalapa during the 230-odd years covered in Table 4, an estimated 325 to 330, or 65 to 70 percent of them, stepped onto the auction block between 1590 and 1610.[25]

The timing of Jalapa's trends correlate even more closely with the conjunction of events in Africa and Europe than the more unevenly supported trends for Mexico as a whole. The period of heavy trading in Jalapa coincided almost perfectly with the nadir in the district's population decline, 1610. With market incentive high, Jalapa planters and merchants responded predictably and imported large numbers of African slaves. Despite local demand, the trade still could not have grown as rapidly as it did without ideal conditions in the supply and delivery sectors of the commerce. Jalapa represented one of many growing American markets. Fortunately for this parochial demand side of the broader Atlantic commerce, circumstances remained optimum in Africa and Europe as well. From 1595 onward Portuguese slave traders began to appear for the first time in the district. Between that date and 1600 Bermúdez Gorrochotogui found six of them, as well as one merchant from the Portuguese island of Madeira.[26] Not surprisingly from the timing of events in Africa, all seven of them brought slaves from Central Africa. The six from Portugal itself brought Angolans; the Madeiran brought Congolese. During the height of Jalapa's participation in the trade, Central Africa eclipsed West Africa as the major source of incoming slaves, just as data for other parts of Mexico suggest.

Although the beginning of the peak in the Jalapa trade coincided almost exactly with the development of optimum conditions for the growth of the Atlantic slave trade in Africa and Europe, the quick decline in the district's purchase of Africans did not. The post-1610 decline in the Jalapa trade seemed to occur a decade or so too early to fit the general trend for Mexico as a whole. More importantly, it occurred at a time when conditions in Africa and Europe seemed most propitious for the continuation of the commerce.

Some students of the Atlantic exchange in Africans suggest that European rivalries diminished the slave trade. But little consensus exists on when this disruptiveness began to take effect. For example, some argue that evidence from slave-ship licenses points to a post-1630 Mexican withdrawal from the trade. Between 1623 and 1639 the number of slavers licensed to ply the trade with Mexico dropped by as much as 50 percent from the level of the previous twenty-seven-year period. But licenses represent only an indirect means of measuring the volume of the trade. Many who received these *asientos* never applied them, others transported many more Africans than their licenses permitted. Beyond these problems with the legal trade, contraband traffic in slaves appeared widespread. Thus *asientos* provide at best only crude indices of measurement of trade volume.

European disruption within the state bureaucracy's administration of the commerce does, however, offer partial support for the reliability of the Jalapa pattern as representative for much of the rest of New Spain. From the very outset crown officials and Seville merchants only reluctantly allowed Portuguese participation in the trade. After 1580 the two countries may have united under the same crown, but both peoples still saw themselves as economic rivals. Seville served as the hub of Spanish-American commerce, and its merchant guilds correctly accused Portuguese asientists of undercutting Sevillians' virtual monopoly over Spain's overseas exchange. Seville merchants consistently fought Portuguese control of the slave trade. Their opposition strengthened at the turn of the seventeenth century and continued to grow.[27]

But state intervention in the operation of the trade probably represented only a secondary reason for the early decline of the trade. Decreasing numbers of slaves imported into Jalapa and other locales after about 1610 or 1620 embodied but one manifestation of the viceroyalty's general retreat from Atlantic commerce that accelerated just a few years later and continued throughout most of the century, but more will be said about this later. In any case, New Spain's withdrawal from the slave trade proved more a result of Mexican than European or African conditions.

Shortages of cheap native workers created the New World market for African slave labor. Highland Meso- and Andean-America represented slight modifications to this general rule. In these areas the indigenous labor force prevailed but under severe demographic

Table 3. Origins of Slaves Sold in Jalapa, 1578–1810

Origin	1578–1610	1611–1640	1641–1670	1671–1700	1701–1730	1731–1760	1761–1790	1791–1810
Upper West Africa								
Arara	5	3	—	—	—	—	—	—
Banol	5	4	—	—	—	—	—	—
Biafara	13	8	—	—	—	—	—	—
Bran	23	—	2	—	—	—	—	—
Cape Verde	5	—	1	1	—	—	—	—
Carabali	4	—	1	—	—	—	—	—
Fula	1	—	—	—	—	—	—	—
Wolof	5	2	—	—	—	—	—	—
Guinea	—	—	—	—	—	—	—	5
Mina	1	—	—	—	—	—	—	2
São Tome	2	—	—	—	—	—	—	2
Xoxo	2	—	—	—	—	—	—	—
Zape	7	—	—	—	—	—	—	—
Subtotal	73	17	3	1	—	—	—	9
Central Africa								
Angola	219	47	66	2	—	—	—	—
Bambamba	1	1	—	—	—	—	—	—
Congo	8	4	2	1	—	—	—	9

Cazanga	1	—	—	—	—	—	—	—
Loango	1	5	—	6	—	—	—	—
Matamba	—	—	6	—	—	—	—	9
Subtotal	230	57	74	9	—	—	—	9
Southeast Africa								
Cafre	—	—	—	—	—	—	—	1
Subtotal	—	—	—	—	—	—	—	1
Bozal	16	—	—	1	—	—	—	1
Africa Total	319	74	77	11	—	—	—	20
Creoles	25	48	52	69	61	57	58	28
Unlisted	87	59	56	3	4	6	2	—
Total	431	181	185	83	65	63	60	48

Source: Gilberto Bermúdez Gorrochotegui provides 208 cases of slave sales for the period 1578–1600. Although he does not distinguish by origin over time during this period, he does provide a bar graph of the number of sales per year for each of the twenty-eight years. "Jalapa en el siglo XVI" (Master's thesis, Universidad Veracruzana, 1977), vol. 1, 175, 175(*bis*). The cases for the years 1601–1678 are drawn directly from notarial records for the district: (1601–1610) ANJ, vol. 1600–1608, leaves 167–545v; ANJ, vol. 1609–1617, leaves 8–184v; (1611–1620) ANJ, vol. 1609–1617, leaves 186–225v; ANJ, vol. 1617–1620, leaves 108–137; (1621–1630) ANJ, vol. 1621–1630, leaves 47–197v; (1632–1645) ANJ, vol. 1632–1645, leaves 119–210v; (1641–1650) ANJ, vol. 1641–1650, leaves 286–576v; ANJ, vol. 1645–1651, leaves 93–359; (1651–1660) ANJ, vol. 1651–1663, leaves 3v–350v. For decade 1661–1670, Fernando Winfield Capitaine, *Esclavos en el Archivo Notorial de Xalapa, 1668–1699*, 33–42; decade 1671–1680, Ibid., 43–49; decade 1681–1690; Ibid., 51–66; decade 1691–1700; Ibid., 66–105; decades 1701–1810, Carroll, "Mexican Society in Transition," 169, 318–321.

Table 4. *Number of Slaves Purchased in Jalapa by Capital Outlay by Average Price per Five-Year Period, 1581–1690*

Years	No. of Slaves	Capital Outlay (pesos)	Average Price (pesos)
1581–1585	21	8,690	414
1586–1590	7	2,500	357
Peak trade period			
1591–1595	38	17,140	451
1596–1600	123	48,060	391
1601–1605	116	36,405	314
1606–1610	107	35,373	331
Peak subtotal	384	136,978	357
1611–1615	14	5,712	408
1616–1620	25	9,725	389
Total	451	163,605	363

Source: See the appropriate decades in the source materials for Table 3.

stress. Peter Bakewell convincingly argues the adequacy of native Mexican labor throughout the colonial period, and conditions in Jalapa certainly support this conclusion.[28] In the face of severe population decline, especially between 1577 and 1625, and against the backdrop of earlier decimation of the Caribbean island native population, Iberians in Jalapa must have feared history might repeat itself. From their vantage point, they perceived the need to import large numbers of Africans between 1580 and 1615. When the drop in the native population abated and local labor could meet colonial demands, Spanish Jalapans reacted quickly. Most local producers withdrew from heavy involvement in the slave trade before 1620. In the rest of Mexico, only lightly populated but economically productive areas, such as far-off northern silver-mining regions and, in central Veracruz, the disease-ridden lowlands, as well as the coast and the sugar-growing province of Córdoba to the south, continued to import Africans. In these settings the same two prerequisites for the trade continued to apply. Spaniards demanded Africans as long as the local economy generated enough capital to afford them and as long as whites feared an impending shortage of indigenous labor. But such conditions represented exceptions to the norm after 1620. Jalapa, like most of the rest of Mexico, had outgrown its need for expensive African slaves. The district lay close to the coast and possessed a healthy climate due to its elevation. Jalapa's location and role in international trade meant that it experienced and adjusted to European diseases earlier than many other parts of Mexico. Probably no later than 1610 the area's native population began to survive in the altered local disease environment. This gave planters anywhere from five to ten years to perceive developing demographic trends and respond to them. Recognizing the end of a demographic crisis, Spaniards in Jalapa cut their slave purchases to a small fraction of what they had been in the previous twenty years. They bought a few Africans every now and then, but the bulk of the area's labor load shifted to free persons. Elite Afro-Jalapan slave workers performed critical skilled and menial tasks because they represented persons that their owners could depend upon for as long as they lived. Other owners maintained slaves merely as public symbols of wealth. And in slaves' cost lay the second reason Jalapans and the general Mexican public quickly replaced imported slaves with free wage labor.

Spaniards in Jalapa had spent a great deal of money on Africans during the province's brief participation in the Atlantic slave trade. In 1620, when a horse cost fifteen pesos and a small urban house two hundred pesos, Spaniards paid between three and four hundred pesos apiece for each African they imported to labor in the region. The trade drained thousands of pesos in capital out of the local economy. Table 4 clearly illustrates the capital intensiveness of slave labor.

During the peak years of Jalapa's involvement in the trade, free inhabitants of the area spent nearly 137,000 pesos on African labor, and that represents only the total for the legal trade. No doubt more capital fled the district through contraband commerce in slaves. These figures by no means suggest that African slave labor did not yield a profit. On the contrary, it must have produced handsome returns, otherwise the labor system would not have enticed so many successful planter-merchants including those in Jalapa to use it. Slaves represented the most expensive single item on the inventories of many of the province's seventeenth-century estates, plantations such as Mazatlan, Almolonga, Santísima Trinidad, Concepción, and Rosario. They cost more than the land, the equipment, and the buildings.[29] At times capital stood in such short supply that even transient slave merchants had to extend credit. In 1606 Don Melchor de Moral, the owner of the *ingenio* of Mazatlan, bought a prime twenty-year-old slave for 550 pesos. The Portuguese trader had to accept 280 pesos down and the promise of remittance within a year for the $270 balance. When Don Miguel de Avnon bought a block of seven Angolan slaves three years later at $400 apiece, he too fell short of cash. The two Veracruz merchants selling them had to settle for $800 down. Don Miguel promised within a month to pay the remainder in sugar valued at $4000. When the owner of Nuestra Señora de la Concepción, Don Juan Díaz de Matamoros, bought a lot of fifteen Angolan slaves in 1610, he paid a very cheap $340 each. Don Juan initially put only 160 pesos down. Within weeks he reduced the remaining principal to $2900. Unable to produce the balance, he persuaded the dealer, a Captain Francisco López, to give him another eight months to raise the rest.

Sometimes extensions of credit proved a mistake because buyers never paid off the balance owed. A frustrated slave trader named Balthasar Vásques learned this the hard way. He had to seek aid from local authorities in collecting a debt owed him in 1604. Even then he did not receive cash. The slaver had to accept sugar in payment, but at least he did not go away empty-handed. [30]

The slave trade put heavy strain on Jalapa's money supply. Capital stress probably served as an important factor leading to the area's withdrawal from the commerce after about 1615. Much of the explanation for Jalapa's removal from the trade lay in the same types of local conditions that dictated its participation—demographic and economic pressures. The great plagues that swept through Mexico in the late 1570s also hit Jalapa. Had more slaves been available in the 1580s, Spaniards would have probably purchased them, but conditions had not developed enough in Africa and Europe to meet the rapidly growing New World demand. When Africans finally did become available to Jalapa planters, planters bought their share of them but at very high cost. Planters thought that Africans and their creole descendants represented the only future labor force with enough critical skills and potential for menial labor within sugar and commercial industries. Shortly after the turn of the century, however, these pressures reversed themselves. High cost coupled with decreasing demographic stress more than anything else caused Jalapa to disengage from the Atlantic slave trade. Indian and non-Indian populations multiplied. The 1610–1615 European-induced interruption in the trade merely provided Jalapa planters with a forced pause to reassess this costly solution to their perceived labor problem. During that five-year interim they realized that their fears of a vanishing Indian labor force were exaggerated. Significant numbers of natives relocated on sugar estates and in the provincial capital. [31] In addition, the size of the *casta* (racially hybrid individual) population grew and assumed a greater and greater labor role. Native labor became more reliable and accessible after 1610. At the time Jalapa stopped importing slaves, the area poised on the threshold of economic reorientation away from the Atlantic commerce and toward linkages with other areas in New Spain. The province's retreat from the international slave trade represented the first step in this direction. In 1616, when the crown issued another Portuguese *asiento*, the new *asiento* had little effect on Jalapa. New Spain in general did not reenter the Atlantic slave trade, and neither did Jalapa.

Local Variations in the Veracruz Slave Trade

Some local variation did exist in central Veracruz' participation in the Atlantic slave trade. Córdoba began importing Africans at about the time Jalapa started withdrawing from the commerce, in the first quarter of the seventeenth century. Córdoba did not stop purchasing large numbers of *bozales* until a century later. Adriana Naveda Chávez-Hita recorded 151 African arrivals there as late as the decade of 1700–1709. In the following decade this total dropped to twenty-five. By 1770 sales of *bozales* ceased altogether.

In both districts, slave exchanges involved creoles rather than Africans during the last century of colonial rule. Jalapa steadily retreated from involvement after 1610. Except for a bit of activity on the eve of independence, Jalapa remained outside this dimension of international commerce through the next century. Whites there purchased just twenty-odd *bozales* between 1701 and 1810; during the same period in Córdoba they bought nearly twenty times that number. Córdoba appears to have utilized slave labor more fully than Jalapa did during the last century of the colonial period (see the horizontal and vertical marginal totals in Table 5). Córdoba exchanged four to five times as many slaves as Jalapa during this time, and just as importantly, Córdoba remained a market for African slaves a century longer than Jalapa did. As late as the first quarter of the eighteenth century Córdoba bought nearly as many *bozales* as creole slaves. Such a purchase had not happened in Jalapa since the 1620s (see Table 4). Even after Córdoba stopped heavily importing Africans, it continued to purchase a good number of bondspeople from other regions in Mexico and more distant American sites outside of New Spain. In contrast, two thirds of Jalapa's trade was intradistrict in nature, as local masters merely exchanged slaves with one another. All the evidence in Table 5 indicates that Córdoba remained more committed to the Atlantic slave trade than Jalapa. However, equally apparent is that even in Córdoba the value of slaves dropped as the colonial years drew to a close. The last observation proves significant because economic climates in both regions became very positive at the opening of the eighteenth century (al-

Table 5. *Slave Sales in the Districts of Jalapa and Córdoba, 1701–1810*

	1701– 1730	1731– 1760	1761– 1790	1791– 1810	Totals
Bozal					
Jalapa	0	0	1	20	21
Córdoba	348	56	2	0	406
Creoles					
Intradistrict					
Jalapa	52	49	57	18	176
Córdoba	144	88	22	22	276
Inter-Mexico					
Jalapa	9	8	0	0	17
Córdoba	57	13	5	5	80
Other[a]					
Jalapa	3	4	0	8	15
Córdoba	35	13	4	0	52
Unlisted					
Jalapa	3	4	0	2	9
Córdoba	79	73	100	24	276
Total					
Jalapa	67	65	58	48	238
Córdoba	663	243	133	51	1,090

Sources: I derived the Jalapa figures from Table 3 and Carroll, "Mexican Society in Transition," 169. Totals for Córdoba came from Adriana Naveda Chávez-Hita, *Esclavos negros en las haciendas azucareras de Córdoba, Veracruz, 1690–1830,* 26–31.

   [a]Includes slaves arriving from all other places besides Africa, the district itself, and other parts of New Spain.

though, as will be pointed out later, Córdoba did suffer economic instability during the first half of the eighteenth century). The notion of a mid-colonial period of readjustment (roughly 1630–1720) away from heavy participation in the Atlantic economy and more intense involvement in Mexico's domestic economy that ended in 1730 received far better support from Jalapa's pattern of involvement in the Atlantic slave trade than Córdoba's up until 1720. On the other hand, eighteenth-century patterns of slave exchange in both districts suggest that Bourbon Reform pressures originating in Europe and aimed at retarding capitalistic development in Mexico did not contribute to this end through a revival of the Veracruz-Africa slave connection. This held true despite the fact that New Spain again emphasized European commerce with less restrictive trade policies. By the last quarter of the eighteenth century Spain permitted her colonies to trade with any Spanish port and even allowed a limited amount of commerce with England. But the renaissance of Veracruz' involvement in Atlantic commerce did not include resumption of the African slave trade except in unusual locales, such as Córdoba. The record of Jalapa's involvement, as this essay suggests, represents the more common of the two experiences.

Conclusion

The close parallels in the nature and timing of the forces governing Jalapan and the broader Mexican involvement in the international slave trade invite comparison. Apparently, from this very parochial evidence, the trade did not develop haphazardly. New World markets proved sensitive to Old World production and administrative environments. The slave trade thrived in central Veracruz when all the international pieces of the commerce came together. In other places such as Córdoba to the south, the timing appears to have differed, but the dynamics of the trade remained the same. The importance of the Jalapa case lies in the fact that it more clearly illustrates the high chronological correlation existing between the interconnected dimensions of this enormously complex but important exchange in the development of American societies. Yet, the level of dependency of emerging areas, including central Veracruz, was not as great as some suggest. Planters in Jalapa demonstrated a high degree of economic independence when they receded from the Atlantic slave trade. European pressure played a secondary role to local economic and demographic conditions in arriving at the decision. Adherents to theories of world systems revolving around the emergence of sixteenth-century capitalism do not satisfactorily explain the pattern of Jalapa's involvement in the Atlantic slave trade.[32] In this small setting complimentary sets of forces in Europe, Africa, and Jalapa made the slave trade work; uncomplimentary forces in Jalapa alone made it not work.

3

Regional Production, Market, and Capital Development

FORCES ON three continents shaped the Afro-Mexican experience from 1519 to 1630. Trans-Atlantic pressures had greatest impact during the last fifty years of this period, a time when Africans' presence in New Spain reached its apex. As the era drew to a close, the temporary convergence of intercontinental circumstances split. Only the supply side of Mexico's Atlantic slave connection remained intact. Africa continued to pour forth its life's blood into vessels that carried the continent's sons and daughters across the western seas. New Spain, however, no longer received large numbers of these unfortunates; most arrived at other New World shores.

Societies support themselves through activities that provide for their material needs. Environment, or physical setting, obviously plays a role in defining these activities, and taken as whole, the definition that emerges represents an economic system. The period from 1500–1800 saw profound alterations in western economies. Immanuel Wallerstein suggests three critical dates. Sometime around the turn of the sixteenth century (ca. 1500), feudalistic tributary economies waned. These systems operated in response to sociopolitical forces, namely, social custom sanctioned by law. Producers turned surpluses over to hereditary elites as tribute, taxes, or rent for land usage. In return, elites promised to protect producers from other elites.

Trade-driven economies gradually replaced tribute-based ones. Trade-based profit replaced tribute as the principal incentive for surplus production. With the expansion of European states beyond their continental borders and the establishment of overseas colonial holdings, the commercially fueled system entered a new phase, mercantilism. Heavy state intervention marked this stage of economic affairs. Mercantile European economies centered around the Atlantic basin from about 1550 to 1650.

A third watershed fell sometime near 1650. From that date onward, a new order, capitalism, began to eclipse the mercantilist system in western Europe.[1] Herein, forces of the free marketplace subordinated the role of the state in driving economies. Broad impersonal conditions loosely defined as market, production, labor, and capital sought equilibrium in an atmosphere ruled not by governments but by unrestrained competition for profit. From Immanuel Wallerstein's perspective, the European world system shaped economic growth in less-developed "feudalistic peripheral" colonies in America, for example, Mexico. Events in New Spain and Jalapa around 1630 suggest that this argument is overstated.[2]

Jalapa's economic evolution fairly closely followed that of Mexico's as a whole for two reasons. First, Jalapa's location placed it along the vital Mexico City–to–Veracruz trade route, linking it to the main vein of commerce that flowed between the Mexican and Iberian worlds. Secondly, the nature of its economic development, especially after 1550, made the area very sensitive to broader forces operating beyond the local setting.

The Age of Personal Tribute, 1519–1550

From 1521 onward, two economies coexisted in Jalapa. The Indian system was mixed in nature. It involved subsistence agriculture and surplus barter exchange at the central-Veracruz regional level. Spaniards directed the second system—the "peripheral" economy, to borrow from Wallerstein's lexicon. It aimed at producing surplus goods and profit for export to capitalistic "core" economies in Europe through "feudalistic" policies of coerced labor.[3] Chapter 3 deals almost exclusively with Jalapa's European oriented economy; it does not probe the native Indian system. More specifically, it measures production, market, and capital growth against Wallerstein's core/periphery model of development.

The dual economic make-up of the area presented difficulties from the Iberian perspective. Spaniards' new production sectors often required skilled resident laborers, at least in part, and Indians had little incentive to accept these positions. They would have to leave their culture and kin ties and relocate in Spanish towns or on Spanish estates. There they would engage in arduous labor for remittances that probably earned them lower standards of physical comfort than they enjoyed in their villages. Indians would not accept these conditions willingly, so Spaniards had to coerce them.[4] In the end, Indians escaped the most onerous labor demand of all, slavery.

Jalapa's first stage of economic development remains very shadowy. Little primary documentation for the pre-1570 years has surfaced in local- or viceregal-level archives. What is known about the region's early economy comes from statements by sixteenth-century commentators, such as magistrate Constantino Bravo de Lagunas, who wrote in the 1580s,[5] and clerics, such as Francisco Xavier Clavijero, an eighteenth-century commentator.[6] In addition, several crown letters make mention of the province's economy during the early years. One referred to a need for a royal road through Jalapa to facilitate trade between the coast and the interior. Others recommended construction of a hospital and additional services to accommodate travelers' needs.[7] Finally, early seventeenth-century notarial records and a 1563 correspondence to the king make mention of material tribute in cotton, corn, sugar, jalap, and Indian labor received by Spanish residents.[8] From these accounts, tribute collection from Indians and such services to travelers as lodging and storage appear to have driven Jalapa's urban-based economy. Little evidence exists of direct Spanish control over production.

Spaniards lost little time in establishing sugar agriculture in Veracruz. Mills operated before 1530 in a few areas, including central Veracruz. These decades immediately after conquest proved comparatively uncomplicated ones with respect to economic development. Unquestionably, the level of colony-based fiscal activity expanded tremendously, but the nature of the economy remained much the same. With the exception of the infant sugar sector, Spaniards retained many characteristics of the indigenous economy. As before European arrival, those in political control wielded economic power as well. Elites of both eras set up empires held together by legalized tribute from subordinate peoples.[9] Indians gave Spaniards food, shelter, and other living necessities, just as they earlier had provided the Mexica. Natives also supplied Iberians with a number of commercially marketable items—sugar, silver, cochineal dye, and, to a lesser extent, gold.[10] Indians continued to control production of most commodities; indigenous political leaders, at least at the critical village level, still ruled Indian labor. This pattern was not confined to central Veracruz; others document it for elsewhere, in such places as Oaxaca and the Valley of Mexico.[11] The 1519–1550 stage of economic development did seem to fit Wallerstein's model. Veracruz' economy operated in a feudal fashion.

Personal to Mixed Corporate Tribute–Mercantile Economy, 1550–1630

The first step in this second stage of local economic development involved conversion from personal to corporate tribute incentives for production. In the midst of Indian population decline Spanish administrators searched for causes. The Black Legend emerged from their inquiry. Those in imperial power came to at least partially accept the notion that abuse by Iberian colonists heavily contributed to the alarming death rate of natives. In order to correct this problem, and also to limit the potential for a Spanish-creole challenge to royal authority, crown officials acted decisively. They pressured an important economic support to creole-Spaniards' power—the system of personal tribute that had dominated the character of the colonial economy up to 1550. First, they passed the New Laws in the 1540s redefining the European-based population's relationships with Indians. This legislation restricted and regulated Spanish-creole access to natives' labor. In 1542 the laws struck down Indian slavery. They also recognized the integrity of Indian villages and forbade non-Indians from residing there. Finally, the legislation attacked the *encomienda*, foundation of the personal tribute system.[12]

The crown had multiple reasons for its hostility toward *encomenderos* and the personal tribute system. By midcentury, royal interests fully appreciated Mexico's material wealth.[13] Naturally, the state became increasingly worried about its control over this gushing font of plenty. Besides the obvious threat from European rivals, the king and his advisors perceived dangers from within Mexico itself. Three groups posed potential dangers to royal authority.

African slaves, who began to outnumber Spaniards within the viceroyalty, frequently rose up in localized revolt. But they, like Iberians, lived for the most part as aliens in the new land. They could count on little help from natives when they opposed Spanish power. Moreover, their positions as slaves greatly restricted their revolutionary potential.

Indians presented a potentially more serious threat. They numerically dwarfed their conquerors. Extreme demographic stress, however, diminished the Indian danger to royal authority during the second half of the century. Viceregal and local officials alike realized that natives represented little actual threat to Spanish power. Viceroy Antonio de Mendoza commented about their submissiveness before the mid-sixteenth century. Constantino Bravo de Lagunas of Jalapa expressed the same belief.[14]

By virtue of default, then, colonists, who benefitted most directly from the early personal tribute economy, emerged as the principal rivals of the crown for wealth, influence, and power. As a result, royal officials attacked *encomenderos'* power by rigorously and efficiently collecting taxes and by limiting colonists' access to Indian tribute labor and goods. All over New Spain the *encomendero* class declined. From about 1540 to the end of the seventeenth century the number of individuals that held these labor grants steadily dropped.[15]

The crown had an important corporate ally in its struggle with *encomenderos* over control of Indian tribute. Out of the reconquest of the Iberian peninsula grew a strong tradition of church-state cooperation in Spain. That union was transferred and reinforced in Spanish America.[16] Like royal officials, regular Spanish clergy in Mexico opposed individual colonist's control over native tribute. Clerics restricted colonists' access to Indians in two ways. They encouraged royal *corregidores* (Indian agents) and Indian village constables to remove resident natives from Spanish estates, mines, and towns and return them to their villages or to place them under the care of regular clerics. Priests also publicly criticized settlers' treatment of Indians. Corporate political intervention in the conquest-shaped economy resulted. Through the promulgation of the New Laws beginning in 1542, private Ibero-Mexican settlers' roles in the tributary economy diminished. This legislation severely weakened *encomenderos'* economic power and strengthened the fiscal positions of the corporate state and church. In contrast, mendicant orders, nurtured by the labor and material proceeds of Indian tribute, grew tremendously. During the middle of the first phase in the shift from a personal to a corporate tribute economy (1569) just eight hundred friars resided in all New Spain; by 1650 over three thousand regulars administered to the colony.[17]

Between 1550 and 1630 royal tribute and church *diezmos*, or tenths, had multiple effects on the economy. Both encouraged Indians and free Afro-Mexicans to acquire liquid capital. Participation in the expanding trans-Atlantic commerce represented one area wherein the church and crown encouraged individuals to obtain specie for their taxes. This partially explains the rapid ascension of international trade after 1550 and the consequent strengthening of the mercantilistic force within this evolving mixed colonial economic order. But equally important stimuli for fiscal change came from within Mexico itself.

Spaniards on both sides of the Atlantic faced a very serious dilemma from 1550 to 1610. By then Europeans knew of Mexico's fabulous wealth, but Spaniards needed Indians to tap it for them. Production units largely remained in the hands of natives in return for their surrendering a proscribed portion of production to colonists until 1550. Conquerors demanded tribute, and conquered delivered it. Then this "arrangement" went awry when Indians began perishing at a remarkable rate. At the same time as Hispanic cities sprang up, the non-Indians multiplied in inverse proportion to the natives' decline. Spaniards assumed more and more control of depopulated native lands, and as suggested in Chapter 1, much of the production sector passed from Indian to Iberian control. Added to this turn of events was the discovery of new mining areas in lightly inhabited northern regions, especially Guanajuato and Zacatecas. In other words, production potentials in commercial agricultural, urban industrial, and mining sectors of the economy expanded at the very time that the numbers of Indian controllers of these sectors contracted. Iberians' acceptance of control for select sectors of the production side of the economy thus proved a logical response to both European pressures to increase output and native Mexican demographic stress. Generally, this transfer of control appeared greatest during the second half of the sixteenth century. From 1600 onward, Spaniards preoccupied themselves more with consolidating their gains and increasing production on the units they had than with obtaining new ones. This period marked the maturation of commercial agricultural in areas such as the Valley of Mexico, the Tlaxcala region, Morelia, and Veracruz. Most profit went to Spanish merchants and the crown; a lesser amount went to Mexican producers.[18] Two characteristics identified this early colonial stage of mercantilism. International trade emerged as the principal means of profit within the Spanish colonial half of the economy. This was one of two periods in the colonial years when the European core came closest to dominating New Spain's economic growth. Between 1596 and 1620 the value of Mexico's trade with the mother country was nearly as great as that of all other Spanish-American colonies combined.[19]

Circumstances affecting the entire viceroyalty influenced Jalapa as well. Too few Indians meant too little tribute. Initially, this combination translated to near ruin for the district's Spanish community. A 1580 description of Jalapa adequately sums up the situation: "This population has 639 married tributaries; in Moctezuma's time, before the conquest, they say there were thirty-odd thousand tributaries. . . . The Indians support themselves by growing corn and chilies, as well as by fishing and raising chickens and turkeys; they provide a share of these products and their labor to . . . pay their tribute."[20]

For the better part of a century, between about 1550 and 1630, the Spanish-controlled sector in Jalapa fully integrated into Ibero-America's evolving economic order. Scholars coined the term "mercantilism" to describe the new system. Above all, the new order embodied a political economy within which economic policies enhanced the overall power of the imperial state.[21] Iberian merchants, royal bureaucrats, and church leaders cooperated in promoting this new order. Together they endeavored to promote narrow but high commodity production in such areas as central Veracruz, making them dependent on European imports for the supply of many consumer needs. These strategies facilitated an important step away from a nearly feudalistic tribute system toward a more sophisticated capitalistic order.

Mercantilism, however, differed from capitalism in two important respects. First, mercantilism sought profits primarily from trade instead of from production. And second, the Spanish state and merchant class, instead of free competition, directed the operation of the economy.[22] Jalapa's physical environment and European demands drew the province into this new system. Within two generations commercial sugar agriculture became the codriving force, with commerce, in the area's colonial economy. The volume of local production expanded and markets broadened.

Jalapans founded the largest and most productive plantation in all of Mexico during this period. They called it the Santísima Trinidad, and the wealthy Higuera family owned it. The Trinidad could produce up to two hundred tons of refined white sugar per year, most for shipment abroad.[23] This plantation served as Jalapa's production flagship. It led the way to the area's involvement in Atlantic-based mercantilist economy. During this period, individual Spaniards still collected tribute in goods and labor as they had before 1550. Royal and church officials still exacted taxes. But the supply side of the economy had clearly expanded beyond tribute, even at the corporate level.

Between 1550 and 1630 Jalapa economically lived and died on three branches of mercantilist commerce: exchange of sugar for goods, capital, and African slave labor. These Atlantic activities tightly bound the region to Spanish mercantilism until around 1630.

An Incipient Capitalistic Order, 1630–1720

Jalapa and the rest of Mexico retreated from Atlantic commerce almost as dramatically as they rushed into it. During the decade of the 1620s New Spain's portion of the Americas' trade dropped off sharply. Some attribute the reversal to a labor shortage that restricted production levels of exportable items.[24] Others see European forces at work. And some blame evolutionary development in the Mexican economy.[25] What follows from the discussion of economic change in central Veracruz supports the third explanation.

The *diezmos* represents a crude indicator of the value of seventeenth-century Veracruz production. Partial tithe statistics exist for the archbishopric of Puebla, which included central Veracruz. In 1602 the *diezmos* amounted to about 100,000 pesos. Returns for 1607 exceeded $150,000 and remained at this level until 1624. The years from 1624 through 1640 must have witnessed a general rise in the region's commercial production because the amount collected rose to over $200,000. From 1641 to 1656 tax totals fluctuated between a low of 95,000 pesos in 1644 and a high of nearly 277,000 pesos in 1654.

On the basis of these figures a general curve emerges for this period. It suggests relatively high production in the very early 1640s, steep decline during the decade from 1643 to 1652, and strong rise from 1653 to 1656. A drop in production probably took place in the two decades following 1656. By 1675 the amount collected slipped to around 70,000 pesos. *Diezmos* totals remained remarkably stable for the next twenty years but never reached the previous highs of the 1650s.[26] If these *diezmos* figures truly reflect the general prosperity of commercial agriculture in the central eastern quarter of the viceroyalty, then they do not support the idea of a century of depression from 1630 to 1720.

Pierre Berthe notes sugar cultivation's special sensitivity to capitalist forces.[27] Sugar estates represented highly specialized production units. They grew one crop primarily for European market prior to 1630. They could not become self-sufficient and remain sugar *ingenios* or *trapiches* (small-scale estates with animal-driven mills). When Atlantic trade dropped off, sugar estates faced one of three choices in central Veracruz. They could continue to specialize in sugar alone, in which case they quickly found new demand outlets; they could cease emphasizing sugar and diversify production with crops and livestock; or they could fail. Plantations in Jalapa experienced all three of these alternatives.

When Jalapa's involvement in Atlantic commerce fell off, two powerful market forces began to pressure local merchant-planters. Planters needed new markets for their sugar and new sources of operating capital. In effect, planters simply reprioritized old demand and capital markets.

Jalapa had been an integral part of Mexico's international trade for nearly a century by 1630. Early ties developed between the region and other stops along the trade route, most notably with the port of Veracruz to the east and the city of Puebla to the west. Weaker but important socioeconomic linkages also grew between Jalapa, Mexico City, and Tlaxcala. When the seventeenth century shift in Atlantic commerce hit, Jalapans strengthened their existing economic bonds with familiar associates, often kin, in these Mexican areas. Jalapans' creole kin proved no different than administrators of corporate sources of capital, financiers, and merchants throughout the rest, of the viceroyalty. All sought new outlets for their money, products, and expertise. The combination of long-standing economic and blood ties between local Jalapa merchant-planters and big city "money merchants," as Peter Bakewell calls them, facilitated capital market realignments after 1630. Heightened interregional economic ties led to a stronger regional capitalistic economic base. In other words, Jalapa adjusted to decline in Atlantic trade by expanding markets and sources of capital in Puebla and retracting them in Spain. The economy did not collapse after 1630, it simply shifted direction. Production units that did not negotiate this transition failed.

Large plantations, such as the Santísima Trinidad, proved best suited for an expanding market economy. The Trinidad thrived under the mercantilist climate that dominated up to 1630. The estate produced primarily for apparently limitless foreign demand and only secondarily for markets in the Puebla and Mexico valleys. Most of its vast sums of operating capital came from Spain. After 1630 the Trinidad's modus operandi became dysfunctional. Owners and managers made valiant efforts to keep it solvent, but in the end they failed. To hang on to whatever they could of ebbing Atlantic commerce, they hired salaried business agents in the port of Veracruz. These intermediaries diligently sought European buyers for the plantation's sugar. They were usually relatives who marketed a shipment or two before the fleet returned to Spain. Holds of many a ship that sailed every April in the Armada de Barlovento, as the great treasure fleets were called, held sugar from the Santísima Trinidad. Merchants competed for the right to sell this white gold.[28]

In the seventeenth century, when the Atlantic trade began to slip, Don Sebastián de la Higuera, the third in his line to control the Trinidad, began to redirect his marketing efforts away from the coast and toward Puebla. He had many influential relatives there, and as the second most populous city in Mexico, it offered a strong domestic market that lay relatively close at hand. For the next several decades the Higueras and their descendants, the Higuera y Matamoroses, focused their attention on developing Mexican markets for their sugar. They appointed a whole succession of agents in Puebla, sometimes more than one at a time. Unlike sixteenth-century Veracruz wholesalers, these later agents worked year-round trying to peddle the Santísima Trinidad's sugar, some with permanent staffs of four to five. They not only received commissions but also drew salaries. In 1647 Don Sebastián used the lure of retail rights for Trinidad sugar to gain short-term advantage. His cousin Don Fabian Chacón agreed to lend Higuera 12,000 pesos interest-free just for the right to sell Trinidad sugar in Puebla for at least one year. Higuera agreed to supply Chacón with consignments of 400 to 500 arrobas (5 to 7 tons) of refined sweet white sugar per month not to exceed 4,000 arrobas (50 tons) in a year.[29] From the proceeds of his sales Chacón could divert $2,000 annually to operating funds, including $300 a year to rent a warehouse and another undetermined amount for his staff of four aids. The remainder of the $2,000 became his salary. He might clear $1,000 per year. The highest-paid royal official in Jalapa did not earn as much.

The arrangement failed. Even Chacón, with his staff, could not find enough buyers in the Puebla region to absorb Trinidad's output. In 1648, Don Sebastián appointed a second cousin his agent for Puebla. Higuera sent Don Alonso Gutiérrez Sevallos 400 arrobas of sugar on a trial basis. Gutiérrez had a year to sell them and remit the proceeds.

Puebla had clearly become the principal market for the Santísima Trinidad's production by 1650. Just as importantly, it may have become the estate's main source of operating capital. The terms of Higuera's arrangement with Chacón hint at this. The capital connection with Gutiérrez Sevallos proved less obvious. Don Alonso's uncle was a powerful cleric in the Cathedral of Puebla, the Santísima Trinidad's main creditor.[30] Higuera needed all the influence he could get with the cathedral chapter because he had to borrow throughout the century. Running an estate the size of the Trinidad required a great deal of capital, and debts mounted. Creditors, however, could not seize the plantation nor its sister estate, Nuestra Señora de la Concepción. The Higueras had entailed both at the turn of the century.[31] Nonetheless, they remained vulnerable. Despite all of Higuera's market and capital machinations, the two *ingenios* failed.

The Santísima Trinidad, or El Grande, as the locals called it, operated on the basis of economy of scale. This plantation achieved greater output efficiency by engaging in more systemized mass-production methods. Agricultural units such as this produced a great deal for unlimited markets in order to generate operating income and profits. Prior to 1630, such demand existed in Europe, but with the decline in Atlantic commerce, smaller domestic outlets replaced larger European ones. Moreover, the related decline in silver production not only dried up imperial sources of liquid capital but also, to a lesser degree, Mexican ones as well. Both changes proved detrimental to large estates including the Trinidad.

The Higuera's encountered chronic difficulties with cash flow. Ironically, an expensive safeguard to the estate's survival as a single unit presented multiple legal barriers to its access to capital. Entailment prevented division of Santísima Trinidad. Its owners could not sell parcels of land to bring down and offset operating costs, nor could they incorporate the estate for the same reasons. Worse yet, they paid thousands of pesos to the crown each year in return for royal guarantees that the Trinidad's lands would remain intact. In the previous mercantilistic era, bigness and entailment made sense. Although costly, entailment did prevent division. In the post-1630 economic climate, however, bigness and its guarantee (entailment) probably contributed to the ruin of the Trinidad and other plantations. In the evolving freer market economy, big specialized sugar plantations became less competitive because they needed huge and regular infusions of money. Owners of the Trinidad and Concepción, due to the plantations' entailment, could not reduce their economy of scale. The Trinidad became too cumbersome and inflexible to adjust to a rapidly changing seventeenth century economic scene. In just a few generations after 1630 the great estate stood in ruins, a stark monument to bygone economic conditions.[32] Only a handful of its kind survived the seventeenth century.[33]

In Jalapa, midsize to smaller sugar units seemed better able to navigate the changing economic waters of the times. Owners of many of these lesser estates showed remarkable resourcefulness in reacting to changing conditions. They developed two especially useful tactics.[34] When Francisco de la Orduña took up agriculture in 1609, he began very modestly for the son of Jalapa's only notary public. He bought some land to raise sheep and mules and named his *estancia* San Pedro de Buenavista, or colloquially, Mazatlan, after a nearby Indian village. San Pedro's endurance reflected the entrepreneurial skill of Francisco de la Orduña, of his son Diego who succeeded him in the 1620s, and of his grandson Antonio who followed in 1642. A willingness to grow crops besides sugar proved the key to their success. They also raised livestock, corn, and beans. Mazatlan's owners did not continue to specialize in sugar. In addition they peddled livestock to Puebla's growing urban population. Within the district itself, the Orduñas sold corn to more specialized sugar estates, including El Grande, neighboring Pacho, and Nuestra Señora de los Remedios. By not growing too large and too specialized and by diversifying markets, Buenavista survived the shifting economic directions of the mature and late colonial period.

The Orduña family borrowed from Puebla between 1630 and 1720, just as the Higueras had but in much smaller amounts. Mazatlan never offered the collateral the Trinidad and Concepción estates did. The credit the Orduñas received from the Cathedral of Puebla tided them over rough spots but did not bury them in debt. Moreover, the Orduñas did something that the Higueras, because of entailment, could not do to alleviate cash-flow shortages. The Orduñas attracted capital through limited incorporation. Sometime around midcentury they made Don Miguel de Troja and Captain Don Fernando Ruíz de Córdoba Arrellano junior partners in San Pedro. Neither of the new investors actually helped run the estate; that task remained in the hands of the Orduñas. But de Troja's and Ruíz' money proved important in expanding Mazatlan's operations. Also, the plantation remained small enough and its owners flexible enough to adjust to the changing economic climate.

A second example of incorporation involved an estate called El Rosario. Its foundation dates to 1648 in the midst of economic dislocation. What makes the success of El Rosario all the more remarkable is that, unlike Mazatlan, it continued to specialize in sugar. The Rosario's owners chose strategies other than diversification to make the unit competitive.

Part of the explanation for El Rosario's solvency lies in the nature of its incorporation. It involved kin. Each contributed 5,000 pesos, but Don Joseph Sevallos de Burgos emerged as the senior partner and ran the estate. Other investors included his father, Captain Roque Sevallos de Burgos, the highest-ranking royal official in the province (*alcalde mayor*), and his uncle, the previously mentioned Don Juan Gutiérrez de Sevallos, of Puebla. The economic climate of the time magnified the positive effects of the plantation's liquidity. Money remained tight and therefore went further in midcentury than it had earlier. This proved true in the acquisition of land. The Rosario group chose a valley site near the Indian town of Xilotepec, just north of the district capital. It had plenty of running water to irrigate the fields and to power an efficient hydraulic milling system. Fernando de la Calva gave them a good price: 12,000 pesos for nearly 2,500 acres of prime cleared fields. They also did well in the construction of buildings and acquisition of equipment. Master carpenter Don Juan López del Piño and his journeyman Don Juan Mexía finished the physical plant in just over a year. It included a water wheel with its aqueducts and a set of grinding stones complete with gear boxes. López and Mexía also constructed the boiling house with its hearths and cauldrons, the drying house, and the *casco*, or residence, of Don Joseph Sevallos. They erected blacksmith, potter, and carpenter shops. Finally, they built huts for the estate's resident slaves and Indians, many of whom had helped López and Mexía with construction, keeping labor costs down. The total bill came to 3,214 pesos, an excellent price for what the owners got.[35] Rosario's partners incurred fewer debts than their competitors, and they entered the market with a modern, more efficient unit of production. These two factors contributed significantly to the survival of the enterprise.

A Return to Atlantic Dependency, 1720–1820

During the near century that spanned 1630–1720 Jalapa's economy responded more to Mexican than European stimuli. And these new domestic motivations sprang primarily from free-market incentives. Profit motive inspired area merchant planters. They adjusted to altering market, capital, and, as discussed in the next chapter, labor conditions. Regional capitalist rather than European mercantilist forces dominated during this stage of Jalapa's economic growth.[36]

Jalapa's midcolonial move toward capitalism did not completely sever commercial ties with Europe; it just deemphasized them. Early-eighteenth-century events again reversed the direction of Veracruz' economic development, and European influences again overrode local economic influences just as they had done in the 1550–1630 period. As a result of the War of Spanish Succession a new ruling house took control in Spain. From 1713 until the end of the colonial period French-rooted Bourbons claimed sovereignty over the Spanish empire. These rulers initiated sweeping imperial reforms aimed at strengthening Spanish America's economic and political ties with the mother country.[37] Mexico, as the richest of Spain's New World possessions, became a primary target of this design, and central Veracruz weighed heavily in imperial plans.

In 1718, Philip V, first of Spain's Bourbon monarchs, designated Jalapa and Portebello, on the isthmus, as the two largest trade-fair sites in all Spanish America. With the advent of the first fair in 1722, the village of Jalapa became a clearing house for goods from three continents. On the average, vessels that plied this trade held over five thousand tons of merchandise.[38] At a time when prime agricultural land sold for eight pesos per hectare, a mule for fifteen, and a modest stone house and urban lot for two hundred, the total value of merchandise exchanged at each of these events ranged in the millions of pesos.[39] For example, the recorded worth of European goods alone at the 1757, 1773, and 1778 expositions totaled 23 million, 26 million, and 27 million pesos respectively.[40] Items from the Far East and other parts of the New World carried at least equal value. Fifty million pesos represents a conservative estimate of the average worth of goods that changed hands in this small provincial capital. The sheer magnitude of commerce meant that individuals at all levels of the urban society, from the poorest laborer to the wealthiest entrepreneur, felt its impact.

During fair times people and materials stretched the physical limits of the town. Nonperishable commodities filled the streets for want of space to store them. Armed guards watched over them twenty-four hours a day, seven days a week. Jalapa's streets may not have been paved with gold, but they were often stacked with silver. Merchants and officials arranged bars of the metal in neat piles on the town square. Less durable commodities including silk, porcelain, spices, textiles, books, firearms, tools, cochineal, vanilla, cacao, and sugar filled all available covered space.[41]

The fairs operated intermittently. Spanish officials intended to celebrate them every two years and have them last an average of three months. Between 1736 and 1756 none took place. However, royal officials held five during the subsequent generation ending in 1776.[42]

Most of the wealth exchanged during these events did not stay in Jalapa. It left with the merchants that departed after each fair. Yet, some capital inevitably found its way into the local economy and encouraged the expansion of the area's sugar industry. In 1746 five hundred individuals resided on Jalapa's sugar plantations; by 1777 the number more than doubled to nearly 1,300.[43] Moreover, the fairs renewed interest in European markets. By 1750 eight plantations produced for export: Mazatlan, Almolonga, L'Encero, La Orduña, Lucas Martin, Pacho, San Antonio, and San José.[44]

Then the crown began to rethink its trade policies. Rumors spread about the possible abolishment of the convoy system and the Jalapa trade festivals with it. By 1772 everyone involved in commerce knew that the fairs would soon end. Investment dried up, and commercial estates fell on hard times. In 1773 Almolonga went up for sale. Its owner had died, and his heirs wanted to divest themselves of a capital-draining enterprise on the eve of potential financial collapse for the district. They were not the only uneasy ones. Few serious buyers showed interest in the property. At that time, Jalapa did not appear like a place to invest capital.

After several months of waiting for a buyer, the heirs decided to lease Almolonga. They clearly saw this as a temporary arrangement because at the same time they tried to liquidate the estate's slaves and equipment. Under these conditions the plantation's upkeep inevitably suffered. Renters faced the insecurity of losing their leases through sale of the property. They had to cope with the reality of steadily diminishing stock and slaves. These conditions encouraged tenants to squeeze as much profit as possible from the arrangement and ignore the long-range effects of their actions. Neighboring San Antonio fell into disrepair under similar circumstances.[45] In the end, two full years passed before the heirs finally sold Almolonga. By this time it lay in near ruin. The sellers had to shut it down and renovate, but the repairs did not last. In 1788 Don Lino Carraza, a Spanish merchant who came to Jalapa on a trade *flota*, finally bought the estate. He had to invest large sums acquired from an inheritance and his wife's dowry before Almolonga could resume production.[46]

Ancient Pacho proved the only *ingenio* to weather these economic hard times in relatively good shape. The tenacity and hard work of its indomitable owner, a Spaniard by the name of Miguel de Iriate, helped. Like Carraza, Iriarte left a career in Atlantic commerce to become a planter and public official in Jalapa. Unlike Carraza, however, Iriarte retained good European-market connections through his brother José, a Seville merchant. This tie offers the most probable explanation for Pacho's remarkable stability.[47]

Economic insecurity gripped Jalapa from the mid-1770s until the mid-1790s. Then Atlantic commerce once again paced commercial agricultural expansion that lasted a generation. From 1794 onward conditions in the world sugar market offered a very attractive outlet for latent investment potential in Jalapa. Slave rebellion broke out on the western half of the island of Santo Domingo and did not end until Haitian independence in 1804. Haiti had produced more sugar than any place in the world up until 1796. The rebellion shut down its plantations. As a result, Haiti's former markets in Europe opened to other producers, and prices driven up by scarcity provided added incentive to grow sugar for European markets.[48] Concurrently, Cuba's fledgling sugar industry experienced difficulty. Hostilities between Spain and England during the Napoleonic Wars disrupted the island's trans-Atlantic shipping. Cuba also reaped poor harvests between 1795 and 1799.[49] In response to all these dislocations in the supply side of the world sugar economy, Jalapa investors, like those in other Mexican sugar-growing regions, put their money into plantations. As Humboldt observed just a few years later in 1803: "The cultivation of sugar cane has made such rapid progress these last years that the exportation of sugar at the port of Veracruz actually amounts to more than half a million of arrobas."[50]

A late Bourbon reform added further impetus to the resurgence of Jalapa's sugar industry. In 1794, Charles IV lifted the royal ban on American production of sugar brandy. Until that time the law required sugar growers to export molasses to Spain for distillation into spirits, which Spanish merchants then returned to Mexico for sale. The king replaced these restrictive trade regulations with a simple tax on each barrel produced in the New World. This proved advantageous for both the crown and Mexican sugar producers. England's navy made the old system inoperative. The new tax system avoided the risky and expensive Atlantic exchanges while at the same time providing needed capital to support and maintain royal colonial government during times of disrupted communications. Most importantly from the perspective of Jalapan sugar interests, it legally opened to Mexicans an important, previously closed dimension of the sugar by-product market. Jalapa growers found this last concession especially beneficial. The darker, less-refined sugar they produced with their middle- to small-sized mills proved ideal for liquor manufacture. Now Jalapa planters could convert their lower-quality sugar into brandy for both Mexican and international markets.[51] Aquardiente imports into New Spain dropped from 29,695 barrels in 1802 to only 7,999 in 1808. Import levels climbed again between 1811 and 1819, but this almost certainly reflected the effects of the War for Independence. After the conflict the pre-1810 trend toward increased levels of production for home and international consumption continued, and the colony's balance of trade improved. In 1824 Mexico imported a mere 2,920 barrels of sugar brandy, one-tenth of the total for 1802.[52]

Jalapan investors took part in the late colonial and early national period sugar boom. The number of operating plantations in the district doubled between 1791 and 1813. Old mills including the Ingenio Chico and Rosario reopened, and new plantations came into existence—the Arenal, Esquilón, Pocapa, and Zozocola. Most new estates produced on a small scale, about a hundred barrels of brandy per year. The Zozocola, owned by Don Miguel Fernández provides a typical example. From April through September of 1814 it averaged just under eleven barrels of aquardiente per month.

Assessed value of the large commercial agricultural units within the district rose to nearly three million pesos by 1813. Hoarded specie flowed into circulation reviving mercantile activity. Producers marketed in Spain, in such interior urban centers as Perote and Puebla, and locally.[53] Stepped-up commercial activity, in town, stimulated the growth of jobs and formation of capital. Jalapa served as an important link in Mexico's chain of international commerce just as it had since the sixteenth century. A glance at the parish death records verifies that. They list many an anonymous *casta* muleteer from Mexico City, Valladolid, Puebla, Querétaro, Guanajuato, Tlaxcala, Guadalajara, and even Guatemala who died at some point along the royal road that wound through the district.[54] Men including Don Francisco Franceschi and Dionicio González lent money to "friends," with interest of course. Modest urban construction occurred for the first time in twenty years. The town council authorized the expansion of its meeting hall and the construction of a new jail. Members ordered the construction of by-ways to link expanding *barrios* to the urban complex. The city leaders even debated drainage projects for the low-lying *barrios* on the eastern fringes of town. In the end, they voted against this last improvement as too costly. Nobody of great importance lived there, just a group of *castas* and Indians; they would have to settle for roads.[55] Retail trade within the capital grew because of increased demands from prospering residents.

Soon after 1810 heightened commercial activity again fled the province. Low but persistent levels of independence fighting occurred in the area from 1811 to 1821. Actually, less disruption occurred than in many other areas. The worst economic consequence concerned special taxes to support a garrison charged with protecting travel along the royal road. Merchants and planters complained bitterly about levees for troops who did nothing but patrol the royal road and sit in their barracks while small bands of rebels operated uncontested in the countryside.

Most of the district's residents did not join the actual fighting for either side. As neutrals, they found themselves caught in the middle of the conflict. Royal officials taxed them in their towns, and rebels taxed them in the countryside. The monthly bill for soldiers totaled 4,000 pesos. And to make matters worse, international commerce, one of the area's main sources of capital, became erratic. Periodically, rural sugar plantations had to close down. Insurgents forced Almolonga to suspend operations for a full two years in retaliation for Don Lino Carraza's alleged Spanish sympathies. Communications between the rural and urban sectors broke down and sugar production suffered. Francisco Franceschi complained about having to close down several of his plantations while his remaining few estates could barely produce enough to cover operating costs. Fernando Pacheco could no longer continue his mercantile activities for lack of capital. He blamed his problems on the monthly war tax. He claimed to have lost money he had lent out because his debtors did not have the specie to even keep up with their interest payments. Business at his town store fell off for lack of stock. He had to quarter and feed royal soldiers in his home while his aquardiente factory stood idle for want of cane to distill. In short, Franceschi's, Pacheco's, and the district's prosperity waned during the rebellion.

Generally, however, local entrepreneurs were not quite as destitute as they claimed. Most of the specie they lost in taxes eventually made its way back into their pockets. After all, they supplied the provisions that the taxes paid for. They lost products and labor not capital. In fact, most investors withdrew their money from circulation. The area's internationally linked sugar industry became the principal casualty of the independence conflict. By February 1815, only three plantations still produced sugar: Orduña, Coatepec, and Ingenio Chico (Estanzuela).[56]

In the end, the war caused more disruption than destruction. People complained about the loss of contact with the rural areas but said little about loss of life and property. Few fled the district or sought refuge in the urban center guarded by the royal garrison because rural towns and villages did not become battle sites.[57] Royalists abandoned them to insurgent forces too small to occupy them. Under these circumstances the countryside remained a relatively safe place if one remained neutral in the fighting, and most did.

In 1817 the crown pulled many of its troops out of Jalapa, easing the local tax burden. From that date onward the town council devoted less and less attention to the matter, as they again turned to ordinary civic matters, such as funds for the Women's Hospital and those drainage ditches for the newer town streets in the barrios.[58] The next four years leading up to independence may have been uneasy, but they were not bloody. Actual violence in the district of Jalapa remained relatively light compared to other areas, for example, Córdoba, the Bajío, Morelos, and Oaxaca. Census reports indicate growth rates well above pre-1720 levels.[59]

When independence came in the spring of 1821, it had limited effect on Jalapa. The only noticeable adjustments were the familiar realignment of markets. Jalapa's aguardiente continued to meet Mexican demand, but its international markets shifted from Seville to New Orleans.[60] By the end of the year the new national town council collected 630 pesos in taxes on brandy production. At three pesos per barrel this amount meant that local estates legally produced 210 barrels. During the following year production rose to 250 barrels. And by 1823 planters paid taxes on 271 barrels.[61] Local notarial records also reveal heightened interest in the industry. Fig-

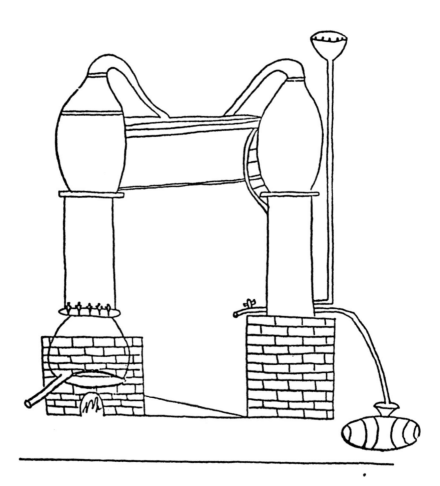

Figure 2. Steam-operated aguardiente distillery, Jalapa, 1830 (a tracing from ANJ, vol. 1830, leaves 255v–258). Unfortunately, the
source did not explain how the device worked. It did, however,
describe the materials used in fabrication. Both tanks were made
of copper, as was the tubing; the furnace door was made of iron.
The builders guaranteed that the device would distill at least eight
barrels of aguardiente per day.

ure 2 is a tracing of an 1830 set of plans for a new machine to distill aguardiente by steam. Don Antonio José Paredo ordered it, and Don Francisco Azcorve contracted to build the still for two thousand pesos including parts and labor. Both were Jalapa merchants.

Conclusion

John Coatsworth places the Bourbon Reform period in proper economic context. He explains that heightened imperial regulations encouraged resubordination of Mexico's economy to the greater Atlantic commercial system between 1720 and 1820. The reforms discouraged entrepreneurial activity in the domestic economy that had flourished during the previous century. Spain placed great emphasis on the export of such products as silver, cochineal, and, in central Veracruz, sugar for European markets. As in the second stage of economic development (1550–1630) the state drained off many of Jalapa's material and labor resources. These processes quickened with the Napoleonic Wars (1799–1814), and the negative economic effects for Mexico mounted.[62]

The relationship between the state and local economic development in Jalapa generally supports Coatsworth's interpretation of the Bourbon era. In this regional setting the reforms ushered in a greater political and economic presence of the Iberian imperial system. From the middle of the eighteenth century onward, royal planners sought to increase revenue from the colonies. Initially, Bourbon monarchs tried to achieve this end by more diligently applying the policies of their Hapsburg predecessors. For example, Philip V restricted trade linkages in order to gain greater control over the commerce. The Jalapa trade fair grew out of this early strategy. Thus, the district became unusually tied to measures that ran counter to the traditionally perceived spirit of the Bourbon Reforms—freer trade. However, when the reforms are seen as means rather than as ends, the apparent anomaly of the Jalapa trade fairs becomes more explainable. The trade monopoly and the freer trade that followed it represented different approaches to the same goal, the increase of revenues from Spanish America to the mother country.[63]

In any case, these eighteenth-century switches in Spanish trade policy had more impact in Jalapa than in many other settings within the viceroyalty. First the trade fairs accelerated local economic change. Then from 1777–1793, when market and supply links with Europe weakened, Jalapans again strengthened ties with Mexican cities, for example, Puebla and Mexico. To achieve these economic realignments, Jalapan entrepreneurs used social leverage. They enlisted the cooperation of their creole neighbors and relatives living in other parts of New Spain just as they had during the 1630–1720 period. In using social bonds to strengthen economic ones, they followed a common pattern throughout the colonial American experience. Creole kin from Maine to Argentina behaved similarly during times of economic stress. They helped each other reprioritize markets, reorganize production, and find new sources of capital. These adjustments proved difficult and required a good deal of innovativeness. Merchant planters experimented in response to new situations. Days of heady expansion and unlimited supplies of labor had passed. Afro-Jalapans got caught up in this period of trial and error. Their experiences during the late seventeenth and early eighteenth centuries became more uneven than in the two previous stages of Jalapa's economic development. In this position of uncertainty some of them enjoyed improved conditions, others did not, but all labored mightily, whether by choice or not, to keep the region's economy afloat.

4.

Afro-Veracruzanos and Changing Colonial Labor Patterns

FROM 1519 TO 1550 in central Veracruz persons of African descent helped to sustain three production sectors of the regional economy through coercion as slaves. They toiled in the carrying trade, in urban service occupations, and in the sugar industry. Some did so within the small town of Jalapa. There they acted as domestic servants in the eight to ten European households.[1] Virtually no record of these slaves' experience has survived. A larger number of bondspeople labored in the countryside on the area's sugar estates.

Some have claimed that certain aspects of sugar culture, including production modes, occupational divisions, and work patterns, remained both constant and universal across the Americas. One of these universalities involved the use of African slave labor. Herbert Klein has noted that sugar plantations relied so heavily on slave labor that they absorbed around 40 percent of all American bondspeople by the middle of the eighteenth century. Klein went so far as to say that "no American society seemed capable of exporting sugar except with use of African slave workers."[2]

On the other hand, sugar's heavy reliance on slave labor represented somewhat of an anomaly. Plantation agriculture required a complex system for integrating "technology, management, and labor."[3] These conditions appear incompatible with slave labor because they depend so heavily on the cooperation of the labor force. Workers needed such incentives as wages to integrate into complex production modes. Slaves, because of their bondage, should have lacked the necessary will to function within sugar culture. Yet they clearly did throughout the New World. In early central Veracruz, sugar functioned as an exception to the existing production rule. Most units of production remained in the hands of tribute laborers (Indians). Thus, little contradiction existed except in the fledgling sugar industry. A feudal tribute relationship between production and labor modes represented the norm during the "personal tribute" years (1519–1550) described in the last chapter. During this early period forced African labor and Indian sugar workers probably co-operated because of a combination of positive and negative incentives, close managerial supervision, standardization of labor tasks, and a certain degree of socioeconomic cooptation.[4] Unfortunately, one can only speculate this because of the paucity of surviving records from the first half of the sixteenth century.

Sugar proved the only Veracruz industry that heavily utilized African slaves at this time. Indian tribute labor also performed plantation tasks from the outset, as did *indios naborías*, persons who left their villages and became permanent resident workers on sugar estates. Indian slaves comprised a third category of native labor. Finally, a few Spaniards assumed managerial roles in the labor force.

In sum, a variegated labor force sustained sugar during this early period of development. Tribute, slave, and resident Indian laborers supplied the bulk of the workers, but they proved ill-suited to many of the specialized work needs of sugar plantations because of the nature of their labor contracts with Spaniards. This type of agriculture employed a great deal of technology, especially in the refining process. Grinding mills required sophisticated combinations of human, animal, or even more technologically complex water power to turn millstones and presses. Growers had to build and maintain ovens along with huge copper cauldrons, skimming tools, drying forms, and a whole series of winches and pulleys. These endeavors led to other trained occupations such as blacksmithing, carpentry, and pottery making. Finally, the estate needed carts and draught animals to transfer sugar from one stage of operation to the next. The fabrication, maintenance, and use of these items required a great deal of know-how. Mistakes cost time and money. Indian slaves might have acquired these skills but for two reasons. They, like the general Indian population, died in large numbers until about 1610, and as a result the crown abolished native slavery in 1542.[5] Resident Indians proved too few and vulnerable to rely on. Tribute Indians did work to a degree. They successfully performed most of the menial tasks. They, however, proved ill-suited to the more skilled jobs. *Encomienda* and *repartimiento* Indians lived in their villages and rotated Spanish estate service.[6] Their transiency within the labor regimen discouraged the acquisition and retention of necessary knowledge that went into producing sugar.

Due to the loss of resident Indian slave laborers and the shortcomings in rotating tribute workers, Spaniards began to train African slaves in sugar agriculture. Cortés himself probably integrated African slaves into the Veracruz labor force sometime before 1530. In 1534 he imported one group of Africans for his mill at San Andrés Tuxtla (in southern Veracruz). Later he had more sent to his great estate of Tlaltenango in Cuernavaca.[7] Veracruz emerged as a center for the early industry. New estate owners followed developing labor precedent. The royal accountant Don Rodrigo de Albornoz founded a plantation near Cempoala in 1535. He purchased 150 slaves to work it.[8] During that next decade Spaniards built five more estates in the Orizaba region including a huge plantation belonging to Viceroy Antonio de Mendoza. He simply called it the Ingenio de Orizaba, or Orizaba Mill. Its generic name was appropriate given its huge size. This ingenio became the working place and home to over a hundred African slaves.[9] Iberians founded other pre-1550 Veracruz plantations at Rinconada, Tepecuan, and Capotitlan.[10] Three things made these enterprises somewhat unique for the times: they required Spaniards to make huge capital investments in production units at a time when Europeans relied on the Indian production sector; the plantations produced for profit in both European and Mexican markets at a time when Spaniards needed only to collect Indian Tribute to prosper; and estate owners utilized a mixed Indian-African work force when the former was virtually free and the latter was very expensive.[11]

Despite the cost, slave labor appeared to have advantages over Indian labor. For one thing Spaniards thought African workers more productive than indigenous workers. Because of their slave status, which made them more exploitable, and because of their demographic characteristics at least as far as longevity, gender, and age were concerned, Spaniards saw African slaves as individually capable of more output than Indian or casta workers.[12]

In balance, however, the personal tribute stage of economic development operated by the will of the conquerors. Exigencies of the market place, such as labor and production efficiency, counted for little in governing feudalistic economic conditions that prevailed in the area during the early colonial years.[13] But the impact of Spanish will proved limited. The European-influenced tribute economy never completely eclipsed the relatively independent and larger Indian peasant economy. Many of the trappings of modern fiscal orders remained absent or not well developed. For example, the use of specie came slowly. This symbolic medium of exchange remained relatively unimportant among native peoples for years after Spanish-Indian contact. When Europeans first introduced coins to Mexico City natives, they threw them into the lake that surrounded the metropolis. It took a generation before Indians overcame their skepticism and used specie. Even then, they merely allowed it to function alongside pre-Columbian barter in their commercial exchanges.[14] Sugar culture, mining, and *obraje* industries represented important but narrow enclaves of European-based economic influence. Thus, the period from 1521 to 1549 witnessed a mixed European-shaped, indigenous-controlled economy. During the next phase of development, change accelerated resulting in fuller growth of the European-based dimension of the economy at the expense of the native Indian one.

Corporate Tribute, Mercantilism, and African Labor, 1550–1630

Afro-Veracruzanos' role within the mixed corporate-tribute–mercantilist phase of economic development grew between 1550 and 1630. They filled a perceived void in the labor pool at a time when the Indian population reached its nadir. More than labor-saving technology, more than Spanish workers, more than regulated Indian labor, Africans plugged the gaps left in the work force created by dying Indians. This represented a time when the mercantilist-driven European economy more fully exploited the tribute-driven Veracruz economy.

African slave labor had many attractive features for this stage of economic development. The coercive nature of slavery remained compatible with the feudalistic tribute system operating in central Veracruz. At the same time, certain features of slave labor made it more productive than Indian tribute labor. For one thing, slaves proved better suited to the region's protoindustrial sugar culture. Through the Atlantic slave trade, masters could choose workers capable of producing the greatest number of foot-pounds of labor: young adult males.[15] These age and gender characteristics appeared in the post-1550 ranks of Cortés' Cuernavaca slaves.[16] There, males outnumbered females by a margin of two to one, and over 50 percent of both sexes fell between fifteen and forty years of age.[17] On the Ingenio de Orizaba, male slaves outnumbered female slaves by nearly the same margin, but the percentage of the fifteen to forty year olds proved even greater. This highly productive age group comprised over 60 percent of the slave population.[18]

Herbert Klein adds general support to the notion of efficient slave labor. He states that in all Latin America and the Caribbean even slave children worked in the fields alongside their parents, as did aged bondspersons. In his estimation, 80 percent of the slave community, regardless of age and gender, participated in the work force, as opposed to 55 percent of the population in current Third World societies.[19]

By 1608 two hundred African slaves toiled on the Santísima Trinidad near Jalapa. They represented the mainstay of the resident work force performing most skilled and arduous tasks involved in the delicate refining process.[20] During planting and harvesting times perhaps as many as six hundred nonresident Indian tribute and wage laborers augmented blacks' work.[21] Another local estate, San Miguel de Almolonga, produced a coarser form of less-refined sugar called *piloncillo* for export as early as 1572.[22] It too employed a combination of resident African slaves and seasonal Indian wage earners. Seven or eight other estates operated within the region. All required massive capital inputs for construction and operation; all produced the same commercial crop; all depended on resident African slave labor to perform skilled tasks; and all sold primarily to European markets.[23]

A combination of the demographic crisis within the Indian population and the imperial state's response to that crisis dictated African slave labor's expanded involvement in economic development. This mix of local demographic and outside political pressures also altered the nature of economic growth.

Local and Atlantic forces transformed other dimensions of the regional economy. Europeans began to assume increasing control over the production sector in such industries as sugar. As for markets, Spaniards, through mercantilism, enormously expanded the flow of items in both directions across the Atlantic. Finally, Iberians began to encourage the integration of Indians into the specie-driven colonial economy. As in the early period, the years 1550–1630 witnessed greater levels of activity that fit Wallerstein's profile of a peripheral satellite to a core European economy. Afro-Veracruzanos would continue to play an important labor role in the establishment of the postmercantilist economy. Without them, central Veracruz could not have reached its second (1550–1630) plateau of economic growth as quickly as it did, nor could the colony have effected the transition into its next stage of economic development.

An Incipient Capitalist Order and African Labor, 1630–1720

In Jalapa's urban capital Afro-related persons performed a wide variety of economic functions during the middle colonial period. Most, like Pablo Alfero, continued to serve as domestics. Alfero spent his entire life as a servant in the household of Doña Ana and Don Sebastián de Acosta. In her will Doña Ana thanked Alfero for his long and faithful service. She charged her niece and principal heir to keep him in his old age.[24]

Other slaves worked in less personal capacities for their urban masters. Many labored as stevedores shuttling goods along the winding and steep roads of the hillside city. Matheo, a slave of Doña Magdalena Díaz, did this. He turned his daily wages over to his mistress to support them both. At times town slaves worked alongside Indian wage earners. Two unnamed bondspeople staffing an inn on the central plaza did this. Indians of the provincial capital's *barrio* of Santiago corporately owned the establishment. In 1654 they rented the property to an individual merely identified as Antonio Luis. The absence of a surname indicated he was probably not Spanish, but beyond that one can only guess his racial and ethnic background. Antonio added his two slaves to the staff of the inn and agreed to pay 170 pesos every four months to the Indian *barrio*. Santiago's governor and town council acted on behalf of the Indians in the deal. Juan Díaz de Cueva interpreted for them.[25] The sum represented a large amount of money, indicating that the enterprise must have been a lucrative one. Exactly what role Antonio Luis' slaves played in the operation remains unclear, but they probably had importance since neither of the two Indian servants spoke Spanish. That left Antonio and his two slaves to interact with the paying Spanish-speaking guests.

Some urban slaves held skilled occupations. Spanish carpenters, shoemakers, masons, blacksmiths, and the like would often buy bondservants and train them. Acquisition of expertise tremendously enhanced the profitability of a slave's labor. Juan Baptista Molinar, a Spanish carpenter, apprenticed a number of his slaves. He hired two of them out to Captain Don Sebastián de la Higuera to make repairs on his *ingenio*, Concepción. They worked an entire year, and the bill came to 2,353 pesos, over four times their combined value.[26]

A few bondspeople held positions as household and body servants to rich Spaniards. In these capacities slaves lived and worked in the same physical surroundings as their owners. They may not have had luxurious accommodations, but they probably enjoyed better ones than those of the poorer class of any race.

A number of urban slaves worked as family units. On rare occasions these servant families enjoyed near kin status with their masters. Ana, a creole slave of the wealthy merchant Don Fernando Ybañes, experienced this type of close relationship. She bore four children under the Ybañes roof, and their owners never sold one of them. They all joined the Ybañes' household staff. In her deathbed testament Doña María Jacinta Ybañes expressed the bonds of affection that existed between her family and Ana's. She used such terms as love and loyalty. They would belong to no other. She freed them all and left Ana 300 pesos in cash along with a number of domestic items so the freed woman could set up her own household.[27]

Slaves of less-wealthy masters usually led less-secure lives. Widowed Spanish women found it especially difficult to care for their bondservants. They commonly rented their slaves to others and lived off the fees. Slaves' tasks and living conditions changed with each new contract, requiring frequent adjustments and separations from family. Don Juan Ochoa rented Antonio from Doña Felipa Hernández to help care for the animals he used in his mule train. He agreed to pay Doña Felipa, his widowed mother-in-law, twenty-five pesos per year for the use of the slave but instead tried to exchange the service of two Indian servants in lieu of the money. Doña Felipa was furious. She needed pesos not servants, and she demanded her slave back. Ochoa finally returned him ill and in poor condition. In this case both master and slave had suffered from a renting arrangement. Doña María Hernández who hired out Felipe de la Cruz to a master shoemaker named Bartholomé de Olivera had a better experience. Olivera employed the slave from January through July, 1647. He provided de la Cruz with food and shelter and paid Hernández seventeen pesos. Doña María's slave returned healthy and ready to assume his next money-earning task.

Renting sometimes gave slaves the opportunity to acquire some capital and property of their own. Doña Anna de Vargas leased her slave Juana to another household for domestic work. Somehow prior to the arrangement Juana had acquired a cow. With the consent of her owner, she sold butter and other dairy products from the animal to her renting masters and kept the profits.[28]

In sum, rented slaves and their owners had uneven experiences. Sometimes all profited from the arrangements. The level of a slave's skill, and therefore his or her value, probably enhanced the likelihood of this happening. Indeed, in many instances renting might have brought a slave more physical security than a financially overburdened master's house could afford. At times it even created the opportunity for a slave to make some profit on the side, as Juana's experience demonstrates. Just as likely, however, slave and owner suffered from these transactions. Renting represented a risky business, one most often practiced by absentee owners or masters with limited financial resources. Bondsperson and owner always ran the risk that an irresponsible or unscrupulous renter would damage life and property. On balance, the drawbacks of renting probably outweighed the benefits. In all probability, renting represented a practice that sprang more from necessity than from choice.

Masters used slaves for other things besides labor. Sometimes owners met obligations of various sorts with them. Don Juan Martín de Obreo gave a slave as the most valuable item in his daughter's dowry. Doña Alonsa de Bargas used her slave, María, to pay a debt she owed to Captain Don Carlos Samano y Quinones, the owner of the ingenio of Almolonga. This must have been a distasteful task because María served as the personal body servant of Doña Alonsa's daughter. All three women realized the changes that lay in store for María. She would exchange household for field labor.[29]

Seventeenth-century opinions about the efficiency of slave labor help explain why it did not disappear after the area's involvement in the Atlantic trade dropped off. Jalapan entrepreneurs recognized the need for efficiency in the face of more competitive market conditions that subsequently came into play after 1630. Most still equated efficient production with higher profits. As a result, some masters hung on to their slaves. They pushed them to increase labor yields at a time when they, the owners, appeared less capable of meeting slaves' material needs and even less capable of replacing servants who inevitably perished or became debilitated as a result of the intensified work regimen. Other masters seemed to grasp more fully the changing economic conditions of the times and allowed their slave forces to adjust with them. The Samano y Quinones family that owned Almolonga allowed others to literally run their slaves into the ground during the seventeenth century, probably because of the death of the estate's founder, Captain Don Juan de Samano y Quinones, in 1642. Without a son, his widow first hired someone to administer the plantation.[30] When this arrangement failed, she decided to rent Almolonga. Tenants worked the estate for much of the rest of the century. By 1700 Almolonga lay in disrepair with an all but decimated slave community. The Cevallos y Burgos family, who owned Mazatlan, seemed more enlightened. They paid much more attention to the physical well-being of their slaves, and as a result both their bondspeople and their estate emerged from the seventeenth century in relatively good shape.[31]

On balance, most owners acted prudently. They recognized the efficiency of bondspeople on the one hand and the expense of replacing them on the other. As a result, owners generally cared for the physical needs of their slaves. Moreover, when Jalapa began to abandon the Atlantic slave trade, masters accepted the fact that they could no longer control the sex and age distributions of their workers. Consequently, the slave population, through natural increase, transformed itself from an adult, male-dominated community to one that more closely mirrored the gender and age characteristics of the broader society.[32] By the end of the seventeenth century, domestic rather than international forces shaped Afro-Jalapans' demographic profile. The Almolonga and Mazatlan estates reflected these changes. Each moved toward a balance of the sexes but in different ways. Almolonga accomplished the change by replacing dead slaves with newly purchased women; Mazatlan achieved it through natural increase. In 1675 and 1691 Almolonga's renters had to account for the death of first eight and then fourteen bondservants. These were not aged slaves that had passed away naturally. All but two were young, either children or laborers in their prime years, between fifteen and thirty. Cecilia died at eighteen, Bernarda at twenty-three, Pedro at six, Valantín at four, and Juana at infancy. Given the description of the other slaves on the *ingenio*, the community obviously lived under duress. Geronima had lost an arm, possibly in the presses or perhaps to infection. Several had no sight in one eye, María Cochichi lay sick and near death at thirty-five, so did María Bomba, thirty-four, and Luisa, twelve. The renters appeared more interested in their short-term profit than the long-term benefits of a healthy slave population. When slaves died, these temporary masters invariably replaced them with women undoubtedly because female slaves cost less.[33]

At the outset of the eighteenth century, Almolonga appeared a well-kept and efficiently operating sugar *ingenio*. It had produced sugar since at least 1620. In that year eighteen slaves resided on the estate: thirteen adult males, four adult women, and one newborn child. All but the creole infant son of Balthasar from the Cape Verde region and María from Biafara were native-born Africans.[34] Half a century later, in 1675, fifty-six slaves lived on Almolonga: thirty-one males, twenty-five females, and twelve children. Only a dozen had made the middle passage from Africa. By the last quarter of the seventeenth century, creole slave families dominated the estate's slave community. All the adult women had husbands. Their sons and daughters comprised most of the younger individuals in the slave quarters. These families, however, lacked physical security. Late-seventeenth-century financial exigencies created an environment that threatened slaves' well-being. The estate's demographic characteristics changed, making the slave community appear more like the surrounding broader population's. This similarity, however, masked conditions there. Natural selection alone did not shape Almolonga's demographics: human abuse did so as well. In any case, both represented domestic rather than international factors.

Generally, however, slave populations on most other plantations evolved without the hardship of excessive and deliberate physical mistreatment. Natural forces averaged out the more extraordinary demographic characteristics of slave communities, for example, uneven sex and age distributions. Slowly but inexorably the Afro-Jalapans became more like the broader society in these respects. Earlier, the slave trade caused Jalapa's unnaturally high ratio of males to females. After 1620, district owners had to rely on mother nature in these matters, and she proved far less discriminating than they.

The trend toward sexual balance did undercut the productive capacity of the district's slave population, but the shift toward more natural age distribution reduced productivity even more. Over 80 percent (142 of 177) of the slaves sold in Jalapa between 1601 and 1620 fell into the age range of 15 to 40, persons at the peak of their productivity. The slave community's evolving age structure after 1620 revealed a growing problem for planters. From birth until age five slaves did not contribute to the labor force, they took from it. They depended on others for their maintenance. Very old slaves, eighty and over, also drew out more than they put into the economy. In between these two age extremes fell several other groups that added varying levels of output to the plantation's overall productivity. Area slaves' output began to drop after about 1620. Combined percentages of dependent children and aged slaves went from 8 to 17 percent.[35] Apparently, one of the few remaining advantages of slave over alternative labor systems in the middle colonial period involved the more fixed status of slaves—they stayed physically bound to the work site. Most Indians lived in native villages. Although *castas* did often reside on rural estates, they were not numerous enough before the late seventeenth century to meet all resident labor demands. But this too changed along with slave sex ratios and age distribution. Reflection on the Santísima Trinidad's altering composition of resident population itself displays patterns that had broad implications for the changing utility of the slave labor. For one thing, the free population grew while the slave population constricted. Within the 1640–1659 generation, over 50 percent of the estates' residents held free status; by the 1680s the percentage of non-slaves climbed to over 70 percent.[36]

The growing number of free persons correlated with shifts in the racial make-up of the plantation community. *Castas'* (mestizos, mulattos, and *pardos*) representation rose significantly. Slavery and the color line faded on the Trinidad. If such things happened on El Grande they probably occurred on smaller estates as well.[37] Slave labor became less productive and cost effective due to demographic changes within and without the slave community that occurred after Jalapa's withdrawal from the Atlantic slave trade. This must have helped precipitate the decision to replace coerced slaves with paid Indians and castas.

Nevertheless, bondspersons remained an important segment of the seventeenth-century labor force. Slaves continued to perform crucial tasks in the production of sugar. They remained the master sugar makers on such *ingenios* as Mazatlan, El Rosario, Los Remedios, and Almolonga throughout the century. For example, Pedro, a creole, had his own hut on the last-mentioned plantation. He lived there with Luisa, also a creole, and their three children. Pedro oversaw the entire sugar-making process. He functioned as the most important and skilled worker on the estate. Another native-born slave named Balthazar lived there also in his family hut not far from Pedro's. Balthazar acted as Almolonga's master carpenter. Thomas worked as a journeyman carpenter under Balthazar's supervision. Anton, an aging *bozal*, still functioned as field supervisor despite his nearly eighty years. Juan Veracruz, a creole *pardo* (of mixed African-Indian heritage) slave, labored as a potter. He threw and fired the conical clay forms into which boiled and refined syrup flowed, dried, and hardened into granulated sugar. Finally, another creole named Joseph Ganan served as the resident blacksmith. He forged and repaired needed metal items just as his deceased father had before him. The estate manager hired seasonal workers to perform less-skilled operations. They appeared during clearing, planting, and harvesting times, but they toiled under the supervision of these resident slaves. Almolonga's creole bondspeople worked hard at the only life and home most of them had ever known. Often, they performed arduous and dangerous tasks that required a great deal of skill. Many labored through illness. When the cane needed harvesting, pressing, and refining, timing was everything. Stalks left too long in the field lost much of their sugar content. Over- or undercooked syrup served no use. Skilled slaves saw to it that everything ran on schedule. They made the decisions of when to plant and when to harvest; they refined the sugar; and they prepared it for shipment. At the same time, they maintained equipment and directed free Indian and *casta* laborers.[38]

Transitions from African to creole, black to *casta* slaves, and slaves to free wage laborers occurred in most Veracruz settings between about 1650 and 1700. Córdoba and such areas as the lowlands surrounding the port of Veracruz represented the few variants to Veracruz' norm. In peculiar settings like these such changes in the Afro-Veracruzano experience met with strong Spanish resistance that led to regional instability. Rare sites, including Orizaba, fell somewhere between Jalapa's early and Córdoba's late transition in emphasis from slave to free wage labor. Orizaba lay closer to Córdoba geographically but the latter's demographic characteristics resembled those of Jalapa more than its near neighbor to the east. Orizaba's higher elevation made its climate cooler and healthier than Córdoba's. As a result, its Indian population remained denser than Córdoba's. In Orizaba more favorable demographic conditions reduced pressures on planters to utilize supplementary slave labor. On the other hand, Córdoba's strong slave tradition influenced attitudes in nearby Orizaba. Racist sentiments that permeated the two neighboring districts somewhat mitigated the pace of change dictated by impersonal structural forces including local environmental and demographic patterns in Orizaba. The end result was change at a faster pace than in Córdoba and a slower one than in Jalapa.

The plantation of Tuzpango lay within Orizaba's jurisdiction. In 1717 Tuzpango had 167 bondservants. The inventory listed them as carpenters, masons, potters, weavers, blacksmiths, refiners, and field supervisors, positions similar to those held by Jalapa slaves two generations earlier. Spanish residents included an administrator, a surgeon, and a priest. Indian laborers from the neighboring village of Chiciguila did Tuzpango's most menial tasks such as clearing the land, planting, and cutting the cane, a pattern very like the one that existed in Jalapa during the 1680s. The record did not state the exact nature and terms of the arrangement, but it did reveal two important points. First, Indians still did not reside on the estate in large numbers. Second, wages had replaced tribute as the principal incentive for Indian labor. Because the Indian field hands had to maintain sixty-four fields in cultivation, they must have been very numerous.[39] Apparently, the level of the Indian work remained fairly constant year-round since those that ran the estate staggered planting times for each field. Consequently, sowing and harvesting went on simultaneously (although production may have fallen off slightly during the region's rainy season, which lasted from June through August each year). The Caribbean and Brazilian patterns of an inhuman pace during the harvest period followed by two or three months of near idleness evidently did not apply in the 1630–1720 Veracruz setting.

Slavery endured as did Indian tribute labor, but they generally lost ground to voluntary wage labor in the region's variegated labor system. Moreover, these changes in the labor system came mainly from local pressures in Veracruz. Between 1630 and 1720, native influences overrode pressures from the Iberian core in shaping labor and the rest of the economy in central Veracruz.

Post-1720 Alternatives to Afro-Veracruzano Slave Labor

The decade of the 1720s ushered in yet three more dramatic shifts in Veracruz' economic development. Bourbon Reforms reemphasized market ties and capital ties with the Atlantic mercantilist system. Production areas linked to the export trade received priority at the expense of production areas serving domestic markets. In these three dimensions of the colonial economy Veracruz' drift toward capitalism ground to a near halt during the last century of Spanish rule.

In the labor sector of the colonial economy the Bourbon Reforms had less impact. Coerced labor continued to lose ground to wage labor. This especially held true in the most industrialized sectors of the economy—mining, textiles, and central-Veracruz sugar agriculture. Examination of some of central Veracruz' plantation communities illustrates this trend.

By 1735, Almolonga's resident population in Jalapa had changed dramatically. Of the seventy-odd people living there, just nineteen were slaves, and these had become a smaller percentage of the overall permanent work force. They dropped from 53 percent in 1675 to just over 27 percent in 1735. Moreover, of the nineteen, ten were women, three children under ten, and two seventy year olds. All had entered slavery and Jalapa the same way—through birth. No native-born Africans appeared on the inventory. *Castas* and free persons of all racial backgrounds assumed higher and higher profiles on the estate's census roles after 1650. Pedro, a *negro*, or black, slave, held the post of master sugar-maker. But Juan Moreno, a free mulatto, served as the master carpenter. Miguel Damian, a free *pardo*, drove the estate's herd of pack mules. The master blacksmith, Tomás González, was a mestizo.[40] In 1743 Orizaba's Tuzpango had only 104 slaves as opposed to the 167 it had a quarter of a century earlier. Indian villagers still occupied a prominent place in the labor force. They performed the bulk of field labor, and they continued to work for wages as in 1717. The village governor and the resident estate manager negotiated the contract. This meant that the Indians' bargaining agent was also their political leader, a resident of their village, and tied to them by bonds of common culture and kinship. The natives acted corporately, and this may have given them more leverage in dealing with planters. The contract also allowed villagers to avoid permanent relocation on the estate despite the fact that demand for their labor remained fairly constant year round. Instead, natives rotated their individual service periods. Each labor shift worked for one week, then a new group took its turn on the plantation. This type of arrangement relegated Indians to relatively unskilled chores, for example, cutting cane, removing stubble from the previous crop, and preparing land for replanting.[41] Since they needed no great training to perform these tasks, they could rotate their labor. Such terms allowed Indians greater opportunity to preserve their cultural ways by minimizing individual contact with the Spanish plantation setting. It assured that villagers would spend the majority of their time in their own communities.

The picture that emerges from this case does not portray an easily exploitable indigenous population. Chiciquila residents banded together. They presented a united front against the economic and cultural encroachments of the local plantation. This represents a much different image of Indian-estate relations than the one commonly portrayed for later Porfirian hacienda society, with its supposedly oppressed peon class.[42]

Tuzpango's slave population climbed slightly to 117 in 1791. Despite their increased numbers, they contributed less and less to the plantation's labor force. In 1560 the estate had a male:female ratio of 2:1; in 1717 it dropped to 4:3; and by 1791 females actually outnumbered males by a ratio of 1.5:1.[43] The aging of the male slave population also reflected declining importance of slave labor. In 1717 ninety-one adult male slaves resided on the estate; that figure fell to thirty in 1791.[44]

Just as in Jalapa a half century earlier, Afro-Veracruzano slaves traditionally occupied many of the skilled tasks on the plantation. In 1717 the slave Juan Thomas acted as Tuzpango's master builder; in 1762 Alphonso Leonardo, a free resident of Orizaba, held that position.[45] In 1717 two slaves worked as master cauldron makers. In 1762 two freed laborers worked in these positions. In 1717 a slave held the post of master carpenter; in 1762 a freed laborer served in this capacity.[46] Tuzpango's experience parallels the general outline of the transition from slave to free labor throughout central Veracruz. It differs from our description of Jalapa plantations in but one respect: it happened over two generations later.

The relationship of small farmers and Indian villagers to commercial estates provides another indicator of the lessening importance of slave labor in Jalapa. Sometime near the middle of the eighteenth century large numbers of small farmers and surrounding villagers moved onto Jalapa estates. In the 1770s with the fairs' cessation and the subsequent decline in plantation agriculture, these laborers left the *trapiches* and *ingenios* and returned to their farms and villages. The post-1790 and the postindependence resurgences of the plantation economy again drew them onto the estates.[47] The crown liberalized the African slave trade in hopes of recapturing revenue and control of this sector of the economy.[48] In 1789 Spain allowed other nations to land slaves at American ports, but the strategy failed in Veracruz. There, neither the acceleration of local sugar production, the heightening of European trade, nor the liberalization of imperial trade policies revived slavery during the late colonial period.[49] The curve of colonial slave prices in Jalapa and Orizaba supports this conclusion. The average sale price of a slave halved between 1600 and 1700, and the general slope of the line moved downward from 1620 onward.

Factoring for gender, age, and occupational skill level yielded the same general trend. A transition in the labor system took place between 1675 and 1725 in most of central Veracruz. An unskilled male between the ages of twenty and forty commanded a purchase price of about 325 pesos in 1700. By 1800, a comparable slave brought

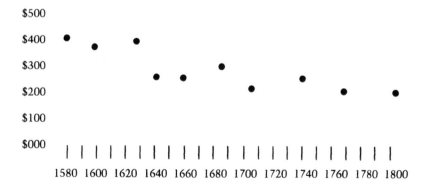

Figure 3. Jalapa and Orizaba slave prices, 1580–1800 (for the period 1580–1790, the same sources cited in Table 3; PATDAT-CCSU).

about 250 pesos. A skilled twenty- to fifty-year-old male sold for around 350 pesos in 1700; by 1800 the price for the same type of slave fell to 250 pesos, about the same as for an unskilled slave. During the second half of the eighteenth century a female of child-bearing age sold for about the same as a male laborer twenty to forty. In fact, women commanded as high a price as skilled artisan men, traditionally the most expensive of slaves. By this time a slave was a slave. They all represented expensively obsolete units of labor.

Changes in age distribution also point to the shrinking significance of slave labor on the Tuzpango estate. As the eighteenth century progressed, the percentage of children grew. In 1560 only 14 percent of Tuzpango's slaves fell under ten years of age, by 1714 23 percent clustered in this cohort; and by 1791 43 percent did so.[50]

Greater numbers of women led to an equalization of the male-female slave ratio. The even sex ratio led to more offspring, and more children should have produced more natural increase for the slave population. But Orizaba's slave community did not grow during these years. The number of Tuzpango's slaves increased at a rate of −.16 percent per annum between 1717 and 1747. From 1742 to 1791 the rate climbed to .27 percent a year but still fell well below the average for the broader population.[51] This suggests that Orizaba slave owners did not make a conscientious effort to substitute natural increase for importation as a means of maintaining the size of the area's slave labor force. Had they adopted this strategy, it should have worked. All the ingredients seemed in place. The slave community had the proper sex and age structure. Disease patterns, the major inhibitor to natural increase in the earlier periods, had grown milder. General prosperity created the means for better living conditions for slaves and should have made natural increase all the more possible. In sum, natural increase represented a viable option for plantation owners in central Veracruz had they chosen to hang on to slave labor. The fact that Orizaba's, Jalapa's, and eventually even Córdoba's populations of bondservants shrank, or at least grew more slowly than the general population, meant that those who controlled labor in central Veracruz during the latter part of the colonial period opted for alternatives to slave workers. This decision accounts for the previously described price, sex, and age changes in local slave populations.

Multiple conditions caused these patterns, as well as the general decline in numbers of slaves. European events contributed to Veracruz' insensitivity to Spanish inducements to reengage in the Atlantic slave trade. The Iberian country's eighteenth-century wars with

England, as well as with Caribbean privateers, proved highly disruptive to the trade. A complicated colonial commercial system also took its toll. It unintentionally impeded the flow of the trade by discouraging its speculative nature.[52] However, demographic and economic conditions, as already pointed out, represented the two paramount reasons for the fall of the Veracruz slave system. Demographic recovery of the Indian and emergence of the *casta* populations created a local labor pool that eliminated the necessity for expensive slave workers. Wage labor simply became cheaper to employ. This conclusion becomes obvious when one considers the relative cost of a slave compared to other contemporary items.

Buying a slave represented a major investment even with the deflated slave prices of the eighteenth century. As late as 1800 a male cost as much as a small but substantial house in Jalapa.[53] The 167 Tuzpango slaves included in the 1717 inventory appraised at 36,000 pesos. The combined value of the next two most expensive items on the list, namely land and buildings, totaled only 41,000 pesos. By midcentury the worth of the estate's bondservants had slipped. In 1747 the value of 104 bondspeople living on Tuzpango came to 15,700 pesos. They had fallen behind land as the single most expensive item on the inventory.[54] Nevertheless, slaves continued to represent a major investment.[55]

The maintenance of slaves also cost money. During a hundred-day period beginning in July and ending in September of 1717, Tuzpango slaves consumed thirty-two bulls. At ten pesos per animal, their meat bill alone came to 320 pesos, only slightly less than the 333 pesos paid out in total yearly wages to Indian villagers who constituted the bulk of the estate's labor force. When one adds the additional costs of 260 pesos worth of corn during the same period, undetermined amounts for health care, clothing, and rations of sugar, and 4,000 pesos for construction of eighteen buildings to house bondspersons, costs mounted. Incidentals including a cup of rum per adult on each major holiday added to the total. Finally, the initial purchase price for some slaves represented a huge outlay. Scarcity drove up the cost of wage labor between 1550 and 1650; abundance had the opposite effect from about 1700 onward. Supplemental slave labor no longer appeared cost-effective.[56]

In sum, a combination of population growth that made cheaper alternative sources of labor available and international obstacles to the Atlantic slave trade that rendered the supply of Africans more uncertain converted slavery into an obsolete institution held over from an earlier colonial era. Those few locales, such as Córdoba and to a lesser degree Orizaba, that for whatever reasons clung to slavery longer than the rest of the viceroyalty paid the price for this persistence in economic dislocation and social disorder.[57]

Conclusion

The evolution of central Veracruz' labor system paralleled that of other dimensions of the economy up until 1720. Yet, labor—more so than production, markets, and capital—proved heterogeneous in nature. Several labor systems operated simultaneously making the area distinct from its neighboring Caribbean island sugar cultures. In Veracruz, emphasis rather than exclusivity distinguished each of the four stages of labor development. From 1519 to 1550 Indian slavery and personal tribute dominated, but both African slavery and wage labor existed. From 1550 to 1630, African slavery rivaled corporate Indian tribute in emphasis. Indian slavery no longer existed, but wage labor did. From 1630 to 1720 voluntary wage labor began to overshadow slavery and challenge Indian tribute for predominance. From 1720 to 1820 slavery slipped further in importance while wage labor rose to even greater dominance. Each of these shifts proved consistent with the overall development of the economy and the source of its main driving force. The first stage derived from a combination of indigenous pre-Columbian influences; the second stage grew from a mix of native demographic conditions and the consequent rise of Iberian involvement in the economy; the third stage represented a reaction to largely domestic demographic and economic conditions; and the fourth stage sprang from indigenous forces despite stepped-up European pressures to encourage a revival of slavery. Indeed, labor represented the one post-1720 dimension of the economy that did not succumb to the World System described by Immanuel Wallerstein. Export industries, such as sugar, and international commerce received priority over other production activities. International markets enjoyed primacy over domestic ones; capital markets shifted to Europe. A climate of general Veracruz economic dependency on Europe, similar to the one that existed from 1550 to 1630, appeared. Labor alone continued to respond primarily to local conditions. Social trends influenced labor's deviation from the previous century's pattern of economic growth, and Afro-Veracruzanos played a significant role in the evolving social environment.

5

Slaves and Social Change, 1570–1720

EUROPEANS BROUGHT social ideas with them to Veracruz. Iberia was in the process of transforming from a feudalist to a capitalist society at the time of American contact. As a result, European social rank still derived in part from seigniorial social relationships between nobles and "lesser born" people. Capitalism added new power groups to the social equation, most notably merchants, bureaucrats, and wage earners. Moreover, it placed greater social emphasis on economic class than seigniorial deference. Spaniards transferred this complex ordering system to Veracruz between 1519 and 1550. In Europe the system functioned well because those that adhered to it made up a majority of the population.[1] In Veracruz, however, Spaniards lived as a small minority during this first stage of colonial development, and their social system had to compete with those of other groups.

Numerically, Indians dominated the landscape. In their communities kinship and seigniorial relationships determined social ranking.[2] Military conquest and consequent tribute also added variables to the indigenous social stratification scheme. By virtue of their numbers alone, Indians' ideas about social ordering impacted on the early colonial society.

African slaves, the third general population in this pluralistic society, lightly contributed to early social development for two reasons. First, they, like Spaniards, made up a small numerical portion of the overall population. Second, they came as slaves, the least powerful segment of the society.

Social Change, 1550–1720

The mid-sixteenth century represented a watershed in colonial Veracruz history. Indigenous demographic crisis resulted in Iberians' assumption of much greater control over the means and modes of production. A consequent change involved greater reliance on African slave labor in an effort to lighten Indians' workload and thereby lower their death rates. Large numbers of imported African slaves arrived from 1570 to 1610 and by 1600 outnumbered Europeans in the region. Their importance within the colonial society greatly expanded. Despite blacks' heightened presence, however, the newcomers still entered Veracruz as slaves, and this status limited their social influence. Vestiges of African social ranking systems lingered to some degree in slave communities, but they had little influence on the broader population.

This mix of unequals in power who experienced social differentiation through coerced labor systems coupled with racial and cultural discrimination produced a hybrid creole social order that helped set important precedents for much of the rest of mainland Latin America. Central Veracruz became a regional stage upon which these different racial and ethnic players interacted and assumed dominant roles in the creation of a social reality that better reflected post-1550 demographic, economic, and political pressures.

The pre-1550 bipartite social order gave way to one that complemented shifting power relationships. A small racially white and ethnically Spanish population assumed social preeminence less on the basis of seigniorial privilege and Indian deference to conquerors than by virtue of racial and ethnic identification. Equal numbers of racially black and culturally West African individuals held a lower social rank. Although they aided Spaniards in the conquest of central Veracruz, Africans did not share proportionately in the fruits of victory because of their slave status. After 1550 their rank lowered further because of their racial and ethnic identification. Indians comprised the remaining portion of the society. Culturally indigenous residents of central Veracruz varied more than their European and African counterparts. Their ethnic heterogeneity, more than their race, defined Indians rank within the post-1550 social order.

During the middle colonial period, biological and social race emerged as the two most critical determinants of social status. The European estate–corporate economic class system still operated, as did the Indian based kinship and conquest fealty system, but within the membership of those two groups only. Race and ethnicity's importance lay in the fact that they operated within and between the variegated social systems of Spaniards and Indians. In this overriding position, race and ethnicity came to dominate the social stratification system from at least 1600 onward. Many of the area's modern social conventions, customs, laws, and beliefs had their roots in events that transpired during the middle colonial period that stretched from 1620 to 1720. From this present vantage point one can glimpse the significance of biological and social race in the lives of Afro-Veracruzanos and those around them. Biological race involved social discrimination on the basis of inherited biological characteristics, most notably skin color; social race involved discrimination on the basis of acquired traits such as language, belief systems, and customs. The importance of race and ethnicity created a social order as complex as the region's labor system.

For Africans, ethnicity, or cultural dissimilarity with the rest of the population, proved a powerful restricter of social status. However, acquired characteristics represented a tenuous divider of power groups. In twenty years a person's ethnicity might change. Nevertheless, culture did count for something in assigning social rank. Colonial Spaniards looked down upon West Africans and Indians alike as "people without reason."

Africans imported into Veracruz did not display the cultural diversity of slaves shipped to many other parts of the Americas. Information already presented in Chapter 2 indicates that Angola supplied the majority of the region's bondservants after about 1580.[3] Cultural homogeneity among such an oppressed group created potential dangers for Iberian masters. Common language and beliefs among related ethnic families facilitated solidarity and communication within the slave community. Such conditions made resistance easier. In order to reduce the threat, Spaniards promoted an inequitable social order that rendered themselves privileged racial and ethnic status by demeaning slaves' blackness and Africaness. Spaniards adopted a similar position toward Indians.

A second possible incentive for Iberians' racial and cultural discrimination against Africans and Indians stemmed from the understandable group pride that filled Spaniards and their creole offspring during this period. After all, had not the conquerors and their immediate forbears reclaimed the Iberian peninsula from infidel Moslem invaders just prior to the discovery of the Americas? Had they not then crossed dangerous seas to subdue millions more pagans for Christianity, the new Spanish state, and their own personal gain? From the mid-sixteenth century onward had they not established an economy that generated enough wealth to make New Spain the most coveted American possession in the Atlantic mercantilist system? In Iberians' minds they had every reason to believe in their own superiority over the peoples they controlled in such places as Veracruz.[4] Sixteenth-century Spaniards probably adhered to an early form of Social Darwinism, a philosophy which argues that some groups, whether defined by culture or race, could more easily achieve material success than others. Conquerors attributed many of their achievements to their higher intellect that reaped them technological advantages—steel, firearms, draught and riding animals, and ships. Africans lacked some, and Indians all, of these technologies. Taking Spaniards' overall perceptions into account, why they viewed their domination of Africans and Indians as the natural order of things is not difficult to understand. As victors Spaniards thought themselves superior to the peoples they dominated. The trick lay in convincing Africans and Indians of this tautological line of reasoning. If accomplished, the two subordinate groups would become their own oppressors and sustain Iberians' hegemony in the region with a level of security that force alone could never achieve. In many ways that is just what happened.[5]

Others had used racism and ethnocentrism as mechanisms of social control long before European contact with Veracruz. Some of the means by which Spaniards applied them in the Americas, however, showed real innovativeness. This proved especially true in the case of racism. Adjacent mainland areas including Veracruz preserved and helped institutionalize the Caribbean islands' precedent of associating slavery with a single racial group, blacks. As America's foremost colony, one that European settlers tried to emulate throughout the hemisphere, Mexico gave great impetus to the use of these social concepts as tools to order the culturally and racially pluralistic New World societies that sprang up.

Slave Community

In the late sixteenth and early seventeenth centuries Spaniards heavily relied on Afro-Veracruzano labor partially out of worry over Indians and partially out of concern for efficiency. Masters and administrators pushed slaves to an extreme. In 1620 slivers of cane sent flying by the force of the huge mill stone left Almolonga slaves Joaquín and Gerónima blinded in one eye. Gerónima's mother lost her right arm in the roller presses. María and Luisa fell ill under the demanding work schedule of the harvest period. María Cochichi lay on her deathbed, stricken with some unidentified disease. No one knew what was wrong with her, but eight slaves had already died of it during the previous year, half of them children.

Injury and disease still stalked slaves who lived on Almolonga in 1675 but not as closely as a half century earlier. Most of the plantation's servants also avoided major injuries. In 1675 only 5 percent of the slaves on the ingenio lived with work-related injuries and diseases. Most slaves endured conditions on Jalapa's estates and lived to ripe old ages. Thirty-five-year-old María Cochichi's illness might have proved fatal, but her father, who visited her bedside, had seen ninety years come and go by 1675. An eighty-year-old male still worked a bit. The slave list included two other octogenarians, Manuel Macaco and Antón. Several more slaves in the inventory fell between seventy and ninety.[6]

The eighteenth century witnessed a good deal of economic change in central Veracruz. During this period of retreat to greater dependency on the Atlantic system, slave labor became a more questionable means of production. This created a good deal of unevenness in conditions within the Veracruz slave community. The *ingenio* of Tuzpango in Orizaba presents a case in point. In 1717 the slaves on the plantation enjoyed a relatively secure material life. Their rations included ample supplies of corn and beef. They lived in permanent structures housing an average of six to seven individuals apiece. Forty-odd years later Tuzpango belonged to an absentee owner, Don Miguel de Sema y Escudero, and that dramatically altered conditions within the slave quarters. In 1754 de Sema rented his estate and slaves for the next twelve years. During that time buildings and equipment fell into disrepair. Fields received too little attention, and the slaves suffered the consequences. Don Gabriel Segura, the renter, decided to take matters into his own hands. To raise money for repairs, he fined the skilled free resident laborers. He then turned on the slaves, whipping them to punish them and to accelerate their work rate. Eight years later Segura attempted to buy Tuzpango. In the mandatory property appraisal that then took place, the effects of his administration became apparent. Tuzpango's soil suffered depletion from repeated over-planting. Buildings needed repair, especially the slave quarters. The slaves themselves suffered from undernourishment, overwork, and general ill health. Segura had even sublet much of the land. De Sema understandably expressed outrage, but renter and seller finally reached an agreement. Segura had wanted a discount price because of the condition of the estate. De Sema threatened to sue Segura for damages unless he paid the full assessed value of the estate at the time he rented it in 1754. Segura gave in and paid the full asking price. Both men's concerns were economic. The suffering of the slaves meant little as long as it did not effect their value. Imagine the sentiments of the slaves when de Sema notified them of the sale. Even Spanish observers on the scene remarked about the consternation of the bondservants. They begged de Sema to reconsider. He simply walked away.[7]

The family provided the social foundation for the general population in central Veracruz. Whether nuclear in nature, as in the Spanish-American community, or extended in nature, as in the indigenous population, the family performed multiple functions, a number of which led to the socialization of individuals. The family taught children their "place" in this complexly evolving social world. It provided psychological support; it offered persons physical security; it engendered a sense of belonging to a caring corporate group. Slavery jeopardized the security of the family. Sale represented one serious threat. Until the eighteenth century children were often separated from their parents in this manner. This fate befell Juana Nicalosa in 1635; Antonio in 1641, and the infant Juan in 1667. All three slaves were less than ten years old at the time of their sale in Jalapa. All three had living healthy mothers at the time.[8]

Children were not the only family members to suffer separation. Of the 260 adult male, adult female, and children slaves sampled from 1575 through 1615, between 60 percent and 70 percent were unattached adults with no apparent family ties. In the next period, 1645–1720, 40 percent to 45 percent of the 375 slaves recorded fell into this unattached category. As late as 1760 a third of the area's servants had no recorded family ties. Not until 1780 did unrelated adults within the slave population drop to a small minority, 9 percent. For at least two thirds of the colonial experience unattached slaves represented the largest single group within the regional population.[9] Lack of family ties within the slave community induced many Afro-Veracruzanos to seek social bonds in the broader population. Slaves of various racial backgrounds did this to a higher degree than any other group.

Afro-Veracruzanos Social Relations with the Broader Population

Afro-Veracruzano slaves' level of social integration into the broader society increased as the colonial period wore on. This trend developed despite formidable social and legal pressures against it. Slavery and racism made cross-racial and cross-ethnic social bonding very difficult. Whites, and perhaps even Indians, engaged in a concerted effort socially to isolate Afro-Veracruzanos. A long-term examination of changes in certain characteristics of the slave population illustrates the limited degree of success that these efforts had.

Only a few African ethnic traits transferred to Veracruz and survived. They sometimes surfaced in such activities as witchcraft, superstition, music, and dance.[10] But on balance, ethnicity created an obstacle to Africans' integration into the broader society. West African cultures fell on a generally unreceptive regional population. European masters assaulted these strange ways on the grounds that they sprang from pagan roots. Language also impeded African's accommodation to the society. Few Ibero-Americans and virtually no Indians spoke West African tongues. Consequently, these dialects impeded communications with other segments of the population. Finally, most Africans had to first forget their native liberty before they could "fit" into the Veracruz slave community. By stripping them of their native culture, Spaniards could then acculturate Africans to a new order that socially induced everyone, including Afro-Veracruzanos themselves, to accept Spanish American racist and ethnocentric notions of social stratification.

The Indian world represented the other possible social outlet for Africans. But in some ways Indian societies extended less welcome to outsiders than Spanish-American society did. Moreover, Spaniards by law and social pressure tried to restrict Afro-Veracruzanos' involvement with Indian villagers. Natives supported this Spanish policy. Like most peoples, Indians did not want non-Indians intruding in their community life. Spaniards tried to force their culture upon indigenous subjects, but their efforts met with only limited success. Native resistance to West African cultural penetration proved even more effective. Many Africans overcame legal obstacles and located in or near indigenous communities throughout the colonial years. But the number of these interlopers remained so small that they made little impact. In the hinterlands, more numerous Indians overwhelmed African influence.

In sum, Africans became ethnically caught between two more culturally dominant segments of the society. Africans had a difficult time using their ethnicity as a defense mechanism against white racism and Indian and white ethnocentrism.[11] This, along with their slave status, created the potential for Africans' social marginality.

Until near the second half of the seventeenth century African-born individuals dominated throughout most of the region's slave community.[12] These individuals suffered a distinct disadvantage in gaining social acceptance by other groups. Spaniards and Indians perceived, in different ways, that Africans posed real threats to their respective niches in the colonial order. Spaniards responded to these threats with a host of laws that stripped power from subject Afro-Mexicans. *Bozal* and creole blacks could not bear arms except under Ibero-Americans' supervision.[13] Spaniards excluded Afro-Veracruzanos, both free and slave alike, from voting and holding public office. Socially, only whites could enter religious orders and belong to certain elite religious, trade, and militia fraternities; nonwhites joined similar but socially inferior organizations.

But racism and ethnocentrism manifested themselves in even more insidious ways. They affected the everyday lives and thinking of the entire population. Perhaps this represented Spanish whites' greatest long-range success in maintaining control over a vast New World empire in the face of their limited human and technological resources. Racism and ethnocentrism helped Europeans to hang on to their possessions for three centuries and aided them in making such regions as central Veracruz very materially productive.

What logic lay behind the influence of race and ethnicity in ordering creole society and stimulating material growth? Much of the answer to this question lay in the social climate Europeans eventually created. Whites based it on two almost contradictory social strategies. First, Europeans used a common religion to bind different groups together into a spiritual community that preached equality in the hereafter in return for inequality in the present. Second, whites relied on racism and ethnocentrism to divide nonwhite and non-Hispanic peoples from one another, thereby inhibiting united opposition to European rule. These concepts provided both a justification and a means for whites' domination over a larger nonwhite population. Spaniards tried to pass down this combination of spiritual and secular beliefs to generation after generation of the general population. They generally succeeded. Even today these notions remain strong within the cultural framework of central Veracruz and the rest of the Mexico.[14] Beyond Veracruz, such ideas helped establish precedents for the growth of a hemispheric social legacy. Regional settings served as experimental arenas for development of peculiar American applications of these two mechanisms of social control. Veracruz was one of the most important precedent setting locales in the early history of the colonial Americas. The region's influence might have been greater if not for the social resiliency of its early African and Afro-American inhabitants.

Choice of marriage partner, godparent, and marriage witness represented three potential opportunities to broaden interracial and interethnic social bonding. Of the three, marriage partnerships represented the strongest social tie. Matrimonial witnesses represented lesser but still strong social links. Colonial Veracruzanos chose these persons carefully. With few exceptions, most selected their closest friends. Parish registries recorded these ties in most cases.

Letters to parish priests and public officials in Jalapa admonishing them to discourage racial intermarriage reflected white ecclesiastic and civil authorities' commitment to racism.[15] Spaniards divided individuals into six basic racial divisions. White denoted light-complected persons of European appearance. Mestizo designated a person of mixed white-Indian racial appearance. *Pardo* defined an individual of black-Indian physical characteristics. Mulatto identified someone of black-white racial background. *Negro* indicated African physical appearance. Finally, Indian, or *natural*, marked a person as having the physical characteristics of the region's indigenous populations.

More ethnically related terms included *bozal*, a *negro* born in Africa, and creole, a person of any racial background born in the New World.[16] A distinction between "persons of reason" and *naturales* sometimes appeared. The application of the word *naturales* did not change; it remained synonymous with Indian.[17] In the early and middle colonial years record keepers reserved the approbation "person of reason" for Spaniards and persons of partial Spanish-white identification only. This phrase initially implied both racial and ethnic differentiation. In addition to Spanish racial heritage it denoted ascription to Hispanic culture. After about 1750 the phrase began to appear after a few Hispanicized *pardos'* names as well. The designation of *pardos* as "persons of reason" appears significant since the two racial strains from which they sprang, *negro* and Indian, originally did not enjoy this distinction. Thus the term "of reason" took on an almost purely ethnic meaning by the mid-eighteenth century.

In the Spanish-controlled urban setting, the late-sixteenth-century incidence of intraracial marriage proved very high. All six groups displayed an overwhelming tendency to wed members of their own race. White Spaniards social policies of divide and conquer appear to have functioned well during the first century of European contact. By the middle of the seventeenth century, however, blacks and Afro-*castas* (*pardos* and mulattoes) joined mestizos in limited noncompliance with these racially based social divisions. From 1645 onward a higher percentage of each of these segments of the population married outside their respective racial groups than whites and Indians combined. This held true in the city and hinterlands alike.[18]

Other types of relationships reflected slightly different patterns of social interaction among races than marriage ties did. Perhaps due to their more casual nature, these encountered less racist and ethnocentric opposition from whites and Indians than intermarriage. For that reason, these less-intense associations displayed higher incidence of interracial bonding than matrimonial ties. Two patterns stand out for these types of bonds. First, the overall average endogamous levels for these relationships changed very little from 1645 to 1715. Second, shifts in these levels proved, as in the case of marriage, virtually identical in urban and rural zones within the region. Whites and Indians remained more aloof; blacks and *castas* showed greater willingness to cross racial lines in forming social circles during the first half of the seventeenth century than three generations earlier.[19] Two attitudes toward race and ethnocentrism surfaced between 1580 and 1645. For whites and Indians racism and/or ethnocentrism remained strong and became institutionalized. Blacks and *castas* placed less emphasis on these two concepts.

Afro-Veracruzanos' social ties with other groups varied at and over different points in time. In this sense, central Veracruz appears more like the Brazilian than the Caribbean island and the later-developing U.S. colonial societies. Shades of black apparently made a difference. One of the most marked changes involved urban Afro-Veracruzanos' association with Spaniards and Indians. As the sixteenth and seventeenth centuries wore on, *pardos* and blacks extended their exogamous ties with Indians; mulattoes moved closer to *negros* and whites. Few members of the three black-related groups seemed to form strong bonds with mestizos.

These patterns persisted into the early eighteenth century. *Negros* displayed the greatest shift by moving away from social links with whites and toward associations with Indians. This probably reflected a decline in the institution of slavery from the mid-seventeenth century onward. In 1645 most blacks lived as slaves, and whites acted as witnesses and godparents for them not out of friendship but out of duty as their owners and overseers.[20] By 1715, the proportion of slaves within the *negro* population diminished, and whites cared less about controlling the lives of the few slaves that remained.

During the middle of the seventeenth century the story in the rural setting appeared much the same as in the urban environment. On the one side stood *negros* and *pardos* linked with Indians; on the other side stood mulattos tied to whites. Here too, none of the black or black-affiliated racial groups showed a strong propensity to establish similar social ties with mestizos. But by the eighteenth century *negros* and mulattoes realigned their social ties. In 1715 a greater balance existed between these two groups' involvement with whites and natives. This proved somewhat surprising since Indians still numerically dominated in the countryside. One would have expected a continued shift toward stronger ties with the indigenous population. However, the 1715 evidence that yields these new *negro* and mulatto social alignments is very limited. These modified social patterns may represent illusory trends.[21]

Whites, as the socially most elite portion of the society, fraternized little with persons of nonwhite racial backgrounds. They formed weak ties with *pardos* and *negros* and only slightly stronger ones with mulattoes.[22]

Apparently, from the above patterns, neither whites nor Indians encouraged bonding with Afro-Veracruzanos. But in the latter's case two circumstances allowed blacks and black *castas* to overcome social bias. Indigenous peoples proved much more numerous than any other racial group within the population. Their sheer numbers placed them at greater probability than whites to form social bonds with *negros* and *pardos*.[23] A small percentage of socially exogamous Indians (about 5 percent) translated into a large percentage of all cases of racially exogamous social bonding. Just as importantly, *negros* and *pardos* more closely approximated the social status of Indians than whites. Some have even argued that in many ways black slaves socially out ranked Indians. Evidence from central Veracruz adds support to this notion.[24]

In the final analysis, white racism offers the most plausible explanation for *pardos'* and *negros'* weaker and mulattoes' stronger association with whites. To Spaniards, mulattos had one racially redeeming feature: they had partial white ancestry. Racist social restrictions existed throughout this period. Racist notions made whites and white *castas* socially exclusive elements within the non-Indian population. To them, race counted for something, and the color line they drew retarded blacks, *pardos*, Indians, and the products of miscegenation between them from heavily interacting with whites and, to a lesser degree, with partially white mestizos.

Afro-Jalapans' noncompliance with these views proves understandable. Whites' and Indians' ethnocentrism and whites' added racism discriminated against Afro-Jalapans. Yet, to a degree, blacks and Afro-*castas* overcame these apartheid social barriers and actually became the most racially outgoing segments of the society by a wide margin. In towns and in the countryside *negros* and Afro-*castas* proved three to four times as likely as whites and Indians to engage in social bonding with persons of different racial backgrounds.[25] In the end, white and Indian efforts to isolate Afro-Veracruzanos may have forced persons of African descent to bridge both worlds, to labor in the area's white setting and to socialize in the Indian environment. These activities, however, represented the exception not the rule for this middle period. Between 1645 and

1715 throughout the district, the majority in all racial and ethnic groups entered into social bonds with persons of similar backgrounds. Later deviations from the norm did not point to racism's and ethnocentrism's failure to socially control subject peoples. They merely portended a much stronger challenge to both control mechanisms in the last decades of the eighteenth century. Whites and Indians created and sustained these instruments of social ordering. Afro-Veracruzanos worked to overcome them throughout the colonial period.

At times, however, whites' degree of control led to social unrest within the slave community. As already noted, a gender imbalance existed among slaves.[26] This forced males to seek out females wherever they could find them, a difficult task indeed. Whites restricted male slaves' access to women of other races because it ran counter to Spaniards' efforts to maintain divisions between subordinate races. This put social stress on the slave community, and it often boiled over into violence.

In 1609, Bishop Alonso de la Mota y Escobar, of the diocese of Puebla, visited the Jalapa region. While returning to the capital from an inspection of some Indian villages in the northern part of the province, he encountered two fleeing Spanish merchants. They told a chilling tale. Just after dark on the previous night a group of men ambushed their party as they camped along the royal road between Jalapa and the port of Veracruz. Their attackers were runaway black slaves, *cimarrones*. The marauders seized the strongbox containing over a hundred pesos. They also took the pack animals. But what they did next best illustrates the level of social tension among slaves that a combination of too few slave women and white racist attitudes caused. First, they killed the Spaniards' twelve-year-old brother. Next, they turned on the Indian servant families accompanying the pack train. As the native husbands helplessly watched, the captors carried off their wives. One of the women clutched her infant, but a *cimarrón* had no use for a captive baby. A man snatched the child from the woman's arms and dashed its brains out on a rock. He then swung the woman onto his horse, and the band rode off.[27]

This incident was unusually violent, but the image that it projects of male slaves' aggressiveness toward Indian women was not atypical. Male slaves commonly harassed native women. Indian females not only represented an outlet for male slaves' sexual frustrations but also provided birth canals to legal freedom for slaves' children.[28] For both these reasons, bondsmen vigorously pursued willing and unwilling Indian women as sexual and marriage partners. Natives lodged frequent complaints with Spanish authorities, but Spanish officials could provide little redress.[29]

Uneven sex ratios caused persistent instability within the Afro-Veracruz slave community. Indians, whites, and free *castas* faced the constant threat of assault by male black slaves. From at least 1550 to 1650 the areas in and around the towns of Veracruz, Jalapa, Orizaba, and Córdoba became hotbeds of illicit runaway-slave activity. Flight, rape, abduction, brigandage, and even revolt heightened racial tensions. Bands of runaway male slaves would congregate in the mountains. From these strongholds they sortied out seeking material goods and women of any race and ethnicity. Sometimes they merely satisfied their sexual urges on the spot and left. At other times they kidnapped the women and forced them into "mountain marriages," as the slaves called them. In such cases the abducted victims spent the rest of their lives wed to their captors and a fugitive lifestyle.

Yanga became one of the most prominent runaway settlements, or *palenques*, in colonial Veracruz. It lay in the vicinity of Córdoba. Its long-time ruler of the same name, a *cimarrón* from one of the port's nearby plantations, founded the hideaway around 1580. He successfully led his men on raids all over central Veracruz for nearly thirty years. During that time his troop captured so many women that the whole demographic nature of the band gradually altered. It changed from a group of highly mobile males to a more sedentary community with a balanced ratio of men to women. The inevitable result of an even sex ratio represented yet another modification in the demographic profile of the group and had significant implications. Children began to appear in the settlement in relatively comparable proportions to those that existed in the general population. Youngsters made the band even less mobile. As a result, raiding grew increasingly less practical while farming and commerce became more appropriate. In a sense, the runaways' marauding lifestyle fell victim to its own success. Children and family responsibilities accomplished what white force of arms could not do. On the one hand, the availability of women within the runaway community removed one of the primary incentives for raiding, and males no longer had to leave the mountain to find female companionship. On the other hand, the duties of family life proved incompatible with raiding and pillaging. Throughout the colonial period many *palenque* settlements in Veracruz died evolutionary deaths as restless unattached male runaways became village husbands and fathers. Whites realized this and reluctantly coopted bands that underwent this type of transformation by granting them freedom and chartering their towns. Yanga evolved into the legal pueblo of San Lorenzo de los Negros. Invariably, these Afro-Veracruzanos settled down to productive lives as nonviolent villagers. Eventually, they even lost their racial distinctiveness as non-Afro-descended people intermingled with them. Within a few generations the town became racially and ethnically indistinguishable from other settlements that dotted the area.[30]

Conclusion

Yanga's evolution from fugitive to legal settlement did not represent an isolated incident. Until well into the eighteenth century, where uneven sex ratios existed in local slave populations, the same set of circumstances repeated themselves over and over again. This cycle contributed directly to the foundation of Córdoba. Even before Yanga's time, the area served as a refuge for runaway slaves. Founding San Lorenzo did not change this, even though part of the bargain with whites was that, in exchange for their own freedom, Yanga and his neighbors had to help catch future runaways for a bounty paid by each slave's master. Evidently, the former slaves did not have as much taste for such activities as white authorities had hoped. This forced Spaniards to found their own settlement in the region. Eighteen white families from the town of Huatusco accepted the challenge and moved to a site they named Córdoba in 1618. This event had a profound impact on south-central Veracruz. It converted the zone from a runaway-slave haven to a slave-worked, white-controlled plantation center. The area went from a climate of outlaw permissiveness and heavy racial interaction to legal enslavement and racism within a half century.

Three interrelated things restricted slaves' social lives: racism, ethnocentrism, and slavery. Biological and social race supported and justified enslavement. Enslavement, in turn, contributed to perceptions of blacks' and Afro-*castas*' social inferiority. Slavery inhibited slaves' ability to actively influence the broader social environment and their place within it. What proves surprising is the degree to which Afro-Veracruzanos did this anyway. At times Afro-Veracruzanos affected the social climate within and without the slave community peacefully through their outgoing social activities. At other times they influenced it through violence. Chapter six will examine two different means by which Afro-Veracruzanos escaped one of these restricters on their social lives.

6

Two Routes to Freedom:
Córdoba and Jalapa

SHORTLY AFTER independence, a national commission on the institution of slavery estimated that only about three thousand bondspeople resided in all Mexico.[1] Yet, bondage remained strong in exceptional locales, for example, Izúcar and Tlapa in the province of Puebla, Tamiahua on the east coast, and Acapulco on the west coast. The institution also continued to flourish in late-developing frontier areas, including Durango, New Mexico, Sinaloa, and Sonora. The few slaves left in most locales experienced a relatively peaceful evolutionary path to freedom in the late colonial period. In the small number of areas with higher slave concentrations bondspersons followed a much more violent and revolutionary course to emancipation.[2]

Slavery, Demographics, and Economy in Córdoba

Córdoba, Veracruz, represented one of the minority settings that still clung to slavery in eighteenth-century Mexico. In 1700 Córdoba, unlike Jalapa and the rest of Mexico, began its heavy reliance on African slave labor. By the end of the century Afro-related peoples comprised nearly 20 percent of the district's population, making them six times more heavily represented than in Jalapa, just eighty-odd kilometers to the north.[3] From that point in time to the end of the colonial period, slavery remained a much more important part of Córdoba's setting than that of most other parts of New Spain. Córdoba became an area dominated by rural life, a place where labor remained scarce and where agriculturalists produced primarily for foreign markets from 1680 to 1740 and for mixed foreign-Mexican consumers from 1740 onward. These conditions provided countervailing pressures on the area's slave system. On the one hand, the scarcity of labor, and most notably cheap Indian labor, added to inertia in pushing for a continuance of slavery. On the other hand, the dislocated international market system made the importation of African slaves more difficult. Córdobans' choice to continue with slavery in the face of these ambivalent circumstances made for one of any number of very peculiar local variants to Veracruz' demographic, social, and political development in the last third of the colonial period.

Whites had difficulty abandoning slavery. It had supported them and their forbearers for four generations. Spanish Córdobans' deep-rooted views of Africans' racial inferiority gave added impetus to the maintenance of the institution. Many Spaniards and other non-Afro-Córdobans saw slaves as subhuman, at best childlike in nature. A 1769 petition signed by virtually all planters in the district reflected the racism that permeated white thought. It asserted that persons tainted with partial African ancestry could not live by reason. "If given freedom, blacks become increasingly more barbarous and bloodthirsty. The only proper condition for them is slavery."[4] These attitudes and the area's traditional identification with slavery helped sustain bondage.

Córdoba's demographic profile also encouraged slavery's persistence. Fewer inhabitants, and especially fewer Indians, resided in the district than in more populous sites, such as Jalapa.[5] This created a greater need for African slave labor. Córdoba planters heavily relied upon bondservants. Table 6 compares estimates for the population of New Spain with those for Córdoba and Jalapa. It reveals one of the principal reasons why Mexico as a whole, and Jalapa as a typical example of that whole, first opted to import Africans and later chose not to. It shows too why Córdoba continued to rely on slavery as other areas abandoned it. At the outset the patterns for all three areas appear similar. Each experienced demographic crisis during the sixteenth century, their populations reaching low points in the first quarter of the seventeenth century. Of the three regions, Córdoba seems to have suffered the most. By 1626 its population dropped to about 1 percent of its 1520 total.

By the end of the century all three areas had achieved about the same degree of recovery. Their respective populations grew to between 16 and 18 percent of their 1520 totals. With the crisis clearly over, incentive for participation in the expensive slave trade vanished. But Jalapa, Córdoba, and Mexico did not all experience this demographic recovery in the same way. Representation of the six basic racial groups within the three populations suggests different means of population growth.

After 1646 Indians' percentage of Córdoba's population dropped

Table 6. *Population Change in Córdoba, Jalapa, and Mexico as a Whole, 1520–1830 (in thousands)*

	1520	1580	1626	1646	1696	1746	1777	1793
Córdoba	72	4	2	3	6	8	10	12
Jalapa	180	8	5	7	9	22	31	29
Mexico	22,200	3,380	800	1,200	1,400	1,400	2,300	4,000

Source: See Appendix 2, pages 168–169.

sharply until at the end of the eighteenth century they counted for just over half the district's residents. Jalapan and the broader Mexican native populations also shrank in proportion to other groups but at much slower rates. By the end of colonial rule indigenous peoples still made up two-thirds of all residents in these areas.[6] Proportionately, Jalapa and most other parts of the viceroyalty could count on greater labor input from local indigenous peoples than Córdoba could. This input eased the general Mexican transition from slave to free labor. In Córdoba, replacement of free Indian for bonded Afro-Córdoban labor proved more difficult.

A noncomplementary two-dimensional commercial agri-economy sprang up in Córdoba during the last century of colonial rule. From about 1690 to 1740 sugar and coerced African labor dominated the scene, a combination that often led to explosive black-white relations.[7] Then around 1740, the area's volatile economic environment became even more charged. Potential wage laborers for the sugar industry started growing tobacco.

Sugar and tobacco agriculture contrasted in many ways. In Córdoba the former strove for economy of scale. Planters tried to achieve greater production through greater efficiency achieved by larger production units utilizing specialized labor. Tobacco *rancheros* (small farmers) took just the opposite approach. They commonly worked small farms in order to keep overhead costs and capital inversion light. Córdoba sugar plantations primarily grew for foreign markets; tobacco *rancheros* produced for domestic consumption. Sugar planters used expensive technology, tobacco farmers did not. And most importantly from the point of this discussion, sugar planters depended on slave labor, and tobacco farmers relied on wage labor. Competition between these two agricultural systems for land and labor undoubtedly added to social unrest that helped to destroy slavery in the district.

Availability of land in late colonial Córdoba provided free wage laborers unusual economic opportunities. Those in Huatusco who sponsored Córdoba's foundation never intended it to develop into a rival sugar-producing area. Through political machinations Huatuscans retarded the formation of large sugar estates in Córdoba until the end of the seventeenth century.[8] Two generations later, when tobacco culture began to take hold in the northern half of the district, sugar growers did not monopolize land to the extent they did in other regions. They had not had enough time. Sugar controlled land in the southern sector of the district only. This provided local voluntary labor with an extraordinary opportunity to raise tobacco on newly settled lands. Consequently, the principal area of competition between sugar and tobacco systems involved labor, more specifically, free wage labor.[9]

In 1765 a second outside influence, as powerful as Huatusco's early opposition to the acquisition of land for large estates, began to hamper sugar growers' efforts to recruit voluntary laborers. In that year the crown granted Córdoba's tobacco farmers an *estanco*, or royal monopoly, on colony-wide production. Both markets and profit expanded for local growers, and the industry boomed attracting larger numbers of free workers.[10] This happened at a time when sugar planters, wearied by the constant threat of slave revolt, might have contemplated a switch to wage labor.

In sum, limitations on Córdoba sugar growers' labor options coupled with a traditional association of sugar culture with slavery, racism, and ethnocentrism explain much of Córdoba's unusually late adherence to a system of slave labor. This adherence cost the region dearly in lives and property. It led to harsh and violent black-white relations that lasted beyond independence in 1821. Whatever the reasons for slavery's resilience in the district, Afro-Córdobans grew increasingly more resentful of their bondage. Denied a peaceful evolutionary path to freedom, slaves violently confronted their masters and the institution that bound them. Afro-Córdobans' restlessness rose as their slave status became more and more unique within their regional setting. Afro-Veracruzanos in neighboring locales enjoyed freedom; Afro-Córdobans still labored under slavery. This realization created a strong motivational force for slaves' contribution to eighteenth-century turbulence within the district.

Slave Rebellion

Rebellion represented the ultimate expression of slave unrest. Slaves in Córdoba and neighboring Orizaba revolted in 1725, 1735, 1741,

1749, and 1768. The 1735 uprising cost a great deal in lives and property. According to the planters, rebel slaves who had applied for amnesty and freedom in return for laying down their arms (in the tradition of bands like Yanga's) instigated this revolt. When royal authorities denied their request because of planter opposition, the fugitives incited general revolt within the "servants'" quarters.[11] Playing upon slaves' resentment of Córdoba's continued commitment to slavery, rebels spread rumors that the king had freed all remaining slaves in Mexico and that Córdoba planters had decided to ignore the decree. Runaways recruited a free mulatto named Miguel de Salamanca. He circulated among the region's slave quarters and spoke of a royal emissary who supposedly visited all the local haciendas and presented masters with the royal order. When owners dismissed the rumor out of hand, they incensed their bondservants. Those on the hacienda of San Juan de la Punta rose in open revolt on June 19, 1735. Their counterparts on many of the adjoining estates soon joined them. Servants deserted plantations en masse and gathered at the *ingenio* of Omealca. By the end of the day an estimated five hundred rebels, about a third of the area's entire slave population, stood in arms. Led by two creole bondsmen from the San Juan de la Punta estate, José Pérez and José Tadeo (alias "the Carpenter"), they fanned out across the countryside, halting white travelers and robbing them. In response, owners commissioned Don Agustín Moreno, a planter and district militia commander, to raise a force and put down the rebellion. He was a harsh man, much feared in the area. But before Moreno could act, the revolt spread beyond Córdoba to the coastal lowlands and the port area.

Local officials sent out an urgent plea for help, and militia units from other districts poured into the area. Despite the expanded commitment of men and supplies, Spaniards had great difficulty in controlling the nearly two thousand slaves that eventually joined the uprising. Tumult ensued for five months. Numerous pitched battles took place. Many Spanish plantation overseers suffered death or injury. Travelers moved through the countryside at great risk. Property loss mounted to unprecedented levels. Sugar and tobacco plants fell to the torch. Buildings lay in ruins; rebels carried off copper caldrons, used in the sugar-boiling process, along with other items. Equally damaging, insurgents prevented workers from entering the fields and sowing the next year's crop. Estimated property destruction alone exceeded four hundred thousand pesos. Adding lost slave personnel, the total soared to over a million pesos, a huge amount for the times. Córdoba approached the brink of economic disaster pushed by the same slave hands that had produced its wealth. Planters in the region had to virtually start from scratch and rebuild their fortunes. Unwisely, they chose to resurrect the same type of society that the rebellion had nearly destroyed. They restocked their slave quarters with captive rebels and purchases from other districts that had already begun substituting free for slave labor. Córdoba emerged from this conflagration no better off than before. The region's planters remained committed as ever to their increasingly more peculiar way of life in a changing Mexico. Córdoba stood as an oasis of slavery and continued to suffer the unstable socioeconomic consequences.

Within six years the district's slaves revolted again. Some witnesses judged the third confrontation of the century as more intense than the one in 1735. But this time planters had prepared. Both sides met at La Palmilla estate to wage the decisive battle. A more quickly mobilized militia than the one fielded in the early stages of the 1735 revolt spelled the difference. Planter forces subdued the rebels with comparatively little bloodshed but with great monetary loss. After their defeat, the runaways sought refuge in surrounding cane fields. This forced drastic measures. With the memories of the 1735 events still fresh in Spaniards' minds, owners did what they felt they had to do: they torched their own crops to deny insurgents hiding places.

Despite repeated economic, social, and political dislocation from three slave revolts in just sixteen years, planters who dominated society in Córdoba emerged from the 1741 uprising still bent on the preservation of slavery. Slaves did not waste time in responding. Rebellion rocked the region for a fourth time in 1749. Eyewitnesses again described the scene as "tumultuous." Slaves on six estates rose up. A Spanish manager on the ingenio of San Antonio died first, killed by his own charges. Other whites soon followed him to the grave. Violent, disorganized skirmishes broke out in many places, and the rebels gained effective control over much of the countryside before authorities finally subdued them. A large number of surviving rebels retreated to the forested hills of Mata Anona, to the south. There they made their stand. Don Miguel de Lieba Esparragosa led the planter militia into battle. Fighting continued for three hours. Dead and wounded from both sides lay all over the site. This time the human costs exceeded the material losses, although Córdoba's Spanish inhabitants appeared to make little distinction between the human and material nature of slaves; to owners slaves often represented both.[12] Planters emerged from the events of 1749 still clinging to local slavery, and slaves responded just as predictably. Bondspeople again ran away and joined others in the rugged lands to the south. Fugitives, in turn, spread unrest.

Maroons repeatedly attacked travelers on the region's roads. Their depredations increased in intensity during the decade of the 1750s.[13] Subversive slave activities also heightened. In 1768 virtually every slave quarter in the district conspired to revolt. The uprising appeared as widespread as the 1735 upheaval but much better organized. Insurrection leaders scheduled simultaneous and coordinated action on all the plantations. They planned to strike during Easter morning Mass, the holiest ceremony on the Hispanic religious calender. Planters' preoccupation with the religious celebrations would make them vulnerable. Fortunately for the masters, a slave loyal to them betrayed the plot, and authorities captured its ringleaders before the planned fighting began. As a precaution, Spaniards temporarily prohibited all contact between slaves of neighboring plantations. Owners did not want to give their servants the opportunity to reorganize resistance.[14]

Intermittent violence continued until the end of the colonial period. Afro-Córdoban slaves coveted the freedom of their counterparts in other parts of central Veracruz and persevered in their struggle to achieve it. Planters' withstood these challenges until the early part of the next century.

Independence and Freedom

When Miguel Hidalgo y Castilla issued his "Grito de Dolores," on September 16, 1810, he and his followers, mainly nonwhite agricultural workers, had less to fight for than the bondspeople of Veracruz. At first slaves did not heavily identify with the conflict. It was figuratively and physically too far removed from their condition. But when Hidalgo realized that few creole Spaniards supported his movement, he turned more fully to the needs of common people. In order to appeal to the masses of Indians, *castas*, and blacks, he abolished the yearly head tax and called for an end to slavery.[15] Because of these and other factors, most notably the conspicuous racial imbalance of his forces (his followers were almost exclusively poor nonwhites) and the random attacks on Spaniards of whatever background (*peninsulares* and creoles alike), his movement acquired overtones of race war. This association may have helped alienate whites and wealthy individuals from his cause, but it had the opposite effect on Mexico's slave population, especially in areas where the institution still remained strong, such sites as Córdoba. In April of 1812, Hidalgo's revolt reached the district, where virtually all the bondservants responded to the call for emancipation. For the next ten years they fought for the cause that promised them freedom.[16]

With Hidalgo's death in 1811, leadership of the Mexican uprising passed first to Ignacio Rayón, the rebel Secretary of State, and from him to José María Morelos y Pavón, an insurgent priest who controlled the south-central region of the viceroyalty. Morelos, of partial African ancestry himself, went beyond Hidalgo's program of colonial reform. After 1813 Morelos called for independence and, among other things, reiterated Hidalgo's abolition of slavery.[17]

Morelos sent agents to agitate in regional pockets that still utilized slave labor. Two of these agents came to Córdoba. Francisco Servino Gómez concentrated his efforts in the slave quarters on the plantations of San José de Abajo and El Portrero. A mulatto called Juan Batista incited slaves on the plantations of Toluquilla, Chiquihuite, and Palma Sola. Lured by the promise of freedom, slaves from these estates fled to the camps of rebel bands operating within the zone.[18] The priests of Maltrata and Zongolica, Don Juan Moctezuma Cortés (the Cura of Maltrata and a direct descendent of the last Aztec emperor) and Miguel Moreno, respectively, commanded two of the largest forces operating in and around Córdoba. Runaway slaves from all over central Veracruz dominated the ranks of their followers. By the end of the year over a thousand insurgents operated within the district.[19] In response to this threat planters joined the royalist camp, and a slave/master split developed in Córdoba, ostensibly over the independence movement but actually over the issue of slavery.

Planters employed their time-honored response to slave revolt. They tried to force servants back into submission. In order to do this, masters recruited free whites, mestizos, mulattoes, *pardos*, and *negros*. They organized their forces into militia units and charged the units with keeping the area's plantations safe. But planters simply did not have the human resources to meet the threat. Spread out all over the countryside, they over-extended themselves. The result proved disastrous. Plantation after plantation fell prey to the guerrilla attacks.

In 1817 fighting somewhat subsided. With the demise of Morelos in December of 1815 and the subsequent collapse of coordinated resistance throughout Mexico, many rebels accepted the offer of amnesty proffered by royal officials in the following year. Those in Córdoba deviated little from this pattern with one major exception— runaway slaves. *Cimarrones* remained in their mountainous hideouts on the periphery of the district. They preferred fugitive to slave status.

The maroons' fears were not unfounded. Having gained the upper hand, Córdoba planters took the offensive. First, they turned their attention to halting defections and resistance from within their slave quarters. Having done this, they began to focus on the recapture of runaways and missing livestock. Planters raised a slave patrol to accomplish these tasks. On the plantations patrols began a campaign of terror aimed at intimidating slaves and diminishing their cooperation with *cimarrones*. The patrols tortured, and in some cases even killed, suspected runaway sympathizers. They regularly subjected female slaves to sexual abuse. They cut rations and other material supplies to intimidate slaves. The patrols also made forays into the surrounding hills in search of runaways and stolen livestock.

The planter offensive met with little success. *Cimarrones* proved too elusive in the rugged foothills. Patrols apprehended few of them. Maroons not only eluded their captors but also continued to cause havoc within the region by burning crops, waylaying travelers, and causing unrest in slave quarters. In 1817 bondspeople on the Concepción de Llave rose up and burned everything on the estate. They then followed maroon instigators to retreats in the hills. Slaves on the Pañuela did the same thing a few days later.[20] Although the level of fighting lowered, it never came to a complete halt during the remainder of the colonial period. Even after independence in 1821, Córdoba slaves refused to come down out of the mountains and take their places in the local slave quarters. They stubbornly clung to their limited freedom and continued to frustrate planters' efforts at rebuilding the area's slave economy. Vicente Guerrero, an old freedom fighter who like Morelos had some African ancestry, became president in 1829. He abolished slavery that same year.[21] Even then Córdoba's *cimarrones* refused to trust regional authorities and lay down their arms. Distant politicians had promised freedom too many times in the past, and local planters had reneged on those promises over and over again. The fugitives stayed at large for years. They did gradually filter back into society throughout the next decade, cautiously, with eyes toward any signs of betrayal. But this time the offer proved genuine. Their own slave resistance had helped shatter the slaveocracy. Córdoba's economy did not recover until after 1840. When it did, slavery belonged to the past. Local Afro-Córdobans had painfully made the transition from slavery to freedom in a revolutionary rather than an evolutionary fashion.

Jalapa and the Evolutionary Path to Freedom

The rise and fall of slavery in Jalapa and most of the rest of Veracruz proved much less spectacular than in Córdoba. Both events primarily resulted from the interplay of mundane factors that effected the lives of all residents in central Veracruz. Slavery, like everything else in the region, was closely tied to constantly shifting local demographic and economic conditions, as well as to occasional outside imperial forces.

When Constantino Bravo de Lagunas described Jalapa in 1580, he continually made reference to the rapidly declining Indian population. His statement about the provincial capital depicted an area in crisis. He attributed this tremendous drop in population to *cocolistli*, which first appeared in 1545 then again in 1576. The last outbreak still raged in 1580 at the beginning of Jalapa's heavy involvement in the African slave trade. He claimed that Indians had only themselves to blame. In his mind their ignorance and stubborn refusal to accept Spanish medical aid accounted for their suffering.[22] Bravo missed the mark in his assessment of the situation. High Indian mortality rates during this period had little to do with their supposed "ignorance." In part, the shock of conquest contributed, as did added labor demands. But the introduction of Old World diseases for which the natives had no natural resistance proved the main cause.[23] As time wore on, Indians adapted to their altered disease environment. By the mid-eighteenth century they succumbed to these epidemics no more often than non-Indians.[24] Smallpox struck Jalapa in 1797, 1813, and 1830. Combined, the three scourges claimed 360 victims.[25] Just as Bravo did two hundred years earlier, eighteenth-century Spaniards blamed the natives themselves for their high death rates. Indians refused inoculation and relied on ancient remedies, for example, *temascales* (a type of steam bath).[26] But late colonial death tolls fell far short of those suffered earlier. Sixteenth-century epidemics lasted for years and carried away thousands; eighteenth-century outbreaks endured for months and killed off hundreds. Fewer Indians died both numerically and proportionately compared to other groups. By this time all segments of the population displayed similar degrees of natural resistance to sicknesses. Disease became less tied to race and ethnicity and more to class and age.[27] The shadow of sickness passed from the Indians to the poor and the young. Burial registries during the 1797 smallpox epidemic support this conclusion. The first recorded victim was Austín Licona, infant son of two poor Afro-*castas*. In this, perhaps the worst of the district's eighteenth-century epidemics, over two hundred individuals perished. Very few of them had acquired enough worldly possessions to leave a will. And in terms of social status, only one had a "Don" before his name. Racially, those who died represented a motley group: whites, such as María Gertrudís Gervacio, Indians, such as Cipriano Jesús, mestizos, such as José Rosales, and Afrocastas, such as little Austín.[28] These new intersocioeconomic and demographic relationships led to greater population stability.

Jalapa's human resources expanded through natural increase and one other mechanism after 1720. Extraordinary economic activity connected with the fairs drew immigrants into the district. As Humboldt puts it, Jalapa grew from a humble region "principally inhabited by Indians, a few Spanish families, and a small number of negroes and mulattoes" into a thriving metropolis.[29] During the 1722–1776 fair period, district population growth accelerated to a rate of over 1 percent per year, nearly double the previous century's rate and higher than the viceroyalty's average.[30] Migration accounted for some of the jump in Jalapa's population increase. Jalapa's capital required a quick infusion of adult labor during the middle third of the century. The town and fair site needed hands to transport goods, it demanded workers to expand urban services, and it required laborers to care for pack animals and materials.

In the sixteenth century economic growth combined with demographic decline resulted in the forced migration of Africans. In the eighteenth century Atlantic economic influence coupled with local demographic increase yielded voluntary European and Mexican migration into the district. Peninsular Spaniards including Don Antonio Serrano, commander of the second and third convoys, and the brothers Don Francisco and Don Ignacio Urrutia arrived.[31] Other Europeans came from Portugal, France, and Italy. Creoles streamed in from such adjacent areas as Córdoba, Jalacingo, Perote, the port of Veracruz, Altotonga, and San Juan de los Llanos. A few traveled from as far away as Puebla, Oaxaca, Zacatecas, Michoacán, Toluca, Tlaxacala, Querétaro, Mexico City, Guadalajara, and the frontier province of Nuevo Santander (Tamaulipas).

These immigrants represented every hue on the racial color spectrum. Profits attracted white Europeans; they hoped to acquire enough capital to broaden their interests beyond the risky business of trade. With investment specie they could pursue more stable enterprises such as dry-goods retailing, urban real estate, and commercial agriculture. Less-ambitious *casta* artisans, skilled laborers, and muleteers arrived to obtain their share of the fairs' profits. Simi-

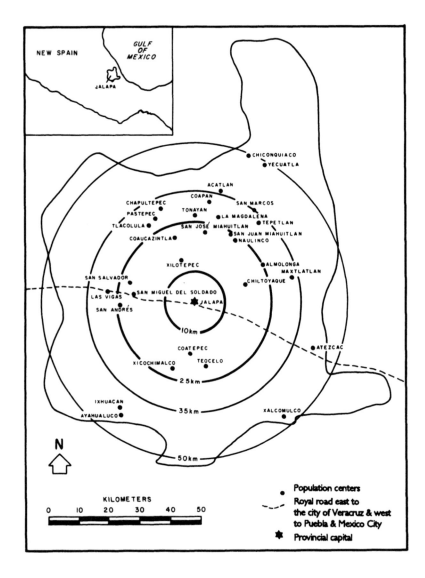

Map 5. Spatial zones of Jalapa, ca. 1700

larly, *indios extranjeros*, or migrant Indian workers, filtered in because of the heightened demand for their labor.

Map 5 offers a spatial view of the specific sites within the district that contributed workers to the capital. Available evidence indicates that moderate voluntary migration within and between the concentric zones did occur during the fair periods. The fairs lured a number of rural dwellers into the town of Jalapa. When the fairs ceased, an out-migration from the capital occurred.[32] Indeed, after the fair periods, many of the district's rural settlements experienced accelerated population growth. Ixhuacán, in the far southwestern highlands, went from just under six hundred to over two thousand inhabitants; Ayahualuco, to the south, grew from around four hundred residents to nearly one thousand right after the fairs.[33] The economic activity appears to have effected the middle zone (26–35 km from the capital) the least, but this conclusion remains tenuous. Indeed, shifts in settlement totals only imply migration; they do not show it. Marriage registries in the capital parish list birthplace for each of the contracting parties and, in the event they came from outside the environs of the town, the date of arrival. This information correlates much more closely to migration trends. It reveals a better picture of the currents of people within the district; it also gives a fuller view of interregional movement.

Table 7 shows the distribution of newcomers to Jalapa marrying in the town parish in three time periods: one just prior to, one during, and one immediately after the fairs. Migrant totals appear at the bottom of the table. In the decade before the fairs, parish registries list nearly twice as many Indian as non-Indian new arrivals. During the decade in the middle of the fairs, the figure for non-Indian newcomers more than doubled until they actually outnumbered Indian immigrants. In the sample after the fairs the in-flow of Indians dropped off more than that of non-Indians. These trends suggest that the fairs did not have a strong effect on natives. The number of incoming Indians rose slightly during fairs and dropped off moderately after them. In contrast, totals for Spanish, *casta*, and black immigrants into the capital climbed after the fairs began and dropped off somewhat after they ended.

Non-Indians from beyond the district appeared most responsive to the district capital's shifting economic conditions. They accounted for nearly 90 percent of all Spanish and *casta* migrants into the capital before and during the fairs. With the cessation of the fairs, the percentage of non-Jalapans dropped and the proportion of rural Jalapans rose among the Spanish and *casta* migrants to the capital.

Table 7. *Zone of Origin and Indian/Non-Indian Status of Individuals Marrying in the Town of Jalapa, 1711–1801*

Zone of Origin	1711–1720 Indian	1711–1720 Non-Indian	1744–1753 Indian	1744–1753 Non-Indian	1792–1801 Indian	1792–1801 Non-Indian
From sites inside 25 km of fair	153	48	122	74	84	106
From sites 25–35 km of fair	5	6	7	3	2	6
From sites 36–50 km of fair	2	0	7	0	1	5
From sites outside the district	15	45	76	187	46	85
Total migrants	175	99	212	264	133	202
Percentage of all persons in the sample	64	36	45	55	40	60

Source: APJ, Matrimonios, Caja 3, Libro 8, leaves 9–119v; Ibid., Entierros, Caja 2, Libro 7, leaves 1–65; Ibid., Matrimonios, Caja 3, Libro 8, leaves 61v–153v; Ibid., Matrimonios, Caja 3, Libro 9, leaves 1–135v; Ibid., Matrimonios, Caja 7, Libro 18, leaves 1–73v; Ibid., Matrimonios, Caja 7, Libro 19, leaves 1–23v.

Note: Correlation coefficients for the immigrant case distribution for the zone supplying the greatest number of intradistrict immigrants to the capital (the area within 25 km of the capital) indicate that Indians comprised a majority of the migrants during the 1711–1720 period. This period yielded an observed Chi Sq. of 54.85 > the critical value of 3.84 @ a 0.05 level of significance. The same held true for the period 1744–1753 (Chi Sq. 11.75 > 3.84 @ 0.05). However, during the 1792–1801 years, after the fairs, migrants from the closest zone to the capital were no more likely to be Indians than non-Indians (Chi Sq. 2.54 < 3.84 @ 0.05). The fair site primarily attracted non-Indian migrants from outside the district during all three decades sampled. This is supported by the following correlation coefficients:

1711–1729, Chi Sq. 15.00 > 3.84 @ 0.05.
1744–1753, Chi Sq. 5.68 > 3.84 @ 0.05.
1792–1801, Chi Sq. 11.61 > 3.84 @ 0.05.

The Fairs and Social Change

Labor needs clearly rose in Jalapa between 1722 and 1778, because of the area's renewed involvement in Atlantic commerce. Had local demographic conditions remained as stressed as they were from 1550 to 1610, Jalapa might have again imported African slaves. By

1700, however, Jalapa, like most of the rest of Mexico, experienced natural population increase. This coupled with immigration pro-duced a cheaper labor alternative to slavery. Resulting social change from this mix of local demographic and imperial economic shifts smoothed the way to Afro-Jalapans' freedom. And all these struc-tural factors caused bondage to die a less-violent death in Jalapa than in Córdoba.

At least partially due to the fair-induced flow of people into the urban zone, officials held a hearing in 1769 to discuss creating a second town parish. Persons with varying racial and ethnic back-grounds were experiencing greater contact with one another as new arrivals took up residence in Indian *barrios* on the outskirts of the capital. Don Francisco de Escalante, a native of Castile, Spain, had relocated in the *barrio* of La Laguna. A merchant, he favored the new parish. He said that families of different racial and ethnic back-grounds lived in formerly all-Indian *barrios*, such as La Laguna. With the presence of these outsiders the *barrio* had grown to the point that the main parish could no longer service it. Don Juan Echevarria, another Castilian merchant, lived in the neighboring *barrio* of Los Berros. He too noted the influx of new *castas* and In-dians into the *barrios*. Isidro de Santa Ana, a mestizo laborer from San Juan de los Llanos to the southwest of the district, resided in the Indian *barrio* of Santiago. He favored the new parish because of population growth. Don Manuel de Rivera, a *pardo* and a lieutenant in the town's *pardo* militia company, pointed out that the fair trade had drawn *casta* muleteers into the district from other parts of the viceroyalty. They lived on the edge of town among the Indians. He feared that without added religious guidance from the new parish non-Indian immigrants would incline the natives toward "loose living."

Crown and church officials worried about the consequences of heightened interracial contact. Those on the hearing committee es-timated that the new parish would serve over twenty-three hundred individuals in the *barrios* on the eastern edge of town. Of these parishioners about fourteen hundred fell within the category of *gente de razón*, or Hispanicized whites and *castas*. Committee members and witnesses alike described Indians in the barrios as *ladinos*, or individuals who had already acquired Spanish cultural traits, such as religion, language, and economic behavior.[34] The social impact of outsiders attracted by the fairs must not be over-stated since they comprised a minority of entries in the marriage registries throughout the fair period. They did, however, comprise a large minority, nearly a third of the entries.[35] While the fairs remained in operation, non-Indians within urban Jalapa's population gained in numerical strength. This growth created a racially and ethnically more fluid environment that benefitted nonwhite groups, including Afro-Jalapans.

In the case of Indians, the fairs' greatest impact fell on two types: those most attuned to pressures exerted by a revived imperially driven economy, the most-Hispanicized Indians, and those physically most accessible, Indians who resided in and around the hub of economic activity—the district capital. Despite their high profits and high employment potential, the fairs apparently did not heavily affect natives beyond a twenty-five kilometer radius of the capital.

Manuel Antonio Ramos represented the type of Indian most influenced by the fairs. He was a Totonoc native from one of the *barrios*, or indigenous neighborhoods, on the outskirts of the capital. The fact that Manuel had a surname indicates a fairly high degree of Hispanization since most Indians possessed Christian names only. Sometime in the early 1770s he moved to the nearby Nahuatl village of Xilotepec, fifteen kilometers to the north. Once there, he sought seasonal work on the nearby sugar estates that drew labor from the village. He found a job on the plantation Nuestra Señora de la Concepción. A Nahua field boss from Xilotepec named Sebastián Fabian (no surname) acted as Manuel's immediate supervisor. Sebastián evidently took a liking to the stranger and introduced him to his daughter, María Pasquala. Manuel was sixteen and María thirteen. A short time later they married.[36] Presumably, each had an effect on the lifestyle of the other.

When the fairs ended, Jalapans faced more than a decade of economic uncertainty. In his introduction to the 1791 census, Vicente Nieto described the shock of losing the fair: "With the opulence and lively commerce of the flotas, the vicinity acquired a luxurious character that it could not sustain with their extinction [*sic*] what profits have been derived from industry and agriculture were inverted into housing and office construction that with the termination of the flotas are empty and useless."[37]

Economic expansion created the potential for heightened interracial and interethnic contact. Cessation of the fairs, as noted in the next chapter, did not fully reduce interaction between groups. Increased interaction, in turn, necessitated modifications in mechanisms of Iberian and creole white social control in the last century of colonial rule.

Conclusion

Jalapa more than Córdoba illustrated the common path to Afro-Veracruzano freedom. In the former, slavery's death primarily came from evolutionary causes; in the latter, it came largely from violent confrontation between masters and slaves. The course of events in both areas flowed more from local than international conditions, although the latter did play a part. In most of Veracruz the eighteenth-century Afro-Veracruzano journey from bondage to liberty proved peaceful because it was directed by reaction to altering local sociodemographic and economic influences. Imperial economic forces did play some role, but Veracruz pressures dominated. In this sense, such settings as Jalapa evolutionarily outgrew slavery. A new labor order based on wage incentives came into place. In general, Mexico made this shift more easily than other areas in the Americas, for example, Brazil, the U.S., and some Caribbean islands. Unlike in those areas, most of New Spain had not relied heavily on slave labor for long periods of time. Even in central Veracruz (Córdoba excepted), a region closely identified with Afro-Mexican slavery, the institution flourished only from about 1580 to 1630. By 1700 it had fallen into decline in all but a handful of areas. Free *pardos* and mulattoes along with other *castas* and Hispanicized Indians replaced African slave laborers. Resident bondspeople no longer dominated plantation populations. As early as 1777 these new groups accounted for over 90 percent of the people living on sugar estates within the district of Jalapa. By 1791 only a handful of slaves resided on the Orduña plantation just north of the district capital.[38] Pacho still maintained a few bondservants as late as 1814. In that same year, however, Pacho's owner, Don Miguel de Iriarte, sold the estate and returned to Spain. Disillusioned by growing local disaffection with the homeland's inability to pacify the countryside in the face of mounting pressure for independence, he decided to sever all his ties with Mexico. Don Miguel tried to sell off his property, including his slaves. In attempting to do this, he came to fully realize the inviability of slavery. He not only found slave values depressed, he had difficulty selling servants at any price. Owners of several other plantations within the district, including San Antonio, Orduña, Tuzamapa, Concepción, Pileta, Encero, and Almolonga, also tried to divest themselves of bondspeople just before independence, and they glutted the local slave market. Frustrated, Don Miguel decided that selling his bondservants was not worth the effort, so he simply freed them.[39]

Other owners proved less ready to write off the value of slaves. Some even encouraged slaves to purchase their own freedom. Raising the necessary funds, however, proved a difficult task. Antonia de la Cruz was forty years old when she made the first payment on her freedom. Before her master and a local notary she counted out one hundred pesos in reales (eight reales to a peso).[40] At her age, still burdened with a 150-peso debt, Antonia faced insecurity. In contrast, her master had rid himself of a bad investment and avoided the responsibility of supporting an aging slave.

Regardless of the motive, the incidence of manumission increased in the eighteenth century. This fact, plus fewer slave sales, and depressed slave prices all reflected the decreasing importance of this extraordinary form of labor. As Humboldt put it in 1805, "The number of slaves in New Spain is next to nothing. . . . Sugar is chiefly the produce of free hands."[41] In 1829, when Mexico legally abolished slavery, owners raised little protest. No major debates appeared in the newspapers or on the floors of either house of the national congress. Compared to later abolition movements in the United States, Brazil, and Cuba, the freeing of Mexican slaves proved a very uncontroversial matter. For all practical purposes, slavery had already died.

In 1821 Agustín Iturbide, commander of the Revolutionary Army, appointed a commission to study the problem of slavery in Mexico. It included some of the most prominent individuals in the country, Francisco Manuel Sánchez de Tagle, the Marquis of Sierra Nevada, Antonio de Gama y Córdoba, the Count of Heras Soto, and the fabulously wealthy and influential entrepreneur José María Fagoaga. They concluded that only about three thousand slaves remained in the country and that the institution had virtually expired. Their final report hardly even addressed the committee's two charges dealing with the institution's historical abusiveness and the then-current status of the slave trade. Neither topic held contemporary relevance. In the case of historical evils of Mexican slavery, the slave population had become too small to warrant attention, and the slave trade had ceased. As a result, the commission turned to more contemporary concerns. It dealt almost exclusively with de facto slave conditions under which small industrial, bakery, and pork shop workers suffered. They also gave special attention to the growing practice of advancing wages as an inducement for Indian workers to sign long-term labor contracts (debt peonage). In order to bring law in line with reality, the commission suggested freedom for all slaves born in the country after independence. The government never put this proposal into effect. Instead, weaker legislation passed. It provided freedom for all slaves brought into the country by foreigners.[42]

Mexico did set up a special fund to purchase liberty for remaining Mexican slaves, but this represented a token gesture.[43] The new government did not have money to spend on compensating owners for the remaining three thousand bondservants. Ceremoniously, local town councils liberated a few slaves each year on the anniversary of independence. One even suspects that this liberating really represented nothing more than a form of political favoritism allowing private individuals to unload poor investments at the expense of the national treasury. Regardless of the motive, it effected only a fraction of a small minority of the general population. One of the largest groups freed totaled just seventeen individuals in 1825.[44] The following year two slaves escaped their bondage in this way.[45] Finally, in 1829, President Vicente Guerrero unconditionally declared an end to Mexican slavery. This act for most areas, such as Jalapa and even Córdoba, merely represented a legal recognition of the path that the Afro-Mexican experience had already taken.

7

Free Afro-Veracruzanos and the Late Colonial Socioeconomic Order

THIS CHAPTER focuses on Afro-Veracruzanos and the meaning and application of race within a socioeconomic context. By the eighteenth century a combination of primarily domestic and secondarily international conditions made slavery a less-viable labor system. These events resulted in the substitution of wage for coerced labor in most locales. With the diminishing importance of slavery came a corresponding alteration in the general Afro-Veracruzano experience. Slaves and their free counterparts found themselves caught up in a changing socioeconomic environment. Some have argued that Afro-Mexicans' racial identification, regardless of their slave/free status, still restricted them to low socioeconomic rank.[1] Others conclude that considerations of social race (ethnicity) replaced biological race as the primary determinant socioeconomic rank.[2] Still others judge that economic class superceded biological and social race as the main factor in ordering socioeconomic status.[3]

Controversy also exists over the cause of persistence or change in the social structure of late colonial Mexico. Those seeing continuity often tie this lack of change to transplanted and persistent European feudalistic socioeconomic systems that endured both out of inertia and intervention by European metropolitan-based political and economic powers.[4] Others link continuity to local changes in means and modes of production involved in the Mexican shift from a more feudalistic to a more capitalistic economy.[5]

This essay attempts, through examination of free Afro-Veracruzanos' evolving social and economic experiences, to shed light on the above questions about the nature and cause of socioeconomic change in the late colonial period.

Significance of Race

As early as the first quarter of the seventeenth century Jalapans commonly used the six racial terms defined in Chapter 5, namely: white, Indian, *negro*, mestizo, mulatto, and *pardo*. Those who constructed and attached these racial identifications to individuals played a central role in maintaining the caste system. Parish priests served as the most active catalogers. Daily they called upon their own judgment in deciding which racial entries to make alongside the names of parishioners. After local clerics, notaries proved the next most important definers and defenders of color lines. In recording commercial transactions of the day, notaries seldom failed to note the races of the parties involved. Whites exclusively served as priests and notaries. As members of the elite group, they remained committed to the concept of their group's racial supremacy. Consequently, most took their duties very seriously.[6]

Racial catalogers did not assign designations on the basis of genetic background. They simply matched persons against popularly accepted somatic norms of the six recognized racial groups. In doing this, catalogers used three basic physical characteristics to define race. In order of significance these included skin color, beard thickness, and facial features.[7] Very little evidence in the central-Veracruz setting suggests that acquired ethnic traits and wealth played as important a role as physical traits in the ascription of race. Thus, in 1736, a Jalapa notary described a female slave as a "white" mulatto, referring to her extremely light complexion. Juan Francisco Díaz appeared *pardo*, or grayish-brown; Juliana de Reyes looked *morena*, or ebony.[8]

Though the ecclesiastical records contain racial references very similar to those found in the notarial records, their color designations seemed less precise. Clerics made these determinations many more times a day than notaries did. Consequently, they used fewer and more standardized racial terms. Whereas a notary might describe a mulatto as being the same shade of yellow as the quince fruit, a curate merely listed him as mulatto.

Vicente González received last rights in 1606. In the margin beside his name the priest wrote *pardo*, but in the textual entry he elaborated. To the prelate's trained eye, Vicente had skin "de color pardo" (*pardo* in color).[9] As time went on, the phrase "de color" dropped from usage. By the eighteenth century it only appeared in a few of the notarial entries. Despite abbreviations in racial terminology, the basis of classification remained the same. Skin color functioned as the most important dividing line separating one group from another.

Emphasis on color led to another step in the development of the colonial terminology. This development involved the distinction between mulattoes and *pardos,* two groups that steadily rose in number throughout the sixteenth and seventeenth centuries. Increasing membership in both groups complicated the system of classification. During the early colonial period (up until about 1600) Spaniards used the term mulatto for all Afro-*castas.* This proved misleading. From the beginning of contact, Africans miscegenated with Indians just as their Spanish masters did. Together these two partners in conquest procreated offspring markedly different from one another in appearance. The children of black-Indian parents appeared darker skinned than the children of white-Indian parents.[10] On April 20, 1671, Diego Hernández, a layman, baptized his dying neighbor. The ecclesiastical scribe listed the dead woman as a "mulatta" but described Diego as "pardo de color."[11] At Beatrís de la Cruz' baptism, the prelate recorded her as black; yet the same priest in the same document listed her father as a mulatto, and her mother as black.[12] Two fraternal twins, María and Josefa Sánchez, had an Indian father and a *parda* mother, but the cleric recorded the first as a *parda* and second as Indian.[13] In a fourth case, a prelate described the child of a white-*pardo* union as a *parda.*[14] Despite this lack of precision in the application of race, racial identification carried with it real socioeconomic significance. Labels attached at birth stuck for life. A cleric classified Pasqual Díaz, Hypolita Antonia, and María Tiburias Rodríquez, all children of either *pardo-parda* or *negro*-Indian parents, as *pardos.* The mulattoes Manuel de la Cruz, Josepha Calderón, Juan Francisco Mejía, and María Rangel each had either *mulato-mulata* or, in rare cases, white-*negro* parents. The same pattern held true for mestizo children, the products of mestizo-mestiza or white-Indian unions. Of the two possibilities, racially alike parents and racially mixed parents, the former appeared most commonly in the documents.[15] This apparently represents yet another example of the catalogers' lack of concern for genealogical backgrounds and their heavy reliance on physical appearance. Otherwise, records would have yielded a higher incidence of mixed offspring coming from mixed parents during the sixteenth and seventeenth centuries.

Race and Spatial Distribution

Spatially, late-eighteenth-century urban society organized itself along the basic racial lines illustrated in Figure 4. Within urban Jalapa and Orizaba the pattern of racial distribution involved concentric bands of residents with progressively more non-Spanish backgrounds, laid over a nucleus with heavy Spanish representation.[16] Six of every ten Spaniards lived within a short radius of the town square, the focal point of Jalapa's colonial economic, social, and political power. Peoples socially subordinate to Spaniards commonly resided in *barrios*, or outer neighborhoods. *Pardos*, mulattoes, and mestizos ranked below Spaniards. This lower rank relegated them to residences on the fringes of the urban core. Hispanicized Indians represented a second subordinate group. They made their homes in the most distant urban *barrios*.

In rural Córdoba, Jalapa, and Orizaba, Spaniards and *castas* commonly lived in a select number of *pueblos* closest to the district capitals.[17] Most Indians inhabited outlying villages, settlements whose racial integrity the crown juridically protected as Repúblicas de los Indios. All groups displayed proportionate representation (vis a vis their percentage in the broader population) on small and large agricultural units.[18] The one major exception to this rule did not involve the free population. Within Córdoba's commercial agricultural slavocracy Afro-*casta* bondservants accounted for two-thirds (67 percent) of the plantation population.[19]

In the rural zones, spatial distribution apparently followed ethnic rather than racial lines. This probably resulted from naturales' dominance in this setting. In the Indian world, social race seems to have counted more than biological race in shaping socioeconomic patterns, a contrast with the Hispanic urban setting in which biological race counted for more.[20]

Race and Occupation

Occupation provides a good indicator of socioeconomic status.[21] In order to measure occupational rank, I used a very simple three-tiered vertical scale that, at least in my mind, reflects attitudes held in colonial Veracruz. Elites comprise the top rank. Within the commercial and sugar cultures of the region this category includes entrepreneurs, plantation owners, and professionals.[22] The Mid-Level rank encompasses medium- and small-sized commercial agriculturalists: *labradores* (mid-sized farmers), *rancheros* (small farmers), and pro-

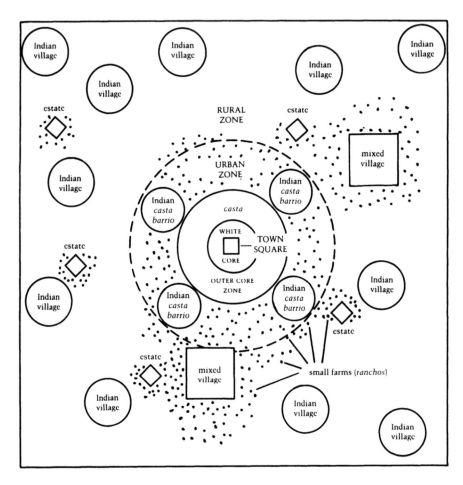

Figure 4. Schematic representation of racial distribution in Jalapa and Orizaba, 1791.

duce farmers. It also includes estate administrators, small merchants (intradistrict-level traders), clerks, students, such low-level
officials as constables and scribes, skilled tradespeople (both masters and journeymen), artists, musicians, teachers, and clerks. Into
the Low-Level socioeconomic rank fall common urban and rural
workers, servants, wood gatherers, bearers, muleteers, and soldiers
below sergeant's rank.

I then compared each racial group's representation within these
three occupational ranks. I assumed that the more even the distribution in all three categories the lower the correlation between race
and socioeconomic ranking by occupation with but two qualifications. First, in drawing conclusions from the data, I took into account the fact that the number of occupational openings increased
from top to bottom on the scale. Second, non-Indian representation
at the low end of the scale is inflated because of the amount of missing data for Indians who fell most heavily in the Low-Level category.
From a total of over six thousand cases collected between 1786 and
1791 in all three districts, the following pattern of occupational distribution emerged for the end of the colonial period.[23]

European and creole Spaniards alike virtually monopolized membership in the Elite category for both the urban and rural zones in
all three districts. Probability of rising to Elite occupational rank
closely correlated to white racial identification. Spaniards also appear to have dominated the ranks of the Mid-Level occupational
category, athough not to the extent they did the Elite one. Spaniards'
representation in the Low-Level rank proved weakest given the high
probability for anyone to fall into this category because of the high
number of occupational openings at this rank and the absence of
Indian data.[24]

Castas enjoyed heaviest representation at the Mid-Level and second heaviest representation at the Low-Level in Jalapa. Córdoban
and Orizaban *castas* displayed the opposite order of predominance.
In these two districts *castas* most commonly held Low-Level positions followed in frequency by Mid-Level ones. This held true in
both the urban and rural sectors.

Indian case distributions present a bit more of an interpretative
problem. Since much of my data for Jalapa and Orizaba came from
the military census counts that did not include Indians, to compile
a meaningful sample of native occupational distribution proved impossible. A 1786 census for rural Córdoba did, however, include
Indians and list their occupations. Moreover, tribute rolls dated at
the turn of the century for all three districts included Indians.[25]
These sources, coupled with qualitative evidence, suggest that In-

dians occupied very few positions in the region's Mid-Level and none in the Elite rank. Instead they appear to have dominated the lowest paying and least prestigious jobs in the urban and rural wage labor force. However, the data supports the earlier conclusion that other groups, including Spaniards, enjoyed over-representation in the Mid-Level rank and that whites dominated Elite positions.

These observations make it tempting to conclude on a basis of distribution patterns for the Mid-Level, and to a greater extent the Low-Level, ranks that race did not strongly correlate with occupational position. Indeed, John Chance and William Taylor deduce this from similar patterns in Oaxaca as does Rodney Anderson for Guadalajara.[26] But at least two possible explanations come to mind for the potentially most critical deviation in the above patterns from a caste system of stratification, namely, somewhat high Spanish representation in the lowest occupational rank. First, although their percentage of all cases in this level proved unexpectedly high (30 to 40 percent of all cases in the category, depending on the zone), the number of Spaniards in the Low-Level versus all three occupational levels proved proportionately lower (20 to 25 percent, again depending on the setting). More importantly, the absence of Indian cases in the Low-Level rank undoubtedly inflated representation for other groups. In rural Córdoba, the only setting that contained Indian occupational cases in this rank, Spanish representation fell well below the group's representation in the other two levels, while Euro- and Afro-*castas* were only slightly less represented in the Low- than the Mid-Level rank.[27] This pattern indicates a strong overall association between race and occupational rank with but one qualification. The high representation of *castas* at the occupational Mid-Level suggests that the association between race and occupational status weakened below the Elite rank on this stratification scale, indicating that the caste system eroded a bit below the white-controlled Elite level. This represents a very tenuous conclusion because the absence of complete totals for Indians skews results at the low and possibly even the middle occupational categories. Examination of social relations within and between the various components of the region's racially pluralistic society sheds further light on the question of race's influence in socioeconomic stratification.

Social Bonding and Race

Social ties that formed in central Veracruz reflected the association of race with social rank. *Padrinazgo,* or godparenting, and marriage witnessing represented two moderately strong types of social link-

Table 8. *Percentage of Change in Afro-Jalapans' Social Alignments by Period and Race*

	1645–1715		1715–1750		1750–1805	
	Urban	Rural	Urban	Rural	Urban	Rural
Negro	38%	32%	70%	83%	20%	30%
Pardo	23%	34%	84%	69%	19%	19%
Mulatto	35%	31%	109%	92%	43%	13%
Total	96%	97%	263%	244%	82%	62%

Source: Same as for Tables A.22 and A.23, Appendix 3. I arrived at these percentages by totaling the percentage differences for each group's interaction with other racial groups in the society between the two adjacent sets of dates for each vertical column above.

ages. Because of these linkages' frequency and relatively casual nature, whites, and perhaps Indians as well, had a difficult time in preventing interracial bonding through these types of activities. Table 8 traces a century and a half of racial interaction through these ceremonies in Jalapa.

Between 1645 and 1715 the three Afro-Jalapan groups more freely engaged in godparenting and marriage witnessing activities with members of other racial groups than did any other segment of the population. Most of their interracial contacts, however, took place with other groups of African descent. *Pardos* served as godparents or marriage witnesses for *negros*. Mulattoes did the same for *pardos* as did *negros*. In addition, all but mulattoes frequently entered into these types of ties with Indians, especially in the urban sector of the district. Few forged these links with mestizos, and even fewer with Spaniards.

The post-1720 fair period ushered in two changes. First, the tendency to make such cross-racial social links strengthened among Afro-Jalapans. Before the fairs, roughly half the members of both Afro-*casta* groups and *negros* engaged in interracial social bonding through *padrinazgo* and marriage witnessing; during and after the fairs nearly two-thirds of them did so. Second, the fairs brought about a higher incidence of Afro-Jalapan interaction with mestizos. As late as 1715 mestizos accounted for an average of only 10 percent of all participants in ceremonies involving Afro-Jalapans. This held true in the urban and rural setting. After 1750 the degree of mestizo involvement tripled in the city and doubled in the countryside. These expanded ties held beyond the fair period and the turn of the century.[28] More generally, the greatest realignment of interracial social relationships took place between 1715 and 1750 while the fairs operated. Table 8 measures the percentage change in nearly eight hundred baptismal and marriage ceremonies between 1645 and 1805. It shows the effect of heightened Bourbon-inspired economic activity on interracial social bonding. The quickened pace of change appears to have had a dramatic effect on Afro-Jalapans' social contact with members of other racial groups. While the fairs operated, the percentage of Afro-*castas* and *negros* engaging in racially exogamous baptismal and marriage-witnessing ceremonies rose sharply. After the fairs these percentages dropped back to their prefair percentage levels.

Marriage and Race

Marriage offers one of the best means of correlating race and social rank. Spouses entered into extended personal contacts that impacted not only on their own immediate status within the community but also upon their future children's standing as well. The analysis below emerged from comparisons of racial identifications for partners in over fifteen thousand marriages within both urban and rural zones of Córdoba, Jalapa, and Orizaba between 1791 and 1802.[29]

In early and middle colonial Veracruz the color line greatly restricted interracial marriages. Over nine in ten Spaniards wed other Spaniards during these years. The same held true for Indians.[30] A handful of biracial marriages and many more illicit unions, however, increased the ranks of *castas*. While miscegenation increased racial categories, it, coupled with a decline in the Veracruz-African slave trade, virtually eradicated one of the original racial and ethnic groups.[31] Black Africans underwent near racial absorption and ethnic assimilation between 1620 and 1750 in central Veracruz. These events coupled with the general climate of change ushered in by the century of Bourbon Reforms beginning around 1720 in Jalapa brought about some modifications in the *sistema de las castas*, or caste system. Racial interaction increased as evidenced by the above *padrinazgo* and marriage-witnessing patterns. What follows attempts to gauge race's importance in the selection of spouses within this late-colonial regional setting.

Córdobans displayed the strongest overall persistence of racial endogamy in marriage of the three populations examined. Orizaba, in contrast, exhibited the sharpest break with the past. In the latter setting nearly as many people married outside their racial group as not by the end of the eighteenth century. The inhabitants of Jalapa fell between these two extremes in their racial preferences when selecting mates. Moreover, just as in the middle colonial period, racial endogamy did not occur much more frequently in the urban zone than in the rural zone.[32] Whites exercised no greater control over this type of activity in their enclave of influence than Indians did in theirs.[33]

Beyond the above general patterns, members of individual racial groups behaved somewhat differently in choosing spouses. At the end of the eighteenth century Indians in central Veracruz married members of their own race more commonly than members of other segments of the population. As in past samples, in over 90 percent of native weddings both parties were Indians.[34] High levels of endogamy even held true in the urban zones of Jalapa and Orizaba. Of those few Indians who did marry outside their race, rural females appear most heavily represented in the cases examined.[35]

Spaniards displayed the second highest degree of endogamy in marriage. Controlling for gender had no discernable affect on this trend. The same held true for the urban/rural residential factor. However, when compared to the middle colonial period, whites' propensity to hold the color line appears to have diminished somewhat by the second half of the eighteenth century. Roughly 10 percent more whites married nonwhites in 1800 than they had in 1645.[36]

Mestizos, like whites, demonstrated a greater tendency to choose marriage partners of another race from at least 1750 onward. This drift away from endogamy proved strongest in rural Jalapan females and among Orizaban mestizos in general.

In Córdoba and Orizaba Afro-*casta* endogamy rates decreased more than any other group's. In the Jalapa setting mulattoes and *pardos* showed slightly more mixed patterns. There, the incidence of urban Afro-*casta* males marrying within their racial group actually increased after the middle colonial period. Conversely, the percentage of urban Afro-*casta* females marrying Afro-*casta* males dropped sharply. After averaging gender differences in urban Jalapa and percentage breakdowns in the other two districts, the urban sector emerged as the crucible of greatest Afro-*casta* racial exogamy in marriage.[37]

Due to the paucity of evidence for free *negros*, I can draw few conclusions about their choices of marriage partners. Based upon the little data available, they appear to have acted very exogamously in these activities. Urban and rural males in Córdoba and rural females in Orizaba married outside their racial group over half the time. Rural Córdoban females proved the only exception to this rule.[38]

The general pattern that emerges from the above analysis suggests relatively high rates of racial endogamy in marriage for whites and Indians and moderately high levels for *castas*. Orizaba proved somewhat exceptional in this respect. There, *castas* married non*castas* nearly 50 percent of the time.

Overall marriage patterns also suggest an erosion of the caste system in late colonial central Veracruz. Increased incidence of interracial marriages among all groups but Indians points to this conclusion. On the other hand, the degree and rate of change in maintaining the color line does not appear that great. For example, in 1645 nine in ten whites wed other whites; in 1800 eight in ten whites married whites. Spanish racial endogamy in marriage had changed little in a century and a half. Just as importantly, the nature of that change proved very limited. Those whites who wed outside their race invariably selected mestizo mates. Indeed, combined white-white and white-mestizo marriage totals accounted for an average of around 95 percent of all unions involving Spaniards in late colonial central Veracruz. If whites strayed from the earlier color line, they did not go far.[39]

Patterns for *castas* and negros generally present a different picture from those of whites and Indians. In the case of mestizos, collapsing their matches with white individuals into the same category as those with other mestizos eliminates much of their racial exogamy in marriage, yielding only slightly lower adjusted percentages than the same procedure produced for whites (95 percent vs. 90 percent).[40] However, this procedure fails to produce the same results for Afro-*castas* or *negros* in two important respects. Even when combined with the most common non-Afro-*casta* group from which Afro-*castas* drew marriage partners in 1800, the totals fail to yield rates of 90 percent or above in half the types of Afro-*casta* marriages measured. In addition, unlike whites, Afro-*castas* showed no consistency in choosing marriage partners from other races. For example, in urban Jalapa exogamous Afro-*casta* men most commonly married *mestiza* women. Urban Afro-*casta* females there appeared to favor whites in their interracial matches. Rural Afro-*casta* males and females alike often selected Indian partners. In the Córdoban countryside Afro-*casta* females chose *negro* spouses almost as frequently as they selected Afro-*casta* ones. *Castas*, and especially Afro-*castas* along with *negros*, did deviate more than Indians and whites from the racially apartheid policies that played such a strong role in spouse selection during the early and middle colonial periods.

Increased imperial intervention in central Veracruz in matters such as the Jalapa trade fairs seems to have speeded social change, but these shifts probably would have occurred anyway as evidenced by the fact that removal of the fairs did not alter the direction of social realignments by race. In these matters the Atlantic-based political economy seems to have played the role of an intervening rather than an independent variable. Heightened European intervention all complicated the meaning and socioeconomic application of race.[41] In the final analysis, the most important consideration in determining the nature and degree of alteration in the social application of race between the middle and the late colonial periods comes down to the rate of change in the racial endogamy in the most extreme form of social bonding-marriage. Table 9 attempts to measure that rate between 1645 and 1800.

Whites, *castas*, and *negros* displayed the greatest drop in marriage endogamy, the highest belonging to the urban based of the latter two groups (−13 percent). Indian rates remained virtually the same over the 155-year period. Moreover, very little change occurred in the combined overall percentage averages for all groups. Trade fair–accelerated rates of lesser interracial social bonding (*padrinazgo* and marriage witnessing) did not lead to comparable increases in racial marriage exogamy. The overall average rates of marriage endogamy for all groups combined dropped just 6 percentage points in 155 years. Racism lost little in influencing choice of marriage partner by the end

Table 9. *Percentage of Endogamous Afro-Jalapan Marriages by Zone and Race, 1645 and 1805*

	1645	1805	Difference
% Whites			
Urban	96	86	−10
Rural	90	79	−11
% *Castas* and *negros*			
Urban	77	64	−13
Rural	82	79	− 3
% Indians			
Urban	96	98	+ 2
Rural	97	98	+ 1
Overall combined % for all groups	90	84	− 6

Source: I derived these percentages from Table A.24, found in Appendix 3.

of the colonial period. In this regional setting at least, race based on physical appearance still played a very important role in choice of spouse.

The above socioeconomic "patterns" help place race in better late colonial context. Change had taken place between the middle and the late colonial periods, especially in the charged economic atmosphere of such places as eighteenth-century Jalapa. Yet, these generalizations, because of their abstract nature, have real limitations in communicating the significance of modifications to the caste system. Human illustrations of these changes at work make their affect more apparent. Real people and race's impact on their lives drives home an important point that the above socioeconomic patterns may have understated. Practical racial categories may have changed, and some racial drift may have occurred as evidenced by a bit more cross-racial social bonding for all but Indians. Nevertheless, race remained a very powerful mechanism of social control in central Veracruz down to the end of the colonial period.

Race and Real People

Francisco Toral immigrated to New Spain as a sailor aboard one of the *flota* ships. Generally, mariners like him enjoyed little respect within Spanish society.[42] Once Francisco reached Veracruz, he decided to stay. Eventually, Toral followed the huge pack trains of goods to the fairgrounds in Jalapa. Once there, he bought some land, not the best plot, but land nevertheless. By 1791 he owned a farm in the village of Banderilla, just a few kilometers west of the capital and adjacent to the royal road leading up onto the central plateau. This purchase represented a significant step up the socioeconomic ladder for a lowly mariner. But Banderilla's proximity to the capital and the royal road did not cancel out its rural nature, and in the countryside Spanish women proved scarce. Accordingly, Francisco married one of the available females at hand, an Indian woman named Hilaria Antonia.[43]

Francisco Toral achieved moderate economic success. As a *labrador*, he ranked in the middle level of the occupational scale described in the previous section. Despite his economic status, he did not enjoy comparable social rank. In the census report of 1791 no socially prestigious "Don" appeared before his name nor did a "Doña" appear before Hilaria's. A second Spanish immigrant, Joaquín Torano, was an urban shopkeeper. This occupation held no more social prestige than a *labrador*. Yet, the word "Don" did precede Joaquín's name in all the records. Despite comparable economic status, Torano enjoyed higher social rank than Toral. Choice of spouse may have had something to do with the difference. Francisco had married an Indian, Joaquín a *mestiza*. In support of this conclusion, María, Torano's spouse, also enjoyed the coveted prefix before her name. The census taker listed her as Doña María Torano. This distinction reflected the slightly altered social alignments of the eighteenth century. Mestizos enjoyed more social status than Indians because of their closer racial proximity to whites.

Spanish women's marriage patterns reinforced this impression. They too, although not to the degree of their male counterparts, displayed a greater tendency to wed outside their race after the beginning of the fairs. In the cases of women for whom family backgrounds are available, most appear to have had four things in common. First, either both their parents or at least their fathers had died by the time they contracted these marriages. Second, they invariably came from poorer neighborhoods, such as the outlying *barrios*. Third, they usually married more affluent members of the non-Spanish population. And lastly, their biracial unions most commonly involved mestizos. Fifteen-year-old María Rodríguez wed a twenty-four-year-old mestizo silversmith who not only owned his own shop but also employed a Spanish apprentice. María had lost both her parents, and she lived on the outermost fringe of the urban core, among Jalapa's Indians and castas.[44] Felipa Ochoa also married a mestizo who, like María's husband, labored as a skilled artisan in his own shop. Again, the couple resided in one of the nonwhite sections of town, the *barrio* of Santiago, where a trade would have reflected a certain degree of wealth and prestige. At the time of their wedding, Felipa's father had already died.[45]

Late colonial whites' more liberal attitudes toward Euro-*castas* did not apply to Afro-Veracruzanos. The actions of a white mother from Orizaba illustrates this point. Mariana Cazares petitioned her parish priest to have the union of her daughter to Francisco Díaz annulled on the grounds that the groom had misrepresented his race to the family. He called himself a mestizo, but his mother-in-law discovered that he was actually a *lobo*, or Afro-*casta*. Since the bride herself did not desire the separation, the ecclesiastical judge ruled in favor of the couple and decided to uphold their marriage. In explaining his judgment, the priest conceded that there may have been some misrepresentation on the part of the groom regarding his racial status, but he also pointed out that both contracting parties were of age and desired to remain together. The frustrated mother's response to the verdict reflected prevailing white racial attitudes: "In view of the notable inequality that exists between the referred-to Francisco and the person of my daughter who is commonly known to be Spanish, pure of all bad blood . . . I convey my repugnance at this ecclesiastical court's verification of the marriage."[46] Mariana could have accepted a Euro- but not an Afro-*casta* son-in-law.

Affluence did not alter whites' aversion to persons of African descent. Francisco Xavier López, an extremely wealthy *pardo*, lived in Jalapa during the last quarter of the eighteenth century. He held the rank of captain in the Militia Company of Pardos and Morenos of Veracruz, which brought with it both good salary and the privileges of the military *fuero* (exemption from civil legal jurisdiction and head taxes). Francisco owned a residence and other properties within the district capital's limits indicating that, like most whites, he had an urban base. One of López' houses sold for four thousand pesos in 1804. The price of a modest wood and stone dwelling in the city averaged only 200 pesos at the time. López maintained mercantile ties with important Spaniards along the Veracruz-to-Mexico City trade route. In addition, he acted as the agent for the executors of Don Luíz Asanio's estate. Asanio had been a prominent Spanish merchant and landholder in the port of Veracruz. López and four white creole creditors foreclosed on the plantation of Don Antonio de la Riva, another resident of Jalapa. When one of López' Puebla merchant clients died, the widow retained Don Francisco to look after her dead husband's commercial interests. López himself commissioned Don Mariano Randón, the *contador*, or accountant, for the Cathedral of Puebla, to act as his financial representative in that city. Don Francisco also led a delegation of nonwhites from Jalapa to the viceregal Audiencia, or advisory and judicial council, in Mexico City. They petitioned for the defense of their rights and special privileges.[47]

Francisco Xavier López' standard of living and economic influence rivaled that of any white elite in Jalapa. As a sign of social respect authors of documents that mentioned him consistently inserted the title "Don" before his name, but they also carefully recorded him as a *pardo*.

The same pattern held true for other prominent Afro-Jalapans, for example, Manuel de Rivera, Juan Morcho, and José Blanco. None of these men ever married white women, none served as witnesses at the weddings of wealthy whites, and none stood as godparents for white children. And no Afro-*casta* gained membership in any of the all-Spanish socioreligiously orientated *cofradías* (lay brotherhoods) of the church. Afro-Jalapans formed their own fraternities along with other nonwhites.[48]

Colonial scribes displayed just as much care in affixing racial

labels to Afro-*castas* of more modest means. They made every effort
to preserve the racial order and to keep each individual in his or
her "proper place." Notarial, church, and town records consistently
referred to small farmers, property owners, and artisans including
Vicente Joseph Domínguez, Diego Antonio Hernández, Marcos de
Arellano, Matheo Cipriano Gutíerrez, and Ana de Castro as *pardos*
right on down to independence.[49]

The experience of Gertrudis de Rivera provides a final example of
how hard whites tried to hold the color line with respect to Afro-
Veracruzanos. She was the granddaughter of a wealthy *pardo*, Don
Manuel de Rivera. In 1817 Gertrudis appeared before the curate of
the Cathedral of Jalapa with her betrothed, Don Francisco Ortíz, a
Spanish corporal in the militia Regiment of the Three Villas (Jalapa,
Córdoba, and Orizaba). They wanted to initiate the lengthy nuptial
rites that the church prescribed. When the prelate asked for her racial status, she feigned ignorance. Undoubtedly the pastor already
knew the answer to his question given the prominence of Gertrudis'
family, but out of deference to her he graciously penned the somewhat ambiguous phrase "appears to be mulatto" in the margin beside her name. Later, after consulting his records, a highly unusual
procedure, he made a corrected marginal notation in the registry. He
listed the bride as a *parda*.[50] Not the wealth of Gertrudis' family, her
pretended ignorance, nor the forty-six years that had elapsed since
the first encountered reference to her grandfather proved enough to
erase her identification with what Veracruz whites judged a "bad
race." She might have successfully misrepresented her racial background except for two crucial factors. Her physical appearance betrayed her; the prelate might not have bothered to check his records
had she looked white. Second, the Riveras had too high a profile in
the community for her ruse to succeed as long as race overrode her
high economic class in designating social rank. Priests performed
many baptisms, funerals, marriages, and confirmations on a daily
basis. All of these actions required paperwork. And in this record
keeping, clerics, more than perhaps any other individuals within the
colonial society, made judgments about racial identification on a
regular basis. In these matters they relied almost entirely upon their
own perceptions. A priest only referred to genealogical references in
official documents when in doubt or when his opinion conflicted
with the word of the subject or with common knowledge.

The late colonial experience of a prominent creole from Jalapa,
Don José Ledesema y Castillo, illustrates the persistent importance
of race for social ordering throughout the colonial period. In 1801,
responding to public questions about his lineage, Ledesema sub-

mitted a 160-page notarized manuscript brief to the town council supporting his petition that the body publicly confirm the absence of "bad blood" and non-Spanish influence in his family background. This remarkable document traced his origins all the way back to seventh-century Spain.[51]

Persistent racial labeling of the population reflected the importance that whites still attached to race. Upper economic status and clear Hispanic cultural identification did not override one's inherited physical characteristics. Race, as based on physical appearance, counted for a great deal in social ranking throughout the colonial period.

Conclusion

The lives of such people as Francisco Xavier López, Don Manuel de Rivera, and Gertrudis Rivera illustrate the socioeconomic consequences of slowly changing demographic trends. All three came from racially mixed backgrounds. They all experienced economic mobility without comparable social change. Spaniards placed limits on late colonial flexibility in the region's socioeconomic life. López and the Riveras and other individuals merely represented firsts among unequals. Although on rare occasions wealthy Afro-Veracruzanos might command financial and commercial patronage from white business associates, they could not expect social equality to follow. Race still outweighed other factors including economic class in determining social station.

The late colonial socioeconomic orders displayed more similarities than dissimilarities with their counterparts in the sixteenth and seventeenth centuries. Whites concentrated in the core of urban areas at the outset of the colonial period, and they continued to do so at its end. Spaniards still monopolized elite occupations from 1550 to 1821 and experienced comparatively light representation in lower occupational positions. Whites expanded their social ties partially to include Euro-*castas* only.

These adjustments did not arise in main from a European-inspired move away from a feudalistic toward a commercial capitalistic economy as some have argued.[52] Chapter 3 already takes issue with this economic interpretation. Shifts in central Veracruz' means of production and the greater economic mobility among *castas* actually proved very light. Moreover, what change did take place affected individuals furthest removed from these events—creole nonwhites. Veracruz' masses of *castas* and Indians came more under the influence of local sociodemographic conditions that through miscegenation created almost a dual reality in the late colonial meaning and application of race. On one level whites continued to hold the color line just as they had always done. The only meaningful change involved a lumping of racially mixed groups into one category—*castas*. Indians generally acceded to this modified *sistema de las castas*. *Castas* and the few remaining blacks within the region ascribed to a more fluid socioeconomic system. This second social order had its greatest influence from the midsocioeconomic ranks on down. In *castas'* social world, race played a much less important role in socioeconomic ranking than other considerations including ethnicity and economic class. This system evolved more in response to altering local sociodemographic patterns that encouraged miscegenation and themselves grew from it. Competition between these two orders would increase social tensions between whites and non-whites from the end of the eighteenth century onward.

8

Adjustment, Independence, Politics, and Race

LINKS EXISTED between the late colonial Bourbon Reforms, the 1810–1821 struggle for independence, and the politics of the early national period. At the international level, the Bourbon Reforms represented a largely successful attempt on the part of Europe to reassert its domination over Mexico. The colony renewed many facets of its involvement in Atlantic commerce. Socially, the Spanish-promoted *sistema de las castas* endured, at least from the upper socioeconomic levels on down to the middle ranks of the society. And politically, the homeland instituted an intendency system that increased its control over Mexico. Chapters 3, 4, and 7, place Afro-Veracruzanos in socioeconomic context within the Bourbon Reforms. This chapter will attempt to put them in political context during this and the early national periods. Beyond this, it probes the relationship between politics and race during the years 1794–1830. Because of Afro-Veracruzanos' strong racial identification, they provide a good test case for the assumption that race continued to correlate with political participation during the Mexican transition from colony to nation.

On February 4, 1821, Agustín Iturbide succeeded in doing what Miguel Hidalgo and José María Morelos had failed to do. Through the Plan de Iguala, Iturbide brought independence to Mexico.[1] He succeeded because he limited his goals. Iturbide sought political control for creole white elites; Hidalgo and Morelos had sought political, social, and economic liberties for all segments of the population.[2] But Iturbide remained sensitive to the popular support that the broader-based movements of his revolutionary predecessors had enjoyed. Due to this sensitivity, he tried to identify lightly his more conservative coup with the early risings for independence. To do this, he invited participation from one of the last prominent pre-1815 insurgents still in the field—Vicente Guerrero.[3] Guerrero brought popularity to Iturbide's revolt not only because of his rebel record but also because he personified the upward aspirations of the non-white masses of Mexico. Racially, he embodied all three stocks that had produced the most rapidly growing segment of the population, the *castas*. He was of mixed black, white, and Indian ancestry.

Guerrero was born in rural Tixtla, within the province of Mexico, of humble parents. Uneducated, he worked as a muleteer for most of his early adult life and as such gained first-hand knowledge of much of southern and western portions of the viceroyalty. In 1821 he struck a bargain with Iturbide, a member of the elite white creole upper class. Guerrero accepted Iturbide's offer of alliance in 1821 toward the same apparent end—independence.[4] Both men, however, apparently had different interpretations of what that meant. For Iturbide and other powerful white creoles, independence merely represented a political break with Spain; for Guerrero and people like him, it meant more. To disenfranchised nonwhites, independence signified a repudiation of the racially and ethnically based inequities of the colonial system.[5]

An interrelated set of power dialectics operated from at least 1800 onward. One of these sets of opposing forces did not have obvious racial overtones: the centralist vs. local interests. Three sets of other opposing forces did have racial and/or ethnic overtones: whites vs. nonwhites, foreign vs. native interests, and overprivileged vs. underprivileged.

National politics represented one arena in which elite white and subordinate nonwhite differences surfaced.[6] White/nonwhite, European (peninsular)/creole politics permeated these issues from at least 1821 to 1830. Afro-Mexicans—Vicente Guerrero, for example—moved at the center of these high-level political disputes wherein secret masonic orders served as vehicles of expression for these opposing factions.[7] Generally, the Scottish rite, *escocés*, supported centralism, whites, and privilege. The York rite, *yorkinos*, publicly aligned themselves with federalism (regionalism), all racial groups, and the underprivileged.[8] The *Aguila Mexicana*, a government newspaper, had *yorkino* leanings. In 1826 its editors published a series of articles linking the Scottish rite lodge with an impending Spanish invasion of Mexico and the resubjugation of the country to colonial inequities. For their part, the Scottish lodge members, through the pages of their newspaper, *El Sol*, denied the charges and personally attacked leaders of the *yorkino* group as rabble-rousing, slanderous atheists who pandered to the wishes of the masses and local interests.[9] An editorial war between both factions had a direct impact on the congressional and state elections of 1826. *Yorkino* propagandists proved the most effective during this campaign. Their candidates won majorities in the national Chamber of Deputies, or the lower house in the Mexican legislature, and in every state legislature save of Puebla and Veracruz. Only in the national Senate, or upper federal chamber, did Scottish rite candidates capture a majority.[10] *Escoceses* bitterly contested the election. They claimed fraud, but in the end their protests counted for little.

During this heated campaign Vicente Guerrero had taken the lead in attacking *escocés* politicians as a pack of unpatriotic elitists. His role in this successful *yorkino* bid for power earned him two things. Guerrero transformed his public image from that of a military hero to that of a skilled politician. In the process he won the respect of the *yorkino* party, which rewarded him with the rite's Grand Master office for all of Mexico.[11]

For the next four years both sides vied for power in national politics, sometimes resorting to extreme tactics—revolt—when legal means failed them.[12] The period from 1827 to 1830 proved especially turbulent. It culminated at the national level in the 1828 presidential election that pitted the nonwhite radical *yorkino* Vicente Guerrero against the white coalition *escocés*–conservative-*yorkino* candidate, Manuel Gómez Pedraza.[13] As the campaign wore on, the debate became more bitter. In September when the votes were finally tallied, Gómez Pedraza won capturing eleven of eighteen states. Guerrero finished a disappointing second. In addition, Gómez Pedraza's moderate coalition captured a majority in the national Senate. Guerrero and radical elements within the *yorkino* ranks gained control of the lower house only.[14]

The radicals did not accept defeat any more gracefully than the *escoceses* had in 1826. Guerrero backers revolted and forced Gómez Pedraza to abdicate. Constitutionally, that placed Guerrero in the presidential chair as runner-up in the election. He served from April 1 to December 28, 1829.[15] This represented the high-water mark of success for the localist, nonwhite, populist forces that Hidalgo had begun to mobalize in 1810.[16]

The anticipated conservative and moderate military response came on December 4, 1829.[17] A wide range of individuals rallied to the call, but they basically had centralist leanings. The conspirators included former Vice President Anastasio Bustamante, the prominent *escocés* politician José Antonio Facio, General Melchor Murquíz, and the *iturbidista* Nicolás Bravo.[18]

Guerrero had no choice. His public support evaporating, his allies falling, and his enemies in the field, he relinquished his presidential powers, recalled the congress, and fled the capital on December 18, 1829. The pendulum had swung again. The moderate *yorkino-escocés* coalition that had supported Gómez Pedraza resumed power. By June of the following year they had purged radical *yorkino* elements from national and state legislatures.[19]

Fundamental issues came into focus during the the populist/elitist political confrontations of the 1820s. They included questions of locus of power, foreign influence, and colonial privilege. An important political strategy also took hold. Revolt became an accepted weapon for use by all competing factions.

A view of Mexican political development from the national level invariably gives the impression of intense competition between political elites. This national view presumes that elites controlled the political destiny of masses of other Mexicans who had become complacent pawns since their short period of activism during the Hidalgo-Morelos years. This interpretation assumes that the select few plunged the country into political chaos during the early national period. An examination of local-level politics demonstrates shortcomings in this interpretation.

Limited evidence exists to suggest that during the first decade of independence, and probably beyond, nonwhites in Mexico took a more active part in politics and that the stands they took on specific issues did not always parallel those taken by white elites. More basic egalitarian objectives moved local masses, and one of these was to rid the country of its colonial legacies of racism and ethnocentrism, notions that historically restricted nonwhites' participation in politics. When the *escocés* politician Carlos Bustamante admonished authorities in 1826 for failing to protect foreigners, his scathing description of the attackers reflected his opinions of the nonwhite common folk involved. He referred to the them as "a savage tribe of Caribs [the offspring of runaway slaves and Indians that inhabited the eastern coast of the isthmus] or orangutans."[20] Bustamante's statement also implies an important political position taken by ordinary Mexicans during this period. They vehemently opposed foreign influence. Traditional conservative white politicians abhorred the *yorkino*'s common tactic of stirring up these Indians and *castas* whom they viewed as "people without reason."[21] During Vicente Guerrero's unsuccessful election bid of 1828 for the presidency, his opponents repeatedly attacked him as El Negro Guerrero, referring to his partial black racial ancestry.[22] However, Guerrero's mixed racial heritage appealed to much of the population that had also suffered the same types of racial discriminations in their own lives. Guerrero's and his party's ascendancy to power represented an extension of that independence-period challenge to white privilege and political monopoly. Guerrero's political base, the radical wing of the *yorkino* party, rested less on the shoulders of such elites as Lorenzo de Zavala, José Antonio de Santa Anna, Ramos Arizpe and more on the backs of nonwhite *castas*. Guerrero rose to prominence on the crest of a populist wave in early national politics, a movement that had its roots in the early 1810–1815 independence movements that he symbolized.[23] Foes' most consistent criticism of him from 182,5 onward referred to his frequent encouragement of nonwhite "rabble" to commit violent political actions. Moderate and conservative elites from Manuel Gómez Pedraza to Lucas Alamán repeated this theme over and over again in their indictments of Guerrero.[24]

Racism in early national politics had its roots in the colonial *sistema de las castas*—the exclusion by law and practice of the nonwhite underprivileged from political participation. Guerrero's national struggles hinted at the relevance of this issue during the 1820S. Events in central Veracruz offer a slightly clearer view of these forces in motion. This regional perspective is appropriate because, according to Brian Hamnett, the independence movement was regionally based and "magnified the pre-existing local conflicts, which, understandably, continued to manifest themselves after the War of Independence proper had finished in 1821."[25] In Hamnett's opinion, racism represented one of the foremost of local social tensions that spilled over into the politics of the early national period.[26]

Jalapa, a hotbed of political activity during the turbulent decade of the 1820s, had clear involvement in national politics. No less than three regional uprisings that effected Vicente Guerrero's national fortunes between 1826 and 1829 sprang from this regional capital.[27] What follows is an examination of race and local politics in this state capital setting.

Local Politics in the Early National Period

The *yorkinol/escocés* split existed as strongly in central Veracruz as it did in central Mexico.[28] Local nativist backlash against foreigners and centralization of political power came at the same time it did in Mexico City and with equal strength.[29] Jalapa lay in the center of Veracruz. Some national figures including Santa Anna came from Jalapa; such others as Valentín Gómez Farías had lived there.[30] Still others including Agustín Iturbide, Guadalupe Victoria, and Nicolás Bravo frequently visited the area. Guerrero himself served there as military commandant for the state from 1826 to 1827.[31] Many of the revolts against national governments between

1823 and 1832 originated in Jalapa (the Plan de Casa Mata, Plan de Veracruz, the Barragán Revolt, the Plan de Jalapa, and Santa Anna's revolt of 1832). An understanding of this regional capital's political life could provide a better understanding of Mexican politics in general, especially the unclear role of *castas* and other common Mexicans during the era.

Afro-Jalapans represented an important and politically active segment of the local *casta* population leading up to and immediately after independence. This coincided with, and perhaps even grew out of, their heightened economic and social activities outlined in Chapters 4 and 7.

In 1794, the crown elevated the *pueblo* of Jalapa to the status of a *villa*. For the first time, residents had the right to elect their own municipal council.[32] Such elections took place at the end of each year and involved four types of offices: *alcaldes* (magistrates), *regidores* (council members), *síndicos* (public defenders), and representatives of outlying subject neighborhoods. The specific number of each of these officials depended upon population size.[33] Privileged whites had the option of purchasing any one of two *regidor* positions from the crown at a price of 225 pesos per year. Voters indirectly elected individuals to all other offices.[34] By law, eligibility fell to males at least twenty-one years of age or to the male heads of households who had resided in Jalapa for no less than five years prior to the election. Non-Christians, "uncivilized" Indians, and persons of African ancestry could neither vote nor hold office. The term for each office lasted two years. Voters elected half of the council on one year and the other half on the following year thereby always insuring a balance between experience and inexperience.[35]

From 1794 to 1821, no known Afro-Jalapan served on the town council despite the fact that a number of prominent persons of African descent lived within the township during the period. The group included the already mentioned Don Francisco Xavier López, Don Manuel de Rivera, Don Juan Morcho, and Don José Blanco. Neither their wealth nor their military status merited them political office. Their race denied them this privilege by law.

An even lower level of local political participation in Jalapa involved the voting process by which town council members advanced to candidacy. At least once per year, usually in December, citizens reported to their parishes to choose an electoral *junta*, or committee. As in the case of the council offices themselves, population size determined the number of *junta* members for individual parishes. Each parish voter submitted as many names as election committee seats. Lists of all those who received even a single vote in the town's

Table 10. *Afro-Jalapans Receiving Votes in Parochial Electoral Juntas, 1820–1829*

Year	Number
1820	1
1821	7
1822	6
1823	12
1824	a
1825	10
1826	10
1827	6
1828	3
1829	8
Total 10 years	63 vote getters

Source: AAJ, Libro 31, leaves 9, 9v, 13, 14–15, 19–20, 23, 24v–26v, 30v–32, 33v, 35–37v, 40–41v, 45, 46, 52–52v, 56–58; AGN, Padrones, vol. 20, leaves 299v, 300, 302, 305, 306, 309, 312, 313, 315, 324, 325, 330, 337; Nieto, *Padrón de Xalapa,* 130, 238; APJ, Bautizos, Caja 6, Libro 19, leaves 291, 337; APJ, Bautizos, Caja 7, Libro 23, leaves 91, 130, 165v, 172v, 173v; APJ, Bautizos, Caja 7, Libro 25, leaves 3v, 18v, 20v, 34v, 43, 48, 86; APJ, Bautizos, Caja 8, Libro 27, leaf 53v; APJ, Bautizos, Caja 8, Libro 28, leaf 39; APJ, Bautizos, Caja 9, Libro 31, leaf 35v; APJ, Bautizos, Caja 3, Libro 9, leaf 140; APJ, Bautizos, Caja 3, Libro 16, leaf 47; APJ, Matrimonios, Legajo 4, 1790–1794, unnumbered *expediente;* APJ, Matrimonios, Legajo 8, 1800–1809, unnumbered loose *expediente;* APJ, Marimonios, Legajo 9, 1810–1815, unnumbered loose *expediente;* ANJ, vol. 1771 y 1772, leaves 86–87, 90–91; ANJ, vol. 1789 y 1790, leaves 177–178, 204, 237–238; ANJ, vol. 1820 y 1821, leaves 330–330v; ANJ, vol. 1822 y 1823, leaves 189–191; ANJ, vol. 1827, leaves 186v–188.

ªVoting lists for the *junta* election of 1824 were missing from the election registry. Only the winners and the town council members they in turn elected appeared in the record for this year.

main parish elections exist for the years 1820–1829. Table 10 shows the number of Afro-Jalapans receiving votes for positions on the parochial electoral *junta* during each of these years.

Only one Afro-*casta* received any votes in the last *junta* election of the colonial period. José Vela, a *pardo* farmer, got one vote. He was the forty-seven-year-old son of a *pardo* father and an Indian mother and married to a local *mestiza*.[36] Since José had limited African ancestry, he may have passed for white in order to qualify for nomination. That would explain why he was the only Afro-*casta* to take part in an election during the last quarter century of colonial rule.

By the time of the next town council elections, December 1821, Mexico enjoyed independence. In that year's balloting the number of Afro-Jalapan candidates in the parochial *junta* contest jumped to seven. The following year six received nominating votes. In 1823, at least twelve persons of African descent collected ballots for *junta* seats. I could not locate voting data for the *junta* election of 1824, but in each of the two succeeding races ten Afro-*castas* participated. Six, three, and eight Afro-Jalapans respectively received votes for the *juntas* in the last three years of the decade. This drop may have reflected a slowing of the populist movement that did not show up at the national level until the ouster of Guerrero in mid-1829.[37]

Other factors indicate that Afro-*casta* participation in the political process increased during the decade of the 1820s. Just prior to the break with Spain and on through the *junta* election of 1822, none of the persons of African ancestry running in these races won posts. In 1820, when José Vela received his lone vote for the *junta*, colonial law barred nonwhites from casting ballots and holding public office. The following year, when this discriminatory legislation no longer existed, three prominent Afro-Jalapans did much better. Don José María Gonzáles received twenty-seven votes.[38] Don José María de Rivera, the son of the mulatto militia officer and entrepreneur Don Manuel de Rivera, polled thirty-two votes.[39] Don José Blanco obtained twenty-seven votes.[40]

Census compilers in 1791 listed José María González as a mulatto married to a *mulata*. He appeared fairly secure, having inherited his father's shoemaker shop plus a limited amount of urban property. He also bought and sold small city lots. González lived just two blocks from the town square in the direction of the Barrio de los Berros. His house fell within the white residential core, the most well-to-do section of town.[41]

The same census takers recorded Don José María de Rivera and Felipa Monasterio as *pardos*. The de Riveras lived near the Gonzálezes, and, like them, resided close to the center of Jalapa on Alba street at the corner of San Miguel. De Rivera's occupation remains unknown, but given his entrepreneur father, the location of his home, the "Don" before his name, and the votes he consistently received in the *junta* and town council elections between 1823 and 1829, he must have had some means.[42]

The percentage of the total vote that Afro-Jalapans received in each of the electoral *junta* elections represented another indicator of the postindependence increase in their political activity. During the decade of the 1820s, Afro-*castas* and *negros* comprised between 5.3 and 5.7 percent of the district's total population.[43] Table 11

Table 11. *Balloting Results for Jalapa Electoral* Junta *Elections, 1820–1829*

Year	No. Votes Received by Blacks	Total No. of Votes Cast	Black % of Total Vote
1820	1	1,689	.0
1821	113	2,236	5.1
1822	29	791	3.7
1823	370	2,863	12.9
1824	—	—	—
1825	267	3,375	7.9
1826	142	2,839	5.0
1827	1,759	7,227	24.3
1828	89	1,557	5.7
1829	51	2,111	2.4

Source: AAJ, Libro 31, leaves 1–2v.

shows the percentage of the total number of *junta* votes cast by persons of African descent during each of these years. In 1820, when the prohibitive Spanish laws against nonwhites remained in effect, Afro-Jalapans' share of the overall vote proved insignificant. The very next year, with the lifting of discriminatory legislation, their percentage of the vote rose dramatically, almost equalling their representation in the overall population.

On a yearly basis the Afro-Jalapan percentage of the vote fluctuated. The only exception to this pattern involved the election of 1827. Some evidence exists suggesting irregularities in this race. In each of the other elections, winning candidates polled between 50 and 150 votes. Those who won in 1827 received from 325 to 375 votes. Moreover, the total number of ballots cast in the 1827 contest represented over twice the number of any other in the decade. This anomaly came on the heels of the populist *yorkino* sweep in national congressional and state elections of 1826. Added to this coincidence in timing, Vicente Guerrero, one of the most prominent *yorkinos* in the nation, just so happened to be serving as military commander for the state of Veracruz. He had his command post in the state capital, Jalapa.

Although the evidence remains circumstantial, a link appears to have existed between the Afro-*casta* political ascendancy in Jalapa and the rise of national populist fortunes. Events in Jalapa also suggest that *escocés* charges of fraud in the national and state elections of 1826 may have had some basis in fact. President Victoria awarded Guerrero his Jalapa post in reaction to a pro-Spanish conspiracy that became public in Mexico City during January of 1827. The plot apparently had some Veracruz *escocés* roots. This complicity, plus the fact that the state as a whole remained one of the last important strongholds of *escocés* and antifederalist power left after the lopsided congressional elections of the previous year, probably figured in Victoria's decision to send Guerrero to Veracruz. Guerrero may have associated his charge with the defeat of pro-*escocés* candidates at all levels in the state-wide elections of 1827.[44] This could explain the unprecedented turnout in the Jalapa town council races of that year. *Yorkinos*, as the party with greatest popular appeal, worked hard to turn out the masses, especially nonwhites. This helps to explain why Afro-Jalapan candidates received a surprisingly large share of the vote (24 percent). On the other hand, the possibility also exists that both the large turnout and spectacular showing of Afro-Jalapan candidates resulted from *yorkino* ballot-box stuffing.

In any case, this contest did not parallel others held during the 1820s. Discounting the 1827 Afro-*casta* percentage of the vote, on the average, persons of this racial identification received more than 6 percent of the ballots cast in the *junta* elections between 1821 and 1829. This figure proved just slightly higher than their percentage of the total population within the district at the time. Thus Afro-Jalapans participated in politics at the local level to a degree that was proportionate to their numerical representation within the general population during the early national years.

Increasing numbers of Afro-Jalapans actually elected to parish *juntas* and to *ayuntamientos* (town councils) during the 1820s provides the final and strongest indicator that independence marked a period of open, as opposed to clandestine, nonwhite participation in politics.

Table 12 shows that initial Afro-*casta* participation in the political process yielded limited results in terms of actual office holding. For the first two years, no person of African descent won a *junta* or an *ayuntamiento* election. Then, in 1823, just the third election year after independence, Don José María de Rivera captured seats on both the electoral *junta* and the town council. These events marked a turning point in local politics for Afro-Jalapans. But these victories did not go unchallenged. Two white members of the *ayuntamiento*, Lic. José Mariano Morales and Don Rafael Velad, tried to have de Rivera's election to the council nullified. The law required that a candidate reside in Jalapa for at least five years immediately prior to his election. De Rivera had lived for five months in Naulinco during

Table 12. *Number of Afro-Jalapans Elected to the Parochial Electoral Juntas and Ayuntamientos of Jalapa, 1820–1829*

Year	Afro-Jalapans Elected to the Junta	Total No. of Persons Elected to the Junta	% Afro-Jalapan Junta Election Winners	Afro-Jalapans Elected to Ayuntamiento	Total No. Elected to Ayuntamiento	% Afro-Jalapan Ayuntamiento Winners
1820	0	17	0	0	8	0
1821	0	17	0	0	12	0
1822	0	17	0	0	7	0
1823	1	17	5.9	1	12	8.3
1824	[a]	—	—	1	6	16.7
1825	3	23	13.0	1	18	5.6
1826	2	17	11.8	1	12	8.3
1827	6	17	35.3	0	11	0
1828	1	17	5.9	1	11	9.1
1829	0	20	0	2	11	18.2

Source: Ayuntamiento de Jalapa, Libro 31, leaves 1–65v.

[a] Voting lists for the *junta* election of 1824 were missing from this election book.

1821. The electoral *junta* met in special session to decide the matter. Its members voted to override the protest by the narrow margin of nine to eight.[45]

In comparison to their percentage of the district's population, Afro-Jalapans enjoyed proportionate representation on both electoral *juntas* and town councils during the first decade after independence. This underscored an astonishing turnaround, especially with respect to the *ayuntamiento*. From its 1794 inception until 1820, not a single known person of African descent served on the council.[46] During the first ten years of the national period, seven Afro-Jalapans won seats on the council.

Although over fifty different persons of African descent appeared on the voting lists during the 1820s, only about half a dozen did so consistently, and even fewer got elected. Don José María de Rivera proved the most successful local Afro-Jalapan politician. He first ran as an electoral *junta* candidate in 1821, receiving a total of thirty-two votes. Fifty-four would have gotten him elected. In the following year, he polled half the needed number of votes. In 1823, he finally did win with 128 votes. When the *junta* met, it elected him to the fifth council seat. He became the first individual publicly identified as an Afro-*casta* to serve on the *ayuntamiento*. De Rivera went on to sit as first council member in 1825. He served as a member of the electoral *juntas* of 1826 and 1827. Finally, in 1829, he won the second magistrate's post for the district, the highest political rank any Afro-Jalapan would attain during the period.[47]

Don Manuel Cruz proved the next most successful Afro-Jalapan politician. The son of a stone mason, he was born in 1787 and spent his childhood on the Castillo ranch just outside the district capital.[48] Don Manuel first appeared on the voting lists in the *junta* election of 1822. He received one vote. In the succeeding *junta* balloting, he improved his showing and garnered seventeen ballots. In 1824, he won the eleventh member's seat on the council. He sat as the only Afro-*casta* on the *ayuntamiento* in 1826. Finally, he served as a member of the electoral *juntas* of 1825, 1826, and 1829.[49]

Just two other Afro-Jalapans held town council seats, Don José Zavaleta sat as seventh council member in 1828. Don Juan Ruiz served as a special representative from the congregation of Molina in 1829. Zavaleta, a shoemaker, came from the *pueblo* of Las Vigas. He wed a *parda* woman from the *barrio* of Calvario on the northeastern fringes of Jalapa.[50] Ruiz married well. Beatrice López was the daughter of Don Francisco Xavier López, perhaps the most respected and powerful *pardo* in Jalapa during the last quarter of the eighteenth century. At their son's baptism in 1810, the widow of Don Manuel de Rivera (also the mother of Don José María de Rivera) stood as the infant's godmother. Don Manuel had served as Don Francisco's lieutenant in the district's *pardo* militia company. Ties between these two influential Afro-Jalapan families had endured into the third generation.[51]

Only a few other persons of African descent won posts on electoral *juntas* during the first decade of the national period. Don José Blanco, a well-to-do farmer, Don Juan Cordera, a bookseller, and Don José Antonio Casas, a bakery owner from the parish of San José.[52] All of these officeholders had things in common. They represented the upper echelons of Afro-Jalapan society. One or two enjoyed elite status but most fell within the Mid-Level socio-economic range. Socially, economically, and now politically they were the firsts of unequals in a more open but still white-dominated setting.

Conclusion

Political control helped white Spaniards maintain their power over other racial segments in the colonial society. Even unto the end of the colonial period, whites successfully excluded Afro-*castas* and other nonwhites from voting and holding public office. Politics represented one of the few areas in which distant Spanish legislation had a constant and significant impact on district-level life in New Spain. Whites held local power, and the imperial legislation protected their position. In this dimension of colonial society, crown and local white interests merged. They worked hand in hand to enforce laws disenfranchising Afro-Jalapans and other nonwhites. But in this case, Spanish laws' effectiveness resulted not so much from far-reaching royal authority, as it did from entrenched local white self-interest.

During the unrest of the early nineteenth century, Hidalgo and Morelos called upon whites and nonwhites alike to seize control of New Spain's political sector in order to bring about much-needed social, economic, and political reforms. Racist and ethnocentric inequities were two of their primary targets for change. They tried to institute an end to slavery and the recognition of racial equality. In doing so, they did not put new forces in motion—they reflected existing ones. An undercurrent of change had already begun to swell up in late colonial society. Nonwhites, and especially *castas*, which included in their numbers the bulk of the Afro-Veracruzano population by 1800, began to assert themselves. The strict racial order of the sixteenth and seventeenth centuries underwent some change under the stress. As pointed out in Chapter 7, this order flexed a bit and lumped all *castas* into a single category that predominated from the lower to the lower middle of the socioeconomic levels of society. Whites held the color line from the upper middle to the top ranks of these scales. The *sistema de las castas* had not died, it had simply adapted to pressures on it within locales like Jalapa. At least partially in an effort to blunt this upward surge of the nonwhite masses, colonial white elites strove to gain control of the independence movement. American whites wanted to divert the inner threat from below outward away from themselves and toward Spain. To a large degree they proved successful, but they paid a price. With independence, creole whites had to face late colonial nonwhite populism without the aid of their European allies. This had a significant effect on life in local settings like Jalapa. These effects became partially visible in early national politics; they were even clearer from the local vantage point. Nonwhites including Afro-*castas* managed to increase their participation in political affairs almost immediately because white opposition forces had split in two. Iturbide's first Mexican Empire could not restrain the popular forces nor was it prepared to placate them. At least partially as a result, it lasted less than three years.[53] It simply did not have enough to offer underprivileged nonwhites.

The nineteenth century ushered in a Mexico undergoing slow

transition from a colonial society with heavy caste emphasis to an increasingly nationalistic society with rising dependence on other mechanisms of control including ethnicity and economic class. These trends appeared to accelerate during the first decade of independence. But in the end such changes proved more evolutionary than revolutionary in nature. White creoles regained the upper hand during the second quarter of the century and reinstituted a large measure of race's influence into the political life of the new nation. Racism remained a very significant factor in socioeconomic stratification as well throughout the remainder of the century. Politically, the hard fought gains of the 1810–1830 generation did not endure. Nonwhites did not win de facto political equality until after 1910. Whites retained a strong vested interest in maintaining racial distinctions. They continued to use their whiteness as a justification for their privileged status. Whites, in trying to preserve their elevated social, economic, and political rank, in many ways patterned the new government after the older Spanish colonial order that competed with more popular and nationalistic forces for change until another populist uprising challenged them again on the hundredth anniversary of Hidalgo's uprising.

Conclusions

THIS STUDY has three planes of focus and two levels of conclusions. The first focus deals with Afro-Veracruzanos alone. It addresses questions about the African origins of the group and the changing nature of its multidimensional experience in colonial central Veracruz.

The second focus is on persons of black descent within broader regional society. On this plane of analysis, blacks are important in so far as they reflect general trends. In this sense, their experience becomes a window into the comparative experiences of the society as a whole.

The third focus is interwoven with the first two. This final focus involves the interplay between local Veracruz and outside Atlantic forces that influenced the lives of all segments of the society as well as the overall development of the region.

Conclusions on the Afro-Veracruzano Experience

Blacks' very presence in Veracruz resulted from an intricate weave of events. European adventurers unintentionally carried new diseases to the New World that ravaged the indigenous population.[1] Microscopic organisms more than conquerors wiped out whole pre-Columbian cities, towns, and villages. As much by default as by design, Spaniards assumed an ever-larger share of Veracruz' means of production—the land. Control of physical resources, however, proved not nearly enough to transform the region into a highly productive unit of empire. Workers had to turn raw materials into items that Europeans wanted. Indians appeared to be dying off, and the long-range prospect of their filling labor requirements seemed unlikely. The region needed a another source of labor to free Indian workers from such arduous tasks as sugar refining. Failing this, the indigenous population would surely perish, just as it had on the Caribbean islands, and with it the hands to produce Veracruz' colonial wealth. Perhaps the substitution of imported labor in these physically demanding occupations would save the natives from extinction. However, if the worst scenario came to pass and the indigenous population disappeared, then substitute laborers would be necessary anyway. Why not have the solution in place, at least in the most critical industries, before the catastrophe hit with full force? This cold logic probably ran through royal administrators' minds during the second half of the sixteenth century as areas including Veracruz faced apparent demographic disaster.

Given contemporary technology, any alternative labor source had to be relatively close to Spanish America. The ocean seas proved hazardous and expensive to cross. The amount of time it took to follow a particular trans-Atlantic shipping lane often made the difference between economic failure and success—a hard economic fact for owners, life or death for black slaves. The shorter the route of transport the better. West Africa lay closer to Veracruz than did Spain or any other part of the Old World. Geography made Africa a more attractive source of imported labor than Europe.

Further, the timing proved right for forced immigration of Africans. Portuguese traders expanded their means of acquiring this most subservient form of labor at the very time Veracruz planters needed it most. Easier Portuguese access to African slaves also coincided with the union of the Portuguese and Spanish crowns. This temporarily gave Spanish colonial administrators access to the machinery of the Portuguese slave trade. Finally, inter-African conflict enhanced Iberian accessibility to potential slaves again at the same time that Veracruz' demand for slaves peaked.

In sum, conditions that coalesced for Africans' removal to such regions as Veracruz developed on three continents, partly by random chance and partly by human design. The conditions resulted in Veracruz' and the rest of Mexico's participation in, and strengthening of, an important dimension of a developing Atlantic commerce between the Old and the New Worlds. From about 1580 to 1620, roughly two generations, New Spain imported more African slaves than any other locale in the Americas. Veracruz represented an important local market for Africans during this period. On the broadest scale, involvement of the richest and most dynamic colony in the Western world provided a powerful impetus to the developing international slave trade. For the nascent economy of New Spain, the infusion of 200 thousand captive workers, at a time when fear of collapse in the

labor pool seemed imminent, proved critical. In the minds of its de-
velopers, Mexico simply could not get enough Africans during this
forty-year period.

But the necessary circumstances for utilization of slave labor
proved fragile and interlocking. Breaking even one of the interde-
pendent links broke the international chain. As early as 1620 three
weaknesses developed in most of central Veracruz' ties to slavery.
One involved the dissolution of Spanish-Portuguese union. Portugal
became independent, and Spaniards lost their advantageous position
within the supply and marketing sides of the Atlantic slave trade.
Even more importantly, changing conditions in Veracruz diminished
the area's demand for expensive imported slaves. New Spain's demographic stress abated. The precipitous drop in the Indian population
began to level off. In locale after locale, the dreaded extinction of natives was obviously not going to happen.

Moreover, despite strong legal and social discouragement of Indian, black, and white miscegenation, such mixing occurred. Race
mixture provided an added means to population growth. This in turn
accelerated the recuperative powers of the domestic labor force.
From the early seventeenth century onward supplemental African
labor became less and less necessary. Finally, Spain's involvement
in continental affairs, economic conditions in Europe, and the homeland's decision to limit Mexico's access to mercury for processing silver to generate enough surplus capital to afford slaves, all disrupted
Veracruz' involvement in the Atlantic trade.

Veracruz' and the rest of Mexico's involvement in the African diaspora only partially resulted from European political and economic
pressures on the colony. For the most part, Veracruz players in this
international activity operated more proactively than reactively.
White Veracruzanos sought foreign labor only when they needed
it. They chose African slaves because 1580–1620 geopolitical conditions made such slaves attractive substitutes for disappearing Indian
workers. When Veracruz' need diminished, planters abandoned the
Atlantic slave trade and eventually even creole black slavery despite
periodic Iberian blandishments to encourage participation in the
trade.

As a result of Veracruz' exit from the slave trade, blacks' lives in
Veracruz were shaped, in the main, by local conditions. Affairs in
Europe and Africa became increasingly less relevant. At least two
consequences of this American experience had profoundly negative
consequences for the entire Western world. One was the linkage of
slavery to a single race. If the Caribbean islands set this precedent in

the first half of the sixteenth century, Mexican areas including Veracruz consolidated it in the second half of the same century. And once this racial tie with slavery knotted, an even more insidious and enduring precedent developed. In order to help subordinate blacks to slave status and to maintain their own hold over other subject peoples, Europeans intensified their reliance on racism and ethnocentrism until these became two important pillars of an extremely inequitable colonial social order. Veracruz served as an important laboratory of experimentation with these mechanisms of social control.

Racism and ethnocentrism emerged as devices used to prevent unified resistance of non-white, non-Hispanic subjects to white Hispanics' domination. This development set the stage for the next phase of the Afro-Veracruzano experience. Ironically, in Veracruz, where blacks unintentionally played an extraordinary role in inspiring these tools of oppression, blacks also played an equally decisive role in limiting their influence. Despite the best efforts of Spaniards to prevent it, the creolization of Africans in Veracruz led to their racial and ethnic blending with the broader society. These two dimensions of amalgamation were ironically encouraged by a marginality imposed on Afro-Veracruzanos through the institution of slavery and through racist and ethnocentric white sociopolitical orders. Afro-Veracruzanos' relationships with other groups in general became so economically, socially, and politically restricted that they had little choice but to try to circumvent prejudicial laws and conventions. Not fully accepted into either the creole Hispanic or the native Indian community, Afro-*castas* and blacks lived in both. As a result, Afro-Veracruzanos consistently represented the most socially outgoing element within the developing regional population. They intermarried with, and in other ways socially bonded with, Indians and non-Afro-*castas* more often than other segments of the population did. This interrelating proved a remarkable tribute to the resilience of their spirit. Afro-Veracruzanos entered a strange and demanding setting restrained from equal opportunity with competing non-Afro-Veracruzano segments of the population. Their slave status, white racism and ethnocentrism, and Iberian law all reduced the level and degree of Afro-Veracruzanos' opportunity within the setting. Veracruz' Afro-American population not only survived this opposition, they made positive contributions to the development of the area in the process. Whereas Spanish and creole whites endeavored to segregate the various racial and cultural components of the population, Afro-Veracruzanos acted to integrate them. Economically,

Africans and their descendents supplemented a rapidly declining native labor force at a time when the region's productivity was expanding dramatically. Afro-Veracruzanos served as the backbone of the skilled labor force in critical industries such as mining, commercial agriculture, and urban *obrajes*. They plied rural trade routes as muleteers and itinerant merchants. In these capacities they represented one of the most productive elements of the colonial economy. Without their labor New Spain could never have reached its preeminent economic position within the New World.

Finally, excluded from the political system, Afro-Veracruzanos led the way in seizing political power from a racially and ethnically discriminatory system. Sixteenth- and early-seventeenth-century *bozal* and creole slaves set precedents for late colonial *casta* and Indian followers of Hidalgo and Morelos who eventually stressed Spanish political control to the near breaking point. Rebellion and other forms of physical opposition to racism and ethnocentrism represented time honored Afro-Veracruzano responses to these divisive elements of colonial life. The record of insurrection in Córdoba attests to the clash between rising expectations of nonwhites and heightened Spanish authority in Mexico at the end of the colonial period. Attempted imperial reforms accelerated ongoing changes that became an inevitable part of regional development by the eighteenth century. Subject nonwhites tolerated drastic administrative responses as necessary to maintain order in the midst of early crisis of conquest and demographic depression. But as these extraordinary conditions gave way to more mundane ones, the elites' reliance on racism and ethnocentrism increased as the remainder of the population grew increasingly restive. Heightened interaction among nonwhites led to both race mixture and to ethnic accommodation ranging from assimilation to cultural pluralism.

As the colonial years drew to a close, whites in power, whether creoles or *peninsulares*, experienced ever more isolation from the beliefs and practices of the majority of the population. Their imposed meaning and application of race necessarily underwent adjustment. At the upper reaches of the society stood a powerful minority, from the middle levels on down stood the masses. The former continued to hold out racial and ethnic identification as important criteria for entrance into their ranks. At the same time, whites lumped multiplying numbers of racially hybrid groups into one category—*castas*. This provided a dangerous point of solidarity for nonwhite, non-Indian groups, the fastest growing segment of the regional population. That solidarity first manifested itself in the wars of independence and then in the populist political activities of the 1820s.

Afro-Veracruzanos moved in the vanguards of both these movements. Like their African ancestors, they pushed to liberalize Veracruz' power structure with regard to race, first through rebellion and later through the legitimate electoral process. At least partially as a result of their efforts, race mixture and cultural toleration became slightly more acceptable. As a consequence, free colored peoples enjoyed greater socioeconomic mobility.

On a regional level, Afro-*castas* and their mestizo and Indian counterparts generally appear to have enjoyed the same expanded opportunities. In the handful of settings, however, where whites more stridently opposed these changes, Afro-Veracruzanos' reactions proved strong, consistent, and often violent. Córdoba fits this exceptional category of local environments. In many ways the district represented a historical anachronism, a late-developing colonial area that appeared a half century behind its neighbors in a number of its socioeconomic characteristics. Planter elites continued to rely on slavery long beyond the institution's viability in adjacent areas. Related racist attitudes remained unusually virulent. Definitions of race changed in other places because racial lines multiplied so quickly that the drawing of distinctions between nonwhite peoples proved difficult. But racism and ethnocentrism remained powerful in Córdoba until the end of the colonial period. There, whites still used them to exercise power over creoles of any nonwhite hue. In this sense whites in Córdoba proved more effective in doing what whites everywhere wanted to do but could not because of fading color lines between themselves and subordinate races. Thus, Córdoba was more in step with the Bourbon period, a time when Spain tried to strengthen its control over Mexico by, at least in part, resorting to these time-proven social tools for exercising power. Peninsular Spaniards displayed strident racist and ethnocentric views in the late colonial period. They often leveled charges of racial or ethnic impurity against their creole white rivals for power and status during the Bourbon period. In so doing, these agents of European influence heightened late colonial white, Spanish reliance on the *sistema de las castas*. The consequent resurgence of mechanisms of social control upon which the older orders rested caused unusual problems for suspect members of the white, Hispanic elite population.

The church supported renewed Bourbon emphasis on race and ethnicity as tools for ordering late colonial society. Bishops sent out pastoral letters to parish priests exhorting them to discourage racial intermarriage. White parents took children to court if they tried to wed colored persons who would taint their "good blood." Colonial officials still referred to Indians and *castas* as "people without reason." Scribes punctuated records with racial references. Hispanics persecuted non-Hispanics for religious beliefs that strayed from European-based Catholicism. There were stepped-up attempts to implement ethnically and racially based head taxes.

The dynamics of racism and ethnocentrism as well as the discriminatory actions that sprang from them had not died by 1700. In fact, they may have enjoyed, in modified form, a late colonial renaissance in Bourbon Mexico. Measures aimed at segregating Indians, blacks, whites, Europeans, Africans, and native ethnic groups were simply no longer as viable as they had once been in most locales. Two centuries of miscegenation and cultural blending had made such tactics less functional. Too many groups had emerged to control. But Spaniards still could more or less discern whites from nonwhites and Europeans from creoles. Upon these less refined distinctions, elites in eighteenth-century Mexico drew racial and ethnic lines that counted for as much at the upper levels of society as similar lines had in the previous two centuries. In central Veracruz, these demarcations were no more clearly etched than in Córdoba. White residents of the district blatantly and vigorously applied these modified forms of racism and ethnocentrism. This proved much less true in Jalapa and probably in most of the rest of Mexico as well. Consequently, Afro-Veracruzanos responded much more peacefully in Jalapa to milder discrimination.

In late colonial Jalapa, Afro-Veracruzanos enhanced the level of social, economic, and political amalgamation of all groups within the local population. In contrast, Córdoban slaves, who could not play this unifying role, revolted over and over again.

During the very last years of the colonial era a combination of forces—Napoleonic Wars in Europe, late imperial directives, and local demographic patterns—altered the options available to Afro-Veracruzanos and other groups within the society. Whites justified many restrictions that emerged, whether small or great, on ethnic (Hispanic/non-Hispanic) and racist (white/nonwhite) grounds. In this increasingly more prejudicial environment Mexicans of all ilks responded just as restricted Córdoban slaves did. They revolted. Thus, Afro-Córdobans represented an ironic subpopulation. This socially, economically, and politically restricted group moved to the forefront of a new regional response to an old set of problems—racism and ethnocentrism. In this way Córdoban slaves led the way and acted in some respects as precursors to later violent respondents to a colonial political system that discriminated against all nonwhites and all non-Spanish-born residents of the viceroyalty.

Blacks in the Overall Society

The Afro-Veracruzano experience fit into a much larger pattern of development in the region, and I have tried to place blacks and Afro-*castas* within that context over a 250-year period. This placement required devoting nearly as much attention to other groups and inanimate forces as to Afro-Veracruzanos themselves. The conclusions were at times surprising, disturbing, even inspiring. Men and women of all races and cultures within this particular setting proved only partially responsible for what happened there. People in colonial Veracruz had limited control over their destiny. The underprivileged view of a regional society as described in these pages reveals a much different outline of changes in social, economic, and political orders than those most scholars have commonly described.

Furthermore, this work's section on economic development suggests a somewhat revisionist interpretation of these events. First, neither royal officials nor white colonists anticipated mid-sixteenth- and early seventeenth-century modifications to the area's economic structure, of which the introduction of Africans in large numbers represented just one part. Second, the period 1630–1720 emerges not as a time of prolonged depression but as an era of economic realignment, a time when the colony's orientation turned inward.[2] Veracruz appears to have receded from the trans-Atlantic economic system and moved toward domestic interregional ties in markets, capital, and production. Iberia's partial retreat from control over material development within the province made this increased interaction of parochial and regional sectors of the domestic economy possible. Thus, as Peter Bakewell speculates, the middle colonial economic period may have proved a time of depression for the imperial mercantile economy, but it represented a time of birth for the free-enterprise system in Mexico.[3]

Bakewell's interpretation, of course, places the eighteenth-century Bourbon Reforms in a different light. While shifts in late colonial policy did liberalize and probably revitalize Veracruz' participation in the expanding imperially promoted Atlantic commercial economy, they did so at the expense of the native incipient capitalist experiment of the previous period.[4] Elite white Veracruzanos accepted this domestic loss as long as most of them materially profited from the reversal in direction and nature of economic growth. But from about 1800 onward the driving force behind these late colonial changes, the Spanish state, placed extraordinary strains on regional economies as a result of the heavy demands placed on that state by

Napoleonic wars. The timing of this pressure affected central Veracruz unevenly. Such areas as Jalapa experienced little dislocation and the local response was mild. In slave areas including Córdoba and Izúcar, Puebla, the impact proved heavier, and the local response was stronger.[5] In such areas frictions heated the political climate to the boiling point during the first decade of the nineteenth century. And those groups that acted most restively were the historically underprivileged who either enjoyed limited opportunity in the late-middle and early Bourbon periods or observed their neighboring counterparts enjoying it. Afro-Veracruzanos comprised a part of this lot.

Two developments pushed parts of Veracruz into open rebellion. The first was the French invasion of Spain. This weakened imperial leadership at a time of colonial crisis. The second catalyst involved the emergence of regional leadership to pull the colony away from the imperial sources of stress. Naturally, that leadership came from the largely nonwhite masses in the persons of men including Miguel Hidalgo y Costilla, Vicente Guerrero, and José María Morelos y Pavón from 1810 to 1815. In central Veracruz these men had their local counterparts. One was the Cura of Maltrata, Don Juan Moctezuma Cortés, a direct descendent of the last Aztec emperor. A second was Juan Bautista, a free mulatto. A third was Francisco Gómez, a former slave.[6] But the correlations of race and ethnicity with underprivilege created the specter of race war, perhaps tinged with class struggle. This identification doomed the first more egalitarian resistance movement that started in 1810 in the Bajío and reached such places as Córdoba in 1811. Creole whites who had grown in power during the middle colonial period and then sacrificed these influences for economic rewards during the later rebirth of the imperial system recoiled for fear that the undiscriminating rebellious colored masses would consume them too. These powerful racial elites joined hands with imperial forces to put down the popular revolt and to literally kill all but a handful of its national leaders. Of the most prominent independence fighters only a few survived, including Vicente Guerrero, Nicolás Bravo, and Guadalupe Victoria.[7]

By 1816 the grassroots revolution had virtually died, but the pressures that had precipitated it had not. Upon regaining the throne with the defeat of Napoleon, Ferdinand VII tried to resume the centralizing political directions of the late Bourbon Reforms[8] but without the carrot of economic prosperity. At the same time liberals in the motherland agitated for more egalitarian conditions throughout the empire. Threatened by both these developments, creole Mexican white elites seized leadership of the colony.[9] But the nature of this second rebellion proved quite different from the first. It was not nearly as democratic. Mexican elites, still wary of the nonwhite masses, strove to limit popular participation in the uprising. They exercised a coup from the top rather than a revolt from the bottom of society. The upper reaches of the socioeconomic strata directed and implemented it.

At least one segment of the underprivileged masses in central Veracruz resisted this movement. Afro-Córdobans and -Orizabans refused to come down out of their mountain strongholds for years after the break with Spain. In the end, however, they too entered a postindependence society that promoted evolutionary rather than revolutionary change. Elites made limited concessions to nonwhites that did little more than recognize some of the gains the latter had made in the middle colonial and late colonial periods. After all, white creoles now stood alone against the nonwhite masses. Creole whites had broken with their Iberian allies in maintaining racist and ethnocentric tools of control. Somewhat weakened by this division in their ranks, white creole elites accepted greater equality from the middle sectors of society on down. Nonwhites and individuals of varying cultural identities enjoyed greater mobility up, down, and across occupational and social scales. Nonwhites and non-Hispanics could obtain better jobs and interact more freely with nonwhites and Hispanics at all but the upper levels of society. Public documents no longer contained racial designations, priests no longer openly admonished parishioners to avoid interracial and interethnic marriages. Whites even offered political concessions. Nonwhites began to participate in politics. Initially, blacks and their descendants, who had experienced total disenfranchisement throughout the colonial period, began to vote, run, and be elected to public office. In Jalapa Afro-*castas*, like other nonwhites, won town council seats in the district capital for the first time. At the national level, Vicente Guerrero narrowly lost a disputed presidential election then actually attained the position when his populist backers forced Manuel Gómez Pedraza to abdicate, making Guerrero constitutionally next in line to serve.

Evidence presented herein to support the above social, economic, and political overviews of colonial change is meager, not nearly enough to warrant their full acceptance. But they are worth consideration for no other reason than they place the chaotic early national period in a much more logical perspective. The way more traditional interpretations present the years from 1720 to 1820 appears incongruent with postindependence events. Could the political and economic disorders between the years 1821 and 1876 have evolved out of the supposed order and prosperity of the Bourbon Reforms? The popular revolt of 1810 lasted five years and then was crushed through the collusion of creole and peninsular white elites who then pulled Mexicans in a quite different direction than their much more revolutionary predecessors of the 1810–1815 period. When the break with Spain did come, it proved relatively conservative in nature. It effected only limited changes in the socioeconomic order.[10] These shifts were far too subtle to cause the dislocations that followed.

What this study hints is that the early national period was not a consequence of the pressures that developed at the end of the colonial period but the changes that took place throughout it. The Bourbon Reforms reversed the natural development of Veracruz and the rest of Mexico. They stifled the progression of regional economies that up to 1720 transformed from tribute to mercantile modes of operation and had begun the process of integrating into an interregional free-enterprise system. At this critical juncture, a revitalized Spain successfully rejuvenated its imperial economy and drew Mexico backward into the orbit of Atlantic trade with the lure of greater temporary prosperity for creole white elites but at the expense of a domestic economic infrastructure that had sprung up during the previous ninety years (1630–1720). The mother country also reasserted its political power through the implementation of the intendency system.

Politically, Spain had resubordinated the colony to centralism at the expense of localism. The consequences of these backward steps in economic and political development were not felt until the late colonial crisis of empire caused by the Napoleonic wars. This proved a time when entrepreneurs in Jalapa and planters in Córdoba lost many benefits gained during the Bourbon economic reforms. At the same time they found themselves saddled with new taxes. Thus Veracruz entered into the early national decades moving backwards in terms of economic and political progress. The results proved devastating. A century-old legacy of renewed over-dependence on the import-export sector of the economy was entrenched. But the economic linkages upon which this legacy rested tore apart with independence. Veracruz' domestic economy had eroded over the previous century; its replacement, Atlantic commerce, was dislocated. The region's economy was bankrupt in structure and in fact. It remained in this state for the next sixty years, until the country as a whole reverted to the developmental direction of the Bourbon Reform period under Don Porfirio Díaz.[11]

Political disorder followed from economic dislocation at the national level. Only two heads of Mexican state served their prescribed turns in office between 1821 and 1876.[12] Laws had to be enacted to force individuals to serve in national legislative and judicial posts. Regionalism, even localism, successfully challenged national authority. Political fragmentation rather than political unity proved the order of the times. For that reason, at the parochial level there was more stability. In such places as Jalapa, Córdoba, Guadalajara, Oaxaca City, San Luis Potosí, and Puebla, the foundations of modern Mexican society were laid. In such regional and local settings, social strides of the middle and late colonial periods endured. At the regional and local levels racism and ethnocentrism continued to very slowly erode. These concepts never totally disappeared, but they did become less and less functional, as the roots of the Cosmic Race, planted in the colonial period, bloomed in the late nineteenth century and received recognition by José Vasconcelos in the twentieth.

Finally, local political and social stability grew into general order through the crucible of change formed by the Porfiriato and the revolutionary years that followed (1910–1929). The order that finally emerged proved one tempered by revolutionary responses to the countervailing tugs and pulls of Mexican development from 1519 to 1929. These especially included vacillations between a self-reliant and independent domestic political economy and a dependent internationally oriented political economy, between a more egalitarian social system and a more racist ethnocentrically and more class-stratified social order. These fitful shifts in direction represent the legacy of the colonial period in locales including Jalapa, Córdoba, and Orizaba all over Mexico, and they continue to influence the national character today.[13]

Appendix 1

Materials Relating to the Afro-Mexican and Afro-Veracruz Slave Trade

AS SHOWN IN Table A.1, the population in New Spain declined dramatically between 1518 and 1625. Table A.2 deals with pre-1580 Afro-Mexicans' African origins. Aguirre Beltrán based his assess-

Table A.1. *Population Totals for Mexico and Jalapa, 1519–1625*

Year	Mexico (in millions)	Jalapa (in thousands)
1518	25.2	30.0
1532	16.8	—
1548	6.3	—
1568	2.7	20.4
1580	—	7.3
1595	1.4	—
1625	.7	4.0

Source: Sherburne F. Cook and Woodrow Borah, *Essays in Population History*, vol. 3, 10, 100–101. I have made a few modifications in Cook and Borah's data. First, I rounded their 1568 and 1595 population totals to the nearest hundred thousand. Second, they give a five-year range for the nadir of Indian population growth, 1620–1625. Since the low point in Jalapa took place in 1626, I took the last year in Cook and Borah's range to make both columns more chronologically compatible.

The 1518 and 1580 totals for Jalapa came from district magistrate Bravo de Lagunas' report, *Relación de Xalapa, 1580*, 9–10, 12, 23–24, 30, 37, 43, 47, 51, 55, 59, 63, 69, 73. The 1568 figure for Jalapa came from Cook and Borah, *Essays in Population History*, vol. 3, 43–45, and Gerhard, *Historical Geography of New Spain*, 376. I derived the 1625 total by taking Gerhard's Indian tributary count of 1,434 for the district in 1626 and multiplying it by a factor of 2.8, suggested by Cook and Borah for the late sixteenth century (*Essays in Population History*, vol. 1, 281–282).

Table A.2. *Afro-Mexican Slave Origins, 1549–1560*

Origin	Aguirre	Boyd-Bowman	Orizaba	Total	Modern Africa Location
North Africa:					
Zafi	1	—	—	1	Morroco
West Africa:					
Senegambia/					
Guinea-					
Bissau	3	3	—	6	General West Africa
Agbenyau	—	1	—	1	
Berbesi	6	10	1	17	Senegal
Wolof	14	13	7	34	Senegal
Gomera	1	—	—	1	(extinct) Senegal
Tucuxy	1	—	—	1	Senegal
Fula	—	—	1	1	Gambia
Mandinga	9	5	6	20	Gambia
Manka	—	—	1	1	Gambia
Calabari	—	—	1	1	Nigeria
Banol	5	9	1	15	Guinea-Bissau
Biafara	14	27	13	54	Guinea-Bissau
Bioho	—	—	3	3	Guinea-Bissau
Bran	23	19	10	52	Guinea-Bissau
Cazanga	1	3	2	6	Guinea-Bissau
Nalu	—	—	3	3	Guinea-Bissau
Gyo	—	1	—	1	Liberia
Arda	—	—	2	2	Dahomey
Cape	—	12	6	18	Dahomey
Ewe	—	—	1	1	Dahomey
Zape	4	—	—	4	Dahomey
Terre Nova	1	3	4	8	East Guinea
Subtotal	83	106	62	251	
Intermediate Zone					
São Tome	—	4	—	4	
Subtotal	—	4	—	4	
Central Africa					
Mani Congo	—	10	—	10	Lower Congo
Angola	—	—	5	5	Luanda
Subtotal	—	10	5	15	
Southeast Africa					
Cibalo	1	—	—	1	Zanzibar
Mozambique	4	—	—	4	Southeast Africa
Cafre	—	—	—	1	Southeast Africa/ India
Subtotal	5	—	—	6	
Total	88	120	67	276	

Table A.2. (*continued*)

Source: Aguirre Beltrán listed two "Mozambique" cases twice. I assume this was in error, and I only counted them once. He also recorded one Portuguese slave in a combined "Zafi-Lisboa" category. I also excluded this Portuguese case. As a result, Aguirre Beltrán's total cohort shrank from 87 to 84 cases (see Gonzalo Aguirre Beltrán, *Población negra de México*, 240).

Boyd-Bowman included thirty-four cases from Havana archives. Whether these were slaves bound for Mexico or whether they were Cuban slaves that he was adding to increase general knowledge of the African ethnic backgrounds of slaves imported to the Americas was not at all clear to me. Because of this doubt, I removed the Havana cases from Table 4. I also deleted his total of six cases for Spanish- and Portuguese-born slaves. I then omitted two other cases, 1 "Bolamon" and 1 "Canicu" because I could not find either group in Aguirre's African tribal index. My adjustments reduced Boyd-Bowman's published total of 164 cases to 120 cases (see Peter Boyd-Bowman, "Negro Slaves in Early Colonial Mexico," *Americas* 26, no. 2 (Oct. 1969): 135).

The Orizaba count came from inventories of the Ingenio de Orizaba found in "Papeles del Conde del Valle de Orizaba," vol. 4a, leaves 19–29, Edmundo O'Gorman Collection, NLBC-UTx.

ments of the numbers and origins of arrivals on just eighty-six slaves listed in the pre-1570 records of Cortés' Tlaltenango plantation in Cuernavaca.[1] Peter Boyd-Bowman added another 123 cases mostly from his investigations in the Puebla and Mexico City archives. Six of his totals, however, came from the published description of the Mexico City notarial archive by Augustín Millares Carlo. This study contributes fifty-one more cases from a 1560 inventory of the *ingenio* of Orizaba in the province of Veracruz. Table A.3 contains seventeenth-century breakdowns of Afro-Mexican slave origins. Aguirre Beltrán's analysis of late-seventeenth-century slave inventories for the Colegios of San Pablo in central Mexico represents one body of information.[2] A number of later studies provide added evidence.

Samples from Tables A.2 and A.3 are chronologically unsystematic. As a result, the timing of events in America and Africa are approximated. Much of the problem probably lies in the nature of the sample. Nearly a thousand cases would be enough to show the 150-year patterns we are seeking if that thousand were randomly sampled from the entire slave population within Mexico during the period. Unfortunately, this was not the case. As the footnotes to each table point out, I made admittedly arbitrary decisions in sorting out the categories from the various samples combined. Finally, the nature of the evidence was not uniform. Some of the cases came from plantation inventories; some of them came from slave sales. In the sample for Table A.2, Aguirre Beltrán's and the Orizaba totals come from plantation communities while Boyd-Bowman's contribution was derived from records of slave sales. For the seventeenth-

Table A.3. *Ethnic Origins of Slaves in the Seventeenth Century*

Origin	Konrad (1639)	Mayer (1632–1657)	Aguirre (late seventeenth century)	Total
West Africa				
Senegambia/Guinea				
Unspecified	—	14	22	36
Wolof	—	—	3	3
Cabo Verde	—	—	2	2
Berbesi	—	—	1	1
Bran	—	—	8	8
Biafara	4	—	5	9
Banol	—	—	2	2
Bioho	—	—	1	1
Xoxo	—	—	1	1
Zape	—	—	2	2
Mina	—	—	1	1
Arara	—	—	6	6
Arda	—	—	9	9
Calabari	—	—	6	6
Terre Nova	—	—	1	1
Subtotal	4	14	70	88 (13%)
Intermediate Zone				
São Tome	—	—	14	14
Subtotal	—	—	14	14 (2%)
Central Africa				
Balala	—	—	2	2
Lunga	—	—	1	1
Anchico	—	—	2	2
Longo	—	—	1	1
Congo	13	10	24	47
Malemba	12	—	—	12
Angola	16	187	271	474
Matamba	—	—	1	1
Banquela	—	—	1	1
Subtotal	41	197	303	541 (80%)
Southeast Africa				
Zozo	—	—	1	1
Cafre	—	—	7	7
Mozambique	9	9	7	25
Subtotal	9	9	15	33 (5%)
Total	54	220	402	676 (100%)

Table A.3. (*continued*)

Source: Konrad includes eight additional cases for groups that I could not locate on any other Mexican slave lists or in any of the secondary works I consulted on West Africa. I did not include them in the above totals (see Herman Konrad, *A Jesuit Hacienda in Colonial Mexico*, 247–248).

Vincent Mayer provides a list of 206 more cases of slave origins from sales in the Parral mining region of northern Mexico between 1632 and 1657, but he did not designate a West African category. Instead he had an "Other" group into which he lumped Calabari, Portugal, Biafara, and Guiana, which included a total of eighteen cases. Since he already had a separate Mozambique listing, I assumed that its inclusion in the "Other" group was a mistake. Of the remaining four origins included in this "Other" category, all but Portugal are located in West Africa. Since the Portuguese complement could not have been that large, I arbitrarily estimated the total to be four slaves, subtracted that number from Mayer's total for the cohort, and listed fourteen West African cases. I left Mayer's Portuguese India as an entirely separate category and did not collapse its fifteen cases into the above table (see Vincent Mayer, "The Black Slave on New Spain's Northern Frontier: San José de Parral, 1632–1676" [Ph.D. dissertation, University of Utah, 1975], 36–37; Aguirre Beltrán, *Población negra de México*, 241; Palmer, *Slaves of the White God*, 23).

Curtin places São Tome in the West African slave group. Given its heavy trade with the CongoLuanda region up until the end of the Angola Wars in 1622, I decided to put São Tomen slaves in an intermediary position between West and Central Africa (see Curtin, *Atlantic Slave Trade*, 113).

century totals in Table A.3, Konrad's and Aguirre Beltrán's figures come from plantation records while Mayer's from slave purchases.

Plantation inventories merely record the origins of slaves residing on the estate. They usually do not state when the slave was actually imported from Africa. In some cases *bozal* slaves had resided on estates for many years, raising the possibility that they are chronologically misplaced in the tables.

Slave sales, on the other hand, did list time of arrival in Mexico, as well as point of departure from Africa. For this reason bills of sale are better suited for determining the timing of changes in the Mexican market, the African source of supply, and European distribution policies.

One final problem with the evidence involved a lack of comprehensive indices for measuring the changing volume of the Mexican trade. The larger samples in the seventeenth-century data may truly reflect an actual increase in the number of slaves shipped to Mexico. Then again, they may be the result of better documentation for this later period, especially in the cases of Konrad's midseventeenth-century figures and Aguirre Beltrán's late seventeenth-century totals in Table A.3. Both lists derive from well-administered Jesuit estates in the Valley of Mexico. The good fathers were noted for their exemplary attention to record keeping. Moreover, these inventories involved large estates. Their greater economies of scale heavily depended on reliable labor in skilled positions. Slaves commonly filled this type of need and as a result were heavily concentrated in these settings. Great estates, such as those represented in Konrad and Aguirre Beltrán's samples, had both the need and the capital resources to rely on slaves. For all these reasons they imported unusually large numbers of African slaves. Thus, information too heavily weighted on these types of large estates could lead to overestimates of the size of the volume of the Mexican slave trade.

Timing for retreat from the Atlantic slave trade appears a bit earlier for Jalapa than for Mexico as a whole. Colin Palmer estimates Mexico's retreat no earlier than 1623;[3] Aguirre Beltrán gives a later date, 1640.[4] Jalapa's trade dropped by about 1610.

Some have argued that European events hampered the slave trade from the turn of the seventeenth century to 1616. Merchants in Seville accused the Portuguese traders of heavily engaging in contraband slaving and thereby undercutting the prosperity of legitimate Spanish commerce with the colonies. Frederick Bowser judges that the crown's sensitivity to Sevillian criticisms may have ironically turned these fears into self-fulfilling prophecies. He speculates that the Spanish state may have harassed Portuguese traders in an attempt to limit the amount of profit the Portuguese could derive from the slave trade and to restrict their illegal commerce. The crown invariably held the number of slaves allowed into its New World possessions to a level well below the demand.[5] Palmer states that this was certainly the case in pre-1620 Mexico.[6] These policies forced the asientists to engage in illegal trade to offset losses they suffered from restrictive royal policies. Spanish concern became so great that in 1611 the state enacted sweeping new regulations that crippled the Spanish-American slave trade for the next five years. The crown required slave carriers to put into the port of Seville for on board inspection before sailing for Spanish America. The ships then had to await the annual departure of the Spanish convoy to make sure that they sailed for designated ports only. Finally, Spain pressured Portuguese traders to sell their slaves to Sevillian intermediaries rather than to higher paying American colonists. Portuguese merchants could only transport slaves to America themselves if they could find no Spanish buyers for their Africans.[7]

The end result of these practices was that no Portuguese traders successfully applied for a license until 1616, and not a single slave ship legally sailed for New Spain until then.[8] Contraband trade did continue, as evidenced by the few slaves traded in Jalapa during these five years, but the flow of Africans into the district decreased a great deal. Even after the *asiento* system started up gain, the Spanish state, prodded by pressure from Spanish merchants, continued harassing Portuguese carriers. Officials delayed and searched their ships and more strictly enforced the rule of entry into only designated ports. This type of activity increased in the next decade as Portugal moved closer and closer to a break with Spain.[9]

Philip Curtin, through a series of modifications to the evidence presented by Pierre and Huguette Chaunu, places the shift in principal place of slave origin from West to Central Africa between 1616 and 1620. For Jalapa that shift came a bit earlier, no later than the period 1595–1600. Perhaps this discrepancy merely results from a local variance in a broader pattern, but as Curtin points out, the Chaunu data contains a great many unknowns. Derived from ship licenses for the slave-carrying trade, their totals contain a high percentage (38 percent) of unknown and "mixed" origins of slaves.[10] Curtin solves the problem by dividing the origins of these two categories equally between West and Central Africa.[11] The Jalapa data suggests that this procedure may have been inappropriate.

Appendix 2

Materials Relating to Demographic and Economic Change

TABLE A.4 helps to illustrate the shifting importance of the Atlantic trade in Mexico's economic development between 1596 and 1635. Table A.5 lists the amounts of sugar and their market values per unit that left the port of Veracruz between 1796 and 1820. This data set has, however, several shortcomings. The first and most important is the lack of comparative totals for earlier years. The second is the missing figures for 1805 and 1814–1819, especially since the latter period encompassed many of the Mexican insurgent years. And third, the British Navy disrupted Mexican shipping for many of the years covered in Table A.5. As a result of this threat from at least 1806 onward, the bulk of Mexican commerce flowed as contraband

Table A.4. *Mexico's Percentage of Spanish Trade with America by Five-Year Periods, 1596–1635*

Years	Percentage of All Spanish-American Trade
1596–1600	48
1601–1605	51
1606–1610	48
1611–1615	54
1616–1620	51
1621–1625	43
1626–1630	29
1631–1635	30

Source: Huguette et Pierre Chaunu, *Séville et l'Atlantique, 1504–1650,* vol. 8, pt. 2, no. 2, 1534–1535.

Table A.5. *Sugar Exports from the Port of Veracruz,*
1796–1820

Date	Arrobas	Value (pesos)	Market Price/Arroba (pesos)
1796	346,361	1,347,231	3.9
1797	60,835	159,834	2.6
1798	79,568	212,691	2.7
1799	150,881	479,062	3.2
1800	87,570	287,277	3.3
1801	9,148	25,157	2.7
1802	431,867	1,454,240	3.4
1803	483,944	1,495,056	3.0
1804	381,509	1,097,505	2.9
1805	—	—	—
1806	25,857	64,642	2.5
1807	5,288	13,220	2.5
1808	19,917	39,834	2.0
1809	241,246	482,492	2.0
1810	119,726	269,383	2.2
1811	95,016	237,540	2.5
1812	12,236	30,575	2.5
1813	7,657	19,142	2.5
1814–1819	—	—	—
1820	7,100	24,850	3.7

Source: Miguel Lerdo de Tejada, *Apuntes históricos de la heróica ciudad de Vera-Cruz,* vol. 3, 368–369.

to other Western Hemisphere ports instead of to Spanish ones (see Lerdo de Tejada, *Apuntes históricos de la heróica ciudad de Vera-Cruz,* vol. 3, 366–371).

Incomplete data and the immeasurable volume of contraband activity make the export trade an awkward yardstick with which to measure Mexican sugar production. The status of the industry in Jalapa represents an admittedly poor substitute because of its limited size. Jalapa's importance to the national industry was secondary when compared to other areas, such as Morelos and the Orizaba-Córdoba region. Moreover, its unusually favorable climate allowed it to escape natural hazards including the drought of 1809 that ruined crops in the intendancies of Mexico, Oaxaca, and San Luis Potosí. (see AGN, Intendencia, vol. 73, *expediente* 14, leaves 14–15). However, its ready access to the port made it a good barometer of European pressure on the colony.

Table A.6. *Slaves in Central Veracruz by Gender, 1560–1700*

	1560–1629		1630–1660		1661–1700	
	No.	%	No.	%	No.	%
Male	358	76	50	70	204	58
Female	112	24	21	30	150	42
Total	470	100	71	100	354	100

Source: The sample for the 1560–1629 period was drawn from the 1560 inventory of the Ingenio de Orizaba in "Papeles del Conde de Orizaba," vol. 4a, leaves 19–29, O'Gorman Collection; the slave sales in Jalapa between 1578–1600, in Bermúdez Gorrochotegui, "Jalapa en el Siglo XVI," vol. 1, 165; and slave sales in Jalapa 1601–1629. For notes on this part of the sample, see the appropriate decades in the source notes for Table 3. The cohort figures for 1630–1660 came from ANJ, 1663–1670, leaves 26v–32; inventory of Rosario in 1663; ANJ, 1663–1670, leaves 118v–124, inventory of Mazatlan in 1664; ANJ, 1663–1670, leaves 358–364v; inventory of Mazatlan in 1667; ANJ, 1699, leaves 640–646, inventory of Mazatlan in 1699; "Ingenio de Almolonga y Rancho de Santa Cruz," bound volume, NLBC-UTx leaves 73v, 107–110; inventory for Almolonga in 1675; "Almolonga," leaves 140v–143v, inventory for Almolonga in 1691; "Almolonga," leaves 151–152, inventory of Almolonga in 1700.

Table A.7. *Slaves by Age in Jalapa, 1640–1700*

Age	1640–1659	1660–1679	1680–1700
1–5	2 (5%)	19 (14%)	11 (12%)
6–14	1	16	12
15–40	19 (50%)	58 (42%)	37 (42%)
41–60	9 (24%)	20 (14%)	13 (15%)
61–70	5	12	5
71–80	1	9	6
81+	1 (3%)	5 (4%)	4 (5%)
Total	38	139	88

Source: The 1640–1659 sample was drawn from ANJ, 1651–1663, leaves 81v–82, 1642 inventory of Mazatlan; ANJ, 1645–1658, leaf 392, 1655 inventory of Mazatlan. The 1660–1679 sample came from ANJ, 1663–1667, leaves 26v–32, 1663 inventory of Rosario; ANJ, 1663–1667, leaves 118v–124, 1664 inventory of Mazatlan; "Almolonga," bound volume, leaves 73v, 107v–110, 1675 inventory of Almolonga. The 1680–1700 sample was drawn from "Almolonga," leaves 140–143v; 1691 inventory of Almolonga; "Almolonga," leaves 151–152, 1700 inventory of Almolonga.

Table A.8. *Residents of the Santísima Trinidad by Status and Race, 1631–1670*

	1631–1640		1661–1670	
	No.	%	No.	%
Status				
Slave	54	35	82	17
Free	89	57	351	75
Missing cases	13	8	37	8
Total	156	100	470	101 (rounded)
Race				
White	54	26	82	19
Indian	64	31	149	35
Negro	47	23	57	13
Mestizo	6	3	26	6
Mulatto	9	4	54	13
Pardo	8	4	40	9
Missing cases	18	9	23	5
Total	206	100	431	100

Source: Archivo Parroquial de Coatepec, Matrimonios, vol. 1 (sic vol. 2), leaves 1–22; ibid., Bautizos, vol. 1 (sic vol. 2), leaves 78–94v.

Table A.9. *Population Totals for Small Farms and Large Estates within the District of Jalapa, 1746, 1777, 1791, 1830*

Location	1746	1777	1791	1830
Small Farms	800	1,443	2,100	1,500
Estates	500	1,297	1,330	2,400

Source: Figures for 1746 came from Villa-Señor y Sánchez, *Theatro americano*, vol. 2, 281–297; those for 1777 from AGN, Historia, vol. 522, leaf 239; for 1791 from AGN, Padrones, vol. 20, leaves 246, 337; and for 1830 from *Estadística del estado libre y soberano de Veracruz*, 80–81.

Table A.6 traces the gradual balancing of the sex ratio within the Veracruz slave population, while Table A.7 demonstrates an increasing balance in age distribution within Jalapa's slave community as the proportion of children grew after 1660. Table A.8 illustrates decline in permanent slave residents on the large Santísima Trinidad plantation in Jalapa during the seventeenth century. Table A.9 im-

Table A.10. *Racial Composition of Córdoba, Jalapa, and Mexico, 1580–1793*

	1580	1646	1696	1746	1793
% Indian:					
Córdoba	—	86.9	58.6	56.9	53.2
Jalapa	92.9	85.1	79.2	72.3	65.8
Mexico	99.0	90.0	—	76.1	69.0
% White:					
Córdoba	—	4.3	9.6	10.5	12.2
Jalapa	2.0	3.8	8.1	11.6	15.0
Mexico	.2	5.3	—	9.4	13.4
% *Negro:*					
Córdoba	—	6.4	18.1	6.5	5.1
Jalapa	2.9	4.1	2.6	1.0	.6
Mexico	.6	.8	—	.3	.0
% *Casta:*					
Córdoba	—	2.4	13.7	26.1	29.5
Jalapa	2.1	7.0	9.1	15.1	18.6
Mexico	.2	4.0	—	14.2	17.6

Source: The same as those described for Tables 3 and 5.

plies the changing importance of large- and small-scale agriculture units in the district of Jalapa during the late colonial and early national periods. It reveals these shifts by comparing population totals on each type of unit between 1746 and 1830.

Table A.10 approximates racial breakdowns for the populations of Córdoba Jalapa, and all Mexico at five time points. These percentages came from rough estimates of population in these three areas. I arrived at these totals through a number of speculative calculations in many instances. Generally speaking, these machinations involved interpolation between a series of figures based on contemporary counts of tributaries, families, or individuals. I did, however, seek corroboration for estimates from descriptive accounts of the area at the time point in question.

Córdoba estimates were derived from a variety of sources. An account of the foundation of the *villa* is in AMC, vol. 2, unnumbered leaves, roll 1, TAMUCC Veracruz Microfilm Collection. Gerhard's *Guide to the Historical Geography of New Spain*, pp. 84–85, provided estimates of sorts for the years 1520–1746. Gerhard summarized a number of counts that were at times incongruous with respect to both units of measure and comprehensiveness of racial groups. As a result his data required manipulation. I converted tributary units to population totals using a factoring formula developed by Cook and Borah and listed in Gerhard (p. 26). I converted family units by using factors derived in Carroll, "Mexican Society in Transition," Chapter 3. Adriana Naveda Chávez-Hita's "Esclavitud negra en Córdoba," pp. 8–11, provides a concise overview of the region's demographic growth from 1618 through the end of the eighteenth century. Finally, a few calculations were merely based on qualitative statements made in Herrera Moreno, *Cantón de Córdoba*, pp. 99–105. Late colonial estimates came from Adriana Naveda Chávez-Hita's "Esclavitud negra en Córdoba"; pp. 77–99; Villa-Señor y Sánchez, *Theatro americano*, vol. 1, p. 264; AGN, Tributos, vol. 43, *último expediente*, leaves unnumbered; Gerhard, *Historical Geography of New Spain*, pp. 84–85. Censuses for the villages of Amatlan de los Reyes Santos, San Antonio de Huatusco, and San Thiago (San Diego) de Totutla exist for the year 1777: Archivo General de las Indias, México, vol. 2578; Ibid., vol. 2580, *expediente* 9. I am indebted to Susan Deans-Smith of the University of Texas, Austin, for making these three counts available to me. A partial census for Córdoba exists for the year 1788. It included household counts for the district's haciendas, but it excluded counts for the *villa* of Córdoba and the region's eight Indian villages. See AMC, "Pardón de los individuos que componen las haciendas y los ranchos de la jurisdicción de Córdoba," vol. 16, unnumbered leaves, rolls 5 and 13, TAMUCC Veracruz Microfilm Collection. Totals for Jalapa province are explained in Carroll, "Mexican Society in Transition," pp. 315–317. Calculations for Mexico as a whole involved the use of different types of sources of information. Many of these are reviewed in Gerhard's *Historical Geography of New Spain*, pp. 22–33. Finally, the basis for the 1777 and 1793 are described in Carroll, "Mexican Society in Transition," pp. 315–317.

Table A.11 indicates that the district's residents multiplied more rapidly during the fair years (1722–1776) than at any other time during the colonial period. By today's standards the 1746–1777 average annual population increase of 1.13 percent was by no means spectacular. But measured against other Mexican areas of the same era, it appears high. Cook and Borah found that the Mixteca Alta region's population grew by a mere .60 percent each year between 1750 and 1830.[1] Günther Volmer discovered that indigenous populations around Puebla expanded at a yearly rate of less than .50 percent.[2] Guanajuato appeared the only region encountered in the literature that displayed more rapid population increase than Jalapa at this time. David Brading and Evelyn Wu estimate that Guanajuato's

Table A.11. *Average Population Growth per Year within the District of Jalapa, 1580–1830*

Date	Percentage
1580–1746	.60
1746–1777	1.13
1777–1784	− .52
1784–1791	− .52
1791–1820	.91
1820–1826	.48
1826–1830	2.06

Source: Population totals upon which these rates rely came from the following sources: for the year 1580, Bravo de Lagunas, *Relación de Xalapa;* for the years 1746, 1777, 1784, 1791, and 1830, Carroll, "Mexican Society in Transition," 105, Appendix 3; for 1820 and 1826, *Estadística del estado libre y soberano de Veracruz,* 65.

Table A.12. *Jalapa District Population Totals by Distance from the Capital by Year, 1700–1830*

Distance from District Capital	1700	1743	1777	1784	1791	1830
0–25 Kilometers						
Jalapa		4,689	7,464	4,689	4,824	10,628
Chiltoyaque		114	193	193	182	271
Coatepec		2,346	1,073	1,943	2,276	5,859
Coaucazintla		264	247	267	247	268
Naulinco		1,203	1,338	1,327	1,450	1,493
San Andres		708	830	830	830	1,150
San José		840	425	425	430	554
San Juan		1,032	764	764	864	400
San Miguel		270	311	301	312	478
San Salvador		204	2,370	629	630	854
Teocelo		216	1,342	1,287	1,290	2,006
Las Vigas		332	470	560	652	1,482
Xicochimalco		2,301	2,028	2,022	2,019	2,026
Xilotepec		432	1,582	1,482	1,582	2,155
Small Farms		800	1,443	2,000	2,100	1,500
Haciendas		500	1,297	1,300	1,330	2,400
Subtotal	7,000[a]	16,251	23,177	20,019	21,018	33,524

Table A.12. (*continued*)

Distance from District Capital	1700	1743	1777	1784	1791	1830
26–35 Kilometers						
Chapultepec		350	347	347	335	224
Coapan		390	381	321	381	343
Magdalena		120	112	112	112	123
Pastepec		210	209	206	350	181
Tepetlan		120	136	120	116	287
Tlacolula		132	132	587	580	853
Tonayan		900	887	881	880	960
Subtotal	2,000[a]	2,222	2,204	2,574	2,754	2,971
36–50 Kilometers						
Acatlan		648	468	468	470	589
Ayahauluco		442	989	583	1,000	1,218
Chiconquiaco		1,416	1,074	1,074	1,080	1,012
Ixhuacan		588	2,105	2,075	2,372	2,487
San Marcos		115	114	114	114	154
Xalcomulco		—	—	—	—	757
Yecuatla		30	467	467	467	624
Subtotal	7,000[a]	3,239	5,217	4,781	5,503	6,841
Total	16,000[a]	21,712	30,598	27,374	29,275	43,336

Source: The data for the first, third, and fourth columns (1700, 1777, 1784) was estimated from a variety of sources containing qualitative rather than quantitative information on the population of the district. These sources included: AGN, Padrones, vol. 20, leaves 295–297; Nieto, *Padrón de Xalapa*, 14–16; González de Cassio, *Xalapa*, 68; Rivera, *Historia antigua y moderna de Jalapa*, vol. 1, 122; Villa-Señor y Sánchez, *Theatro americano*, vol. 2, 282–283; Carrera Stampa, "Las ferias Novohispañas," 328. The figures for column two were derived from Villa-Señor y Sánchez's *Theatro americano*, vol. 2, 281–297. The totals for 1791 were obtained from the Revillagigedo census; AGN, Padrones, vol. 20, leaves 246, 337; Nieto, *Padrón de Xalapa*. The 1830 figures were derived from the *Estadística del estado libre y soberano de Veracruz*, 80–81.

[a] Estimated.

population grew 1.37 percent per year from 1761 to 1860.[3] The findings of these scholars place Jalapa's growth rate in better context. They show the positive impact of heightened economic activity on expansion of the region's human resources. Fair-generated prosperity encouraged natural increase and also attracted immigrants.

Table A.12 indirectly measures the impact of the district capital's influence on other settlements within the district by correlating changes between population totals in each settlement with distance from the capital at different points in time between 1700 and 1830.

Appendix 3

Materials Relating to Afro-Veracruzanos and Socioeconomic Change

TABLE A.13 shows one of the consequences of Mexico's diminishing participation in the Atlantic slave trade—the decline of West African cultural influence in central Veracruz.

Table A.14 gives the percentage of racially endogamous marriages at three points in time for each of the six racial catagories commonly used in colonial Jalapa. The cases were drawn from marriage and baptismal ceremonies. Since white Spaniards had greatest control over urban areas, and Indians exercised strongest influence in rural zones, I separated data for both spaces.

I must also point out the unevenness of the data. The earliest data for this table came from the year 1580; I could not find comparable evidence for the 1519–1579 years. Even in 1580, references to only three racial groups in the urban sector appeared. They were whites,

Table A.13. *Percentage of Central Veracruz Slaves by Origin/ Cultural Affiliation, 1575–1760*

	1575	1615	1675	1700	1760	No. Cases
Creole	33%	14%	51%	76%	98%	540
Bozal	67%	86%	49%	24%	2%	390
No. Cases	235	113	175	193	214	930

Source: I derived this information from plantation inventories and notarial, parish, and census records for the towns of Córdoba, Jalapa, Orizaba, and Jalancingo. The sources yielded 1772 cases spanning the years 1575–1780. Creole/bozal status represented but one of many traits that I designated for each slave entered into a computer file that I titled "PATDAT." The PATDAT file is my computer library at the Texas A&M University–Corpus Christi Computer Center (hereinafter, I refer to this information base as PATDAT-TAMUCC).

Table A.14. *Percentage of Racially Endogamous Marriages in Urban and Rural Jalapa, 1580–1715*

	Urban			Rural		
	1580	*1645*	*1715*	*1580*	*1645*	*1715*
% Whites						
Male	91	95	92	—	90	94
Female	98	97	91	—	90	97
Combined Ave.	95	96	92	—	90	96
% Mestizos						
Male	88	89	95	—	78	72
Female	82	85	84	—	83	78
Combined Ave.	85	87	90	—	81	75
% *Pardos*						
Male	93	69	68	—	71	67
Female	96	73	71	—	81	69
Combined Ave.	95	71	69	—	76	68
% Mulattoes						
Male	—	73	64	—	71	67
Female	—	75	70	—	81	77
Combined Ave.	—	74	67	—	76	72
% *Negros*						
Male	—	71	65	—	77	78
Female	—	76	73	—	73	93
Combined Ave.	—	74	69	—	75	74
% Indians						
Male	—	97	94	—	96	99
Female	—	94	89	—	98	97
Combined Ave.	—	96	92	—	97	98
Average combined %	—	83	80	—	83	81
No. of cases	103	172	357	—	194	318

Source: PATDAT-TAMUCC.

mestizos, and *pardos.* Yet, other racial groups, namely *negros,* Indians and mulattoes, resided in the region. District notarial records list them as early as 1578.

Tables A.14 and A.15 compare and contrast the changing strength of the color line in males and females of the six basic racially identified groups in the selection of marriage partners over time in urban and rural Jalapa. Tables A.16 and A.17 attempt to gauge changes in

Table A.15. *Percentage of Racially Endogamous Marriage and Baptismal Ceremonial Participants in Urban and Rural Jalapa, 1645, 1715*

	Urban		Rural	
	1645	*1715*	*1645*	*1715*
% Whites				
Male	92	92	88	95
Female	84	90	88	92
Combined Ave.	88	91	88	94
% Mestizos				
Male	77	83	77	71
Female	77	73	70	67
Combined Ave.	77	78	74	69
% *Pardos*				
Male	54	62	70	63
Female	56	65	74	67
Combined Ave.	55	64	72	65
% Mulattoes				
Male	62	79	64	64
Female	67	83	72	70
Combined Ave.	65	81	68	67
% *Negros*				
Male	48	49	47	60
Female	58	55	57	70
Combined Ave.	53	52	52	65
% Indians				
Male	95	94	96	98
Female	92	95	93	96
Combined Ave.	94	95	95	97
Average combined %	72	77	75	76
No. of cases	336	714	461	751

Source: PATDAT-TAMUCC.

the influence of race on males and females of the six basic racial groups in the formation of lesser social bonds in urban and rural Jalapa in the middle colonial period. Table A.18 shows the growing strength of the slave family in central Veracruz between 1575 and 1780.

Table A.16. *Urban Afro-Jalapan Social Interaction by Race, 1645, 1715*

Male	Female						N
	Negro	Pardo	Mulatto	White	Mestizo	Indian	
1645							
Negro							
Participants	59	10	8	11	3	20	111
Percentage	53	9	7	10	3	18	100
Pardo							
Participants	10	47	4	1	—	23	85
Percentage	12	55	5	1	—	27	100
Mulatto							
Participants	8	4	34	4	2	—	52
Percentage	15	8	65	8	4	—	100
1715							
Negro							
Participants	24	6	1	—	—	15	46
Percentage	52	13	2	—	—	33	100
Pardo							
Participants	6	68	4	1	3	25	107
Percentage	6	64	4	1	3	23	101
Mulatto							
Participants	1	4	42	3	1	1	52
Percentage	2	8	81	6	2	2	101
Percentage Change Per Year							
Negro	0	.01	−.02	−.05	−.03	.01	±.12
Pardo	−.01	<.01	<.01	0	.03	<.01	±.07
Mulatto	−.03	0	<.01	<.01	−.01	<.01	±.06

Source: PATDAT-TAMUCC.

Tables A.16 and A.17 list Afro-Jalapans' participation in baptismal and wedding ceremonies for the years 1645 and 1715. Below the racial designations are the number of participants and the percentage of the Afro-American group participating with each racial group on the horizontal axis. The second part of the tables gives average change in the percentage of Afro-American interaction with the six basic racial groups within the population. In sum, part one tells with whom they interacted; part two shows the rate and direction of change in Afro-Jalapan social ties.

Note: In the urban zone the overall correlation between race participation in these types of ceremonies was strong in 1645 and 1715. Moreover, the frequency distribution in this table was not random. It yielded the following correlation coefficients:

1645, observed Chi Sq. of 155.31 > the critical value of 27.58 @ 0.05 level of significance.
1715, observed Chi Sq. of 217.66 > the critical value of 27.59 @ 0.05 level of significance.

Table A.17. *Rural Afro-Jalapan Social Interaction by Race, 1645, 1715*

			Female				
Male	Negro	Pardo	*Mulatto*	White	Mestizo	Indian	*N*
1645							
Negro							
Participants	76	10	1	22	1	35	145
Percentage	52	7	1	15	1	24	100
Pardo							
Participants	10	92	8	2	—	15	127
Percentage	8	72	6	2	—	12	100
Mulatto							
Participants	1	8	66	12	10	—	97
Percentage	1	8	68	12	10	—	100
1715							
Negro							
Participants	36	5	1	7	—	6	55
Percentage	65	9	2	13	—	11	100
Pardo							
Participants	2	48	1	3	2	18	74
Percentage	3	65	1	4	3	24	100
Mulatto							
Participants	1	1	35	10	1	4	52
Percentage	2	2	67	19	2	8	100
Percentage Change per Year							
Negro	<.01	<.01	.01	<.01	−.01	.01	±.06
Pardo	−.02	<.01	.03	.01	.01	.01	±.09
Mulatto	.01	.02	<.01	.01	−.01	.04	±.10

Source: See source for A.16.
Note: In the rural zone the overall correlation between race participation in these types of ceremonies proved strong in both 1645 and 1715. Moreover, the frequency distribution of the table yielded the following correlation coefficients:
  1645, observed Chi Sq. of 414.79 > the critical value of 27.58 @ 0.05 level of significance.
  1715, observed Chi Sq. of 216.06 > the critical value of 28.58 @ 0.05 level of significance.

Table A.19 correlates race with socioeconomic rank. It uses an occupational stratification scheme to accomplish this. Basically, it lumps raw occupational data into three basic categories. Inclusion in a category was determined by what I perceived to be occupations of comparable socioeconomic rank within a broad three-range scale. Admittedly, these divisions are based upon my judgement for the

Table A.18. *Central Veracruz Slave Population by Familial Association by Year*

	% Un-attached	% Single Parent	% Married Parent	% Children	No. Cases
1575	73	6	7	14	257
1615	60	9	17	14	117
1645	34	20	3	43	112
1675	48	7	21	24	181
1700	47	5	28	20	202
1720	37	4	33	25	425
1740	41	7	23	29	170
1760	35	11	10	44	213
1780	10	1	51	38	92
Total Cases					1,769

Source: PATDAT-TAMUCC.
Note: Table A.18 divides slaves in central Veracruz into four categories. Unattached persons were those having no familial ties in the document listing the slave. Single parent refers primarily to slave women who were listed with children but without a spouse. Married parent includes adults with a spouse and children identified in the document. Children identifies slaves under age fourteen recorded as having either a single or dual parents. It also includes a small number of recently orphaned children. Cases for the 1575 and 1615 samples represent Jalapa and Orizaba slaves only. The remaining samples came from these first two areas as well as from Córdoba. The lack of Córdoba. data stems from the fact that Spaniards did not found the province until 1618.

times and differ with a number of competent scholars on a number of issues. For example, Rodney Anderson, in his analysis of the early national population of Guadalajara, does not include hacendados in his elite category; I do. Within a more urban setting like Guadalajara, the third largest city in Mexico during the early national period, commercial estate owners might not have enjoyed as high a socioeconomic status as they did in more rural central Veracruz. Moreover, Anderson places greater emphasis on the use of the prefix "Don" and "Doña," not only in an attempt to differentiate between working-class and elite Spaniards but also in support of his conclusion that class was more important than race in determining socioeconomic rank. He argues that, because working-class Spaniards were not accorded this honor while some economically more elevated *castas* were, economic rank outweighed caste in determining social status.[1] The problem with this logic within the central Veracruz context is that the use of this honorific title was never

Table A.19. *Free Population's Socioeconomic Stratification by Occupation, by Race, by District, and by Urban/Rural Zone, 1791*

	Spanish		Euro-Casta		Afro-Casta[a]		Indian		Total Cases
	Urban	Rural	Urban	Rural	Urban	Rural	Urban	Rural	
Elite									
Córdoba	25[b]	21	?	?	?	?	?	?	46
Jalapa	107	35	3	0	3	0	0	0	148
Orizaba	186	23	0	0	0	0	0	0	209
Mid-Level									
Córdoba	18	77	0	22	6	30	0	19	172
Jalapa	393	625	191	408	160	298	c	—	2,075
Orizaba	718	123	335	83	42	2	—	—	1,303
Low-Level									
Córdoba	9	0	0	34	17	66	?	225	351
Jalapa	104	89	168	213	36	16	?	?	626
Orizaba	345	100	412	188	42	2	?	?	1,089
Total cases	1,905	1,093	1,109	948	306	414	?	244	6,019

Source: PATDAT-TAMUCC.

Note: The above distribution of cases reveals significant concentrations of different racial groups at different socioeconomic levels. Of the 403 Elite cases all but six were Spanish whites (98.5%). At the Mid-Level status Spanish whites and Euro-*castas* made up 55% and 30% of the cohort, respectively. Euro-*castas*, however, were evenly distributed between the Mid- and Low-Level categories. Afro-*castas* were most heavily represented in first the Mid- and then the Low-Level categories. This data distribution was not random. It yielded an observed Chi Sq. of 871.94 > the critical value of 5.99 @ 0.05 level of significance.

[a]The number of *negros* was so small that I simply included them in the Afro-*casta* cohort.

[b]Urban data for Córdoba is very scant. Naveda Chávez-Hita makes reference to the Spanish owners of thirty-two plantations, most of whom lived within the *villa* of Córdoba during the eighteenth century. They account for the only Elites listed; I suspect there were others. See Naveda Chávez-Hita, *Esclavos negros*, 73, 87. Lack of figures for the *villa* of Córdoba does not impact on the sample as heavily as it might have for the other two districts because the rural sector of Córdoba's economy was more dynamic than its urban sector by a much wider margin than in the other two districts. Córdoba had a commercial agricultural economy in sugar and tobacco.

[c]Both the Jalapa and Orizaba district cases were drawn from the military censuses of 1791. These counts did not include Indians.

completely governed by race in central Veracruz. During the early seventeenth century, when Anderson concedes that the caste system was an important socioeconomic stratification tool in the colonial feudal economy, the same pattern of "Don" usage, which he interprets as change ushered in by late colonial shifts toward capitalism, existed.

The highest rank in the scheme I constructed is Elite. I collapsed entrepreneurs (persons with diversified economic activities in some combination of international or interregional commerce or estate agriculture), urban real-estate owners (persons who posessed at least five thousand pesos worth of urban property), bureaucrats (notary publics on up), royal and town officials (town council members, military officers), and clerics.

The Mid-Level rank includes such occupations as mid- and small-sized commercial agriculturalists (*labradores* and *rancheros*), agricultural estate administrators, small merchants (intradistrict-level trade), clerks, students, urban bureaucrats, constable on down, skilled artisans (master and journeymen), and teachers.

Low-Level socioeconomic rank represented common urban and rural workers, servants, wood gathers, freight carriers, muleteers, servants, and soldiers below the rank of sergeant.

Table A.20 correlates race with gender and urban/rural residency in free Afro-Mexicans' choice of marriage partner in three central Veracruz districts during the late colonial period.

Table A.21 draws from a variety of census, parish, and tributary records dating from 1777 to 1802. This composite data set was necessary in order to construct estimates for Córdoba for which no complete census appears to exist during this period and to add Indian totals for the districts of Jalapa and Orizaba. The 1791 Revillagigedo military census of 1791 lists all non-Indians in these two areas but does not include Indians since they were exempt from military service.

There is a second difficulty with this evidence. Because I had to draw from several disparate types of records, the units of analysis were often different. For example, some totals, such as those in the 1773 census for the division of the Jalapa parish, were reported in family units. To convert these to individuals, I derived a conversion factor from data that supplied both families and individuals (that is, the tribute records). For Indian families that factor was 4.7; for Afro-*castas* it was 5; for Spaniards it was 6. I simply multiplied family figures by the proper factor to arrive at individual totals. Other manipulations were more direct. Knowing town, *pueblo, hacienda,*

Table A.20. Marriage Patterns of Free Persons by Race, by District, and by Urban/Rural Zone, 1791–1802

Male	Spanish		Euro-Casta		Afro-Casta		Negro		Indian		Totals
	Urban	Rural	Urban	Rural	Urban	Rural	Urban	Rural	Urban	Rural	
Spanish											
Córdoba	25	179	1	24	0	2	0	0	0	0	231
Jalapa	203	309	24	41	8	20	0	0	0	7	612
Orizaba	585	132	95	45	4	7	1	0	1	1	871
Euro-Casta											
Córdoba	1	24	27	207	1	15	0	0	0	5	280
Jalapa	24	41	106	228	9	54	0	0	0	15	477
Orizaba	126	56	332	131	33	40	1	3	7	3	732
Afro-Casta											
Córdoba	0	2	2	15	16	98	1	2	1	8	145
Jalapa	0	4	2	0	71	112	0	0	6	35	230
Orizaba	6	17	10	36	18	35	0	0	2	0	124

ivegro

Córdoba	0	0	0	13	74	4	13	0	0	104	
Jalapa	0	0	1	0	0	0	1	0	0	2	
Orizaba	0	0	0	4	1	1	35	1	0	42	
Indian											
Córdoba	0	1	8	0	5	0	0	?	1,700[a]	1,714	
Jalapa	1	15	4	2	41	0	0	400[b]	3,200	3,663	
Orizaba	1	6	26	9	0	1	35	?	6,000	6,089	
Total	972	786	610	766	188	504	9	89	418	10,974	15,316

Source: PATDAT-TAMUCC.

Note: The correlation between race and marriage illustrated by the distribution of cases in this table is strong. Moreover, this distribution of cases was not random in nature. It produced an observed Chi Sq. of 25597.17 > the critical value of 36.41 @ 0.05 level of significance.

[a] Rural Indian-Indian marriage cases come from the 1800, 1802, and 1803 tribute records for the districts of Córdoba Jalapa, and Orizaba, respectively. See AGN, Tributos, vol. 43, *último expediente*, unnumbered leaves.

[b] The figure for urban Jalapa marriages was derived from the 1773 report on the division of the *villa's* parish. See "División del Curato de Jalapa," W. B. Stevens Collection, Wallet 27, *expediente* 960, leaf 9, NLBC-UTx.

Table A.21. *Free Population Distribution in Córdoba, Jalapa, and Orizaba by Race and by Urban/Rural Residency, 1777–1802*

Location	Spanish	Euro-Casta	Afro-Casta	Negro	Indian	Total
Urban Zone						
Core						
Córdoba	?	?	54	4	100	?
Jalapa	2,081	1,258	247	1	169	3,756
Orizaba	3,319	1,610	342	39	600	5,910
Barrio						
Córdoba	?	?[a]	73	8	900	?
Jalapa	394	55	364	0	1,250	2,063
Orizaba	623	851	80	0	4,000	5,554
Total	?	?	1,160	52	7,019	?
Rural Zone						
Pueblos						
Córdoba	16	0	0	0	8,500	8,516
Jalapa	1,479	1,106	437	1	17,998	21,021
Orizaba	963	523	157	3	24,495	26,141
Ranchos						
Córdoba	33	0	0	0	459	492
Jalapa	173	81	574	1	1,271	2,100
Orizaba	183	187	39	0	1,794	2,203
Estates						
Córdoba	151	139	158	17	152	617[b]
Jalapa	176	130	276	14	734	1,330
Orizaba	232	462	26	126	1,200	2,046
Total	?	?	2,827	214	63,622	?

Source: AGN, Padrones, vol.19, leaves 1–240v, and Ibid., vol. 20, leaves 202–337; AGN, Historia, vol. 522, leaf 239; AGN, Tributos, vol. 43, *último expediente,* unnumbered leaves (I wish to thank John and Jane Tutino for compiling these tributary figures for me); AMC, vol.16, unnumbered leaves, roll 5, frames 1078–1231v; TAMUCC Veracruz Microfilm Collection; AGI, vol. 2578, unnumbered leaves; AGI, vol. 2580, unnumbered leaves (again, I would like to thank Susan Deans-Smith for allowing me access to copies of these censuses for the Córdoba area); "División de curato de Jalapa, " leaf 264; Nieto, *Padrón de Xalapa.*

Note: Missing data for urban Córdoba made analysis of this setting very tenuous. Urban data for the other two districts pertaining to all groups yielded correlation coefficients that indicated that the cases were not randomly distributed. In Jalapa and Orizaba case distributions provided the following statistical results:

Spanish whites, observed Chi Sq. of 2993.71 > the critical value of 3.84 @ 0.05 level of significance.

Euro-*castas,* observed Chi Sq. of 1019.99 > the critical value of 3.84 @ 0.05 level of significance.

Table A.21. (*continued*)

Afro-*castas*, observed Chi Sq. of 13.68 > the critical value of 3.84 @ 0.05 level of significance.
   Negros, observed Chi Sq. of 22.92 > the critical value of 3.84 @ 0.05 level of significance.
   Indians, observed Chi Sq. of 3973.35 > the critical value of 3.84 @ 0.05 level of significance.
Data for the rural zones in all three districts was sufficient. It yielded the following correlation coefficients for the relationship between race and type of rural residence:
   Spanish whites, observed Chi Sq. of 2324.1 > the critical value of 5.99 @ 0.05 level of significance.
   Euro-*castas*, observed Chi Sq. of 1093.26 > the critical value of 5.99 @ 0.05 level of significance.
   Afro-*castas*, observed Chi Sq. of 20.77 > the critical value of 5.99 @ 0.05 level of significance.
   Negros, observed Chi Sq. of 294.77 > the critical value of 5.99 @ 0.05 level of significance.
   Indians, observed Chi Sq. of 82102.9 > the critical value of 5.99 @ 0.05 level of significance.
[a] None of the sources for Córdoba population totals present data on Spaniards or Euro-*castas* (mestizos and *castizos*) for the *villa* of Córdoba itself. One source, AMC, vol.16, unnumbered leaves, TAMUCC Veracruz Microfilm Collection, roll 5, frames 1078–1231v, does list persons of African descent for the *villa*.
[b] Córdoban estate totals for free residents fall far below those in the other two districts because slaves accounted for 67 percent of the residents on these plantations in 1786. See AMC, vol. 16, unnumbered leaves, TAMUCC Veracruz Microfilm Collection, roll 5, frames 1137v, 1143, 1145–1147, 1156v–1163, 1164v–1165v, 1171, 1178v, 1181, 1187, 1188–1190v, 1198–1200, 1205–1210v, 1218–1228.

and *ranchero* totals for the district of Jalapa in 1791 from Table A.12, as well as the non-Indian population distribution from each one of these settings from the 1791 military census, I derived Indian totals by subtracting the non-Indian subtotal from the overall setting subtotal. In sum, Table A.21 represents a crude but probably acceptable latitudinal measurement of sociodemographic conditions at the end of the colonial period.

Tables A.22 and A.23 correlate race with gender and urban/rural residency in Afro-Mexicans' formation of lesser social bonds than marriage in the district of Jalapa during the middle and late colonial periods. Table A.24 supports the overall conclusion that racism remained the most important instrument of social control down to the end of the colonial period. Table A.24 contributes to this conclusion by demonstrating that the vast majority of whites and Indians still married within their racial groups between 1715 and 1805 in the district of Jalapa regardless of whether they resided in urban or rural settings.

Table A.22. *Urban Afro-Veracruzano Social Interaction by Race, 1645, 1715, 1750, 1805*

| | Female | | | | | | |
Male	Negro	Pardo	Mulatto	White	Mestizo	Indian	No.
1645							
Negro							
Participants	59	10	8	11	3	20	111
Percentage	53	9	7	10	3	18	100
Pardo							
Participants	10	47	4	1	—	23	85
Percentage	12	55	5	1	—	27	100
Mulatto							
Participants	8	4	34	4	2	—	52
Percentage	15	8	65	8	4	—	100
1715							
Negro							
Participants	24	6	1	—	—	15	46
Percentage	52	13	2	—	—	33	100
Pardo							
Participants	6	68	4	1	3	25	107
Percentage	6	64	4	1	3	23	101
Mulatto							
Participants	1	4	42	3	1	1	52
Percentage	2	8	81	6	2	2	101
1750							
Negro							
Participants	11	1	1	1	7	3	24
Percentage	46	4	4	4	29	13	100

Table A.22. (*continued*)

Male	Female						
	Negro	Pardo	Mulatto	White	Mestizo	Indian	No.
Pardo							
Participants	1	54	16	16	49	27	163
Percentage	1	33	10	10	30	17	101
Mulatto							
Participants	—	9	29	19	39	6	102
Percentage	—	9	29	19	39	6	100
1805							
Negro							
Participants	7	1	1	—	4	1	14
Percentage	50	7	7	—	29	7	100
Pardo							
Participants	1	62	12	21	39	36	171
Percentage	1	36	7	12	23	21	100
Mulatto							
Participants	1	16	31	7	22	6	83
Percentage	1	19	37	8	27	7	99

Source: For 1645, APJ, Bautizos, Caja 1, Libro 1, leaves 1–42v; APJ, Matrimonios, Caja 1, Libro 1, leaves 43–116v and the last five unnumbered leaves at the end of this book; for 1715, APJ, Matrimonios, Caja 1, Libro 3, leaves 9–119v; for 1750, APJ, Matrimonios, Caja 3, Libro 9, leaves 1–128v; for 1805, APJ, Matrimonios, Caja 6, Libro 17, leaves 49v–195v; APJ, Matrimonios, Caja 7, Libro 18, leaves 1–73v.

Table A.23. *Rural Afro-Veracruzano Social Interaction by Race,*
1645, 1715, 1750, 1805

| | | | Female | | | | |
Male	Negro	Pardo	Mulatto	White	Mestizo	Indian	No.
1645							
Negro							
Participants	76	10	1	22	1	35	145
Percentage	52	7	1	15	1	24	100
Pardo							
Participants	10	92	8	2	—	15	127
Percentage	8	72	6	2	—	12	100
Mulatto							
Participants	1	8	66	12	10	—	97
Percentage	1	8	68	12	10	—	100
1715							
Negro							
Participants	36	5	1	7	—	6	55
Percentage	65	9	2	13	—	11	100
Pardo							
Participants	2	48	1	3	2	18	74
Percentage	3	65	1	4	3	24	100
Mulatto							
Participants	1	1	35	10	1	4	52
Percentage	2	2	67	19	2	8	100
1750							
Negro							
Participants	14	13	2	7	8	13	57
Percentage	25	23	4	12	14	23	101

Table A.23. (*continued*)

Male	Female Negro	Pardo	Mulatto	White	Mestizo	Indian	No.
Pardo							
Participants	9	82	12	22	68	80	273
Percentage	3	30	4	8	25	29	99
Mulatto							
Participants	2	11	18	8	15	11	65
Percentage	3	17	27	13	23	17	100
1805							
Negro							
Participants	9	3	1	2	5	6	26
Percentage	35	12	4	8	19	23	101
Pardo							
Participants	3	75	27	24	53	61	243
Percentage	1	31	11	10	22	25	100
Mulatto							
Participants	—	6	11	3	8	6	34
Percentage	—	17	32	10	24	18	101

Source: For 1645, Archivo Parroquial de Coatepec, Libro 1 (*sic*, 2), leaves 18–72; for 1715, Archivo Parroquial de Coatepec, Matrimonios, Libro 3, leaves 1–148v; APN, Bautizos, Libro 2, leaves 61v–89; APN, Matrimonios, Libro 6, leaves 1–41v; for 1750, Archivo Parroquial de Coatepec, Matrimonios, unnumbered book (1734–1754), leaves 31–31v; APN, Matrimonios, Libro 9, leaves 61–72v; APN, Matrimonios, Libro 10, leaves 103–119v; for 1805, Archivo Parroquial de Coatepec, Matrimonios, Libro 2 (*sic*, 1), leaves 22–24v; Archivo Parroquial de Coatepec, Matrimonios, Libro 5 (*sic*, 13), leaves 19–34v; APN, Matrimonios, Libro 15, leaves 87–97; APN, Matrimonios, Libro 16, leaves 118–131v; APN, Matrimonios, Libro 18, leaves 50–65v.

Table A.24. *Percentage of Racially Endogamous Marriages in Urban and Rural Jalapa, 1715–1805*

	Urban			Rural		
	1715	*1750*	*1805*	*1715*	*1750*	*1805*
% Whites						
Male	92	73	78	94	74	76
Female	91	81	86	97	69	73
Combined	91	77	82	95	72	74
No. of cases	53	98	102	32	59	46
% Mestizos						
Male	95	73	67	92	75	71
Female	84	71	60	80	67	61
Combined	89	72	64	86	71	66
No. of cases	41	104	163	57	100	152
% Pardos						
Male	78	71	64	78	58	60
Female	86	71	63	84	70	57
Combined	82	71	63	81	64	59
No. of cases	48	96	133	106	161	193
% Mulattoes						
Male	76	77	64	84	63	62
Female	86	74	70	84	73	69
Combined	81	75	67	84	68	66
No. of cases	23	37	48	14	19	21
% Negros						
Male	65	39	64	78	64	66
Female	85	75	76	93	51	66
Combined	73	54	68	86	58	66
No. of cases	31	23	7	52	22	11
% Indians						
Male	94	93	87	99	93	92
Female	89	89	83	97	90	94
Combined	92	91	85	98	92	93
No. of cases	408	623	754	873	941	1,286
Avg. combined %	85	73	72	88	71	71
Total No.	604	981	1,207	1,134	1,302	1,709

Table A.24. (*continued*)

Source: Samples were drawn for the decades 1710–1719, 1745–1754, and 1800–1809. The middle years for each of these ten year periods—1715, 1750, and 1805—were then listed on the table. This was done in order to increase the sample size. I reasoned that persons remarrying deserved additional representation in the sample since each tie afforded a separate opportunity to reflect social implications for race. As long as the same ceremony is not doubly represented, the sample does not become biased. Urban figures were derived from the following sources: for 1715, APJ, Matrimonios, Caja 1, Libro 3, leaves 9–119v; for 1750, APJ, Matrimonios, Caja 3, Libro 9, leaves 1–128v; for 1805, APJ, Matrimonios, Caja 6, Libro 17, leaves 49v–195v; APJ, Matrimonios, Caja 7, Libro 18, leaves 1–73v. Rural data was compiled from the sources below: for 1715, Archivo Parroquial de Coatepec, Matrimonios, Libro 3, leaves 1–148v; Archivo Parroquial de Naulinco (hereinafter abbreviated APN), Matrimonios, Libro 6, leaves 1–41v; for 1750, Archivo Parroquial de Coatepec, Matrimonios, unnumbered book (1734–1754), leaves 31–31v; APN, Matrimonios, Libro 9, leaves 61–72v; APN, Matrimonios, Libro 10, leaves 103–119v; for 1805, Archivo Parroquial de Coatepec, Matrimonios, Libro 2 (1), leaves 22–24v; Archivo Parroquial de Coatepec, Matrimonios, Libro 5 (*sic*, 13), leaves 19–34v; APN, Matrimonios, Libro 15, leaves 87–97; APN, Matrimonios, Libro 16, leaves 118–131v; APN, Matrimonios, Libro 18, leaves 50–65v.

Note: These combined averages were weighted more heavily by the male average because there was a greater number of male black marriages with nonblacks than female black marriages with nonblacks in the sample.

Notes

Introduction

1. Gonzalo Aguirre Beltrán has published extensively on blacks in Mexico. He was by far the most prolific and respected scholar in this area. His three most important monographic length studies are *Población negra de México, Medicina y magia,* and *Cuijla, esbozo etnográfico de un pueblo negro.*

2. Colin Palmer, *Slaves of the White God: Blacks in Mexico, 1570–1650.*

3. Gerald Cardoso, *Negro Slavery in the Sugar Plantations of Veracruz and Pernambuco, 1550–1680.*

4. Adriana Naveda Chávez-Hita, *Esclavos negros en las haciendas azucareras de Córdoba, Veracruz, 1690–1830;* Gilberto Bermúdez Gorrochotegui, "Jalapa en el siglo XVI" (2 vols., master's thesis in history, Universidad Veracruzana, Jalapa, Veracruz, 1977).

5. Matthew Restall, *Maya Conquistador,* and his "Alterity and Ambiguity: Spanish and Maya Perceptions of Africans in Colonial Yucatán," paper delivered at the X Reunion of North American Scholars of Mexico, Fort Worth (1999); Francisco Fernández Repetto and Genny Negroe Sierra, *Una población perdida en la memoria: Los negros de Yucatán;* Genny Negroe Sierra, "Procedencia y situación social de la población negra de Yucatán," *Boletín de la Escuela de Ciencias Antropología de la Universidad de Yucatán,* nos. 106–107 (1991): 3–20.

6. Norma Angélica Castillo Palma y Francisco González Hermosillo Adams, "Raza y status, mestizos, mulatos, criollos, españoles e indios y sus definiciones en testamentos coloniales," *Signos* 5, no. 2 (1991): 17–45; Norma Angélica Castillo Palma, "Matrimonios mixtos y cruce de la barrera de color como vias del mestizaje de la población negra y mulata (1674–1796)," paper presented at the X Reunion of North American Scholars of Mexico, Fort Worth (1999).

7. Juan Manuel de la Serna H., "Disolución de la esclavitud en los obrajes de Querétaro a finales del siglo dieciocho," paper presented at the X Reunion of North American Scholars of Mexico, Fort Worth (1999).

8. Brígedo Redondo, *Negritud en Campeche.*

9. María Luisa Herrera Casasús, *Presencia y esclavitud del negro en la Huasteca.*

10. One of Fernando Winfield Capitaine's latest in a long list of publications is *Los Cimarrones de Mazateopan.* Adriana Naveda Chávez-Hita, "Hacendados, tabaqueros y libertos en el desarrollo de la Villa de Córdoba, 1750–1810" (doctoral thesis, Universidad Veracruzana, in progress), and her *Esclavos negros.*

11. Gilberto Bermúdez Gorrochotegui, *Historia de Xalapa, siglo XVII.*

12. Susan Deans-Smith, *Bureaucrats, Planters, and Workers: The Making of the Tobacco Monopoly in Bourbon Mexico.*

13. Brígida von Mentz, *Trabajo, sujeción y libertad en el centro de la Nueva España: Esclavos, aprendices, campesinos y operarios manufactureros, siglos XVI–XVIII;* R. Douglas Cope, *The Limits of Racial Domination: Plebeian Society in Colonial Mexico City, 1660–1720;* Juan Pedro Viqueira Albán, *Propriety and Permissiveness in Bourbon Mexico.*

14. For a clear discussion of these two integrative dynamics, see Alejandro Portes and Robert Bach, *Latin Journey,* 20–26.

15. Ben Vinson III, "Bearing Arms for His Majesty: The Free Colored Militia in Colonial Mexico" (Ph.D. dissertation, Columbia University, 1998); Herman Bennett, "Lovers, Family and Friends: The Formation of Afro-Mexico, 1580–1810" (Ph.D. dissertation, Duke University, 1997; Ann Arbor: U.M.I.); María Elena Cortés de Jacome, "La memoria familiar de los negros y mulatos, siglos XVI–XVII," in *La memoria y el olvido,* Segundo Simposio de Historia de las Mentalidades, 125–133.

16. Solange Alberro, "Herejes, brujas y beatas: Mujeres ante el Tribunal del Santo Oficio de la Inquisición en la Nueva España," in *Presencia y transparencia: La mujer en la historia de México,* ed. Carmen Ramos Escandón, 79–94; Susan Kellog, "Gendered Images of Ethno-Race in Colonial Mexican Texts," *Journal of Women's History* (in press), and her "African Women in Central Mexico, 1648–1707: Their Testaments and Their Lives," paper delivered at the X Reunion of North American Historians of Mexico, Fort Worth (1999); Steve Stern, *The Secret History of Mexico: Women, Men, and Power in Late Colonial Mexico.*

17. At the outset it is necessary to define the terms *race* and *ethnicity,* as I apply them in this study. Race depends on inherited biological traits that distinguish one group from another; ethnicity depends on acquired or cultural characteristics that differentiate one group from another. However, it is important to note that the particular traits which identify biological race and cultural ethnicity have the potential to vary in time and place. (See Julian Pitt-Rivers, "Race in Latin America: The Concept of *Raza,*" in *Race, Ethnicity, and Social Change,* ed. John Stone, 329.)

18. Naveda Chávez-Hita, *Esclavos negros;* Cardoso, *Negro Slavery;* Cheryl Martin, *Rural Society in Colonial Morelos;* Nancy Fariss, *Maya Society under Colonial Rule;* John Chance, *Race and Class in Colonial Oaxaca.*

19. William Taylor, *Landlord and Peasant in Colonial Oaxaca;* David Brading, *Miners and Merchants in Bourbon Mexico, 1763–1810,* and his *Haciendas and Ranchos in the Mexican Bajío, León, 1700–1860;* Peter

Bakewell, *Silver Mining and Society in Colonial Mexico: Zacatecas, 1546–1700*; Eric Van Young, *Hacienda and Market in Eighteenth-Century Mexico: The Rural Economy of the Guadalajara Region, 1675–1820*; Brian Hamnett, *Politics and Trade in Southern Mexico, 1750–1821*.

20. I have since published an article which provides a much clearer picture of evolving social conditions in central Veracruz than Chapter 7 of this work does. Whereas Chapter 7 only suggests the coexistence of three separate overlapping and competing white, Indian, and *casta* social orders by the late colonial period, this 1995 piece explicitly outlines them and their operation. See Patrick J. Carroll, "Los mexicanos negros, el mestizaje y los fundamentos olvidados de la 'Raza Cósmica': Una perspectiva regional," *Historia Mexicana* 44, no. 3 (enero–marzo 1995): 403–438.

1. The Human and Material Consequences of Indian and European Contact

1. Alfonso Contreras Arias, *Mapa de las provincias climatológicas de la República Mexicana*, XVIII; Alejandro de Humboldt, *Ensayo político sobre el reino de la Nueva España*, edited by Juan A. Ortega y Medina, 19–30; Bernardo García Martínez, "Consideraciones Corográficas," in *Historia general de México*, edited by Bernardo García Martínez, vol. 1, 9–15.

2. Eric Wolf, *Sons of the Shaking Earth*, 8; García Martínez, "Consideraciones," 40; José Lobato, *Consideraciones generales sobre la geografía, meteorología, y climatología de la zona intertropical de la República Mexicana*, 8–15.

3. Manuel Carrera Stampa, "Las ferias Novohispanas," *Historia mexicana* 2 (January–March 1953): 336–337; Charles Gibson, *The Aztecs under Spanish Rule*, 361–362.

4. Humboldt, *Ensayo político*, 534–536; *Jornal económico y mercantil de Veracruz* 1 (10 April 1806): 163; Leonardo Pasquel, *Biografía integral de la Ciudad de Veracruz*, 263–267.

5. *Jornal económico y mercantil de Veracruz* 1 (10 April 1806): 160–164; Francisco González de Cossio, *Xalapa*, 68–69.

6. Lesley Byrd Simpson, *Many Mexicos*.

7. González de Cossio, *Xalapa*, 26–28; Nigel Davies, *The Toltecs*, 108–111; Manuel Rivera, *Historia antigua y moderna de Jalapa*, vol. 1, 6–7; Felipe Montemayor, *La Población de Veracruz*, 14, 39.

8. Andre Gunder Frank, *Capitalism and Underdevelopment in Latin America: Historical Studies of Brazil and Chile*. Frank focused on capitalist European contact with "feudal" Latin America and its political and economic consequences. His model, however, may have limited application for the pre-Columbian Aztec domination of such areas as central Veracruz. Frank argued that foreign penetration led to a series of "metropolis-satellite" ties primarily aimed at transferring production surpluses from satellite areas (in this case, the Jalapa region) to metropolises (in this case, Tenochtitlan). The end result, he concluded, was underdevelopment for the satellites.

9. González de Cossio, *Xalapa*, 28–29; Peter Gerhard, *A Guide to the Historical Geography of New Spain*, 373; Toribio de Motolinía, *Memoria-*

les, 396; Rivera, *Jalapa,* vol. 1, 10–12; José Luis Melgarejo Vivanco, "Historia Antigua de Coatepec," in *Coatepec,* compiled by Leonardo Pasquel, 27–31; Frederick Peterson, *Ancient Mexico,* 168, 170–180; Jacques Soustelle, *The Daily Life of the Aztecs,* translated by Patrick O'Brian, 59–73.

10. Rivera, *Jalapa,* vol. 1, 10–12; Bermúdez Gorrochotegui, "Jalapa," vol. 1, 130–133; González de Cossio, *Xalapa,* 29; Wolf, *Sons,* 140–141, 149; Alonzo de Zorita, *The Lords of New Spain,* translated by Benjamin Keen, 113–117; Gerhard, *Historical Geography,* 373.

11. J. D. Chambers, *Population, Economy, and Society in Pre-Industrial England,* 51; E. A. Wrigley, *Population and History,* 77–80.

12. Bernal Díaz del Castillo, *The True History of the Conquest of Mexico,* translated by Maurice Keating, 67–69; Constantino Bravo de Lagunas, *Relación de Xalapa, 1580,* 69n; Sherburne F. Cook and Woodrow Borah, *Essays in Population History,* vol. 1, 10–12; Soustelle, *Daily Life,* 8–9.

13. Peterson, *Ancient Mexico,* 103–105; Soustelle, *Daily Life,* XIV–XV, 10–28; Angel Palerm, *Agricultura y sociedad en Meso-America,* 194–195.

14. Díaz del Castillo, *True History,* 206.

15. Bravo de Lagunas, *Relación de Xalapa,* 10. Translating tributary into absolute population counts was done by a conversion factor of 3.74, derived from a division of tributary figures into population figures when both were available. For a more complete discussion of this method, see my dissertation, "Mexican Society in Transition: The Blacks in Veracruz, 1750–1830" (Ph.D. dissertation, University of Texas at Austin, 1975), 51; Archivo General de la Nación, Mexico City (hereinafter abbreviated AGN), Tributos, Vol. 43, *último expediente, passim;* Cook and Borah, *Essays,* vol. 2, 180–181; Gibson, *Aztecs,* 136–141.

16. Bravo de Lagunas, *Relación de Xalapa,* 10–11.

17. Ibid; *Papeles de Nueva España,* vol. 5, 100, 106, 108–120; Rivera, *Historia de Jalapa,* vol. 1, 63–72.

18. Martin also found this pattern in Morelos (see Martin, *Rural Society,* 59–60).

19. Notario Eclesiástico de la Parroquia del Sagrado Corazón, Jalapa, (hereinafter abbreviated APJ) Caja 1, Libro 2, leaves 1–53, 82–106.

20. Other studies will have to test this thesis. The records for Jalapa are too inconsistent to conduct such testing. Some priests and ecclesiastical scribes faithfully recorded birth places of registrants, others did not.

21. Bravo de Lagunas, *Relación de Xalapa,* 11, 15.

22. James S. Olson, *The Ethnic Dimension in U.S. History,* 102–106, 194–195; Leonard Dinnerstein et al., *Natives and Strangers,* 160; Humbert Nelli, *Italians in Chicago,* 156; Pitt-Rivers, "Race in Latin America," 332.

23. Martin, *Colonial Morelos,* 47.

24. AGN, Mercedes, vol. 2, leaves 177v–178; "Ingenio de Almolonga y Rancho de Santa Cruz," Nettie Lee Benson Latin American Collection, University of Texas at Austin (hereinafter abbreviated NLBC-UTx), bound volume, leaves 1–3v, 10, 12–13v, 17–18v, 139–140; Archivo Notorial de Jalapa (hereinafter abbreviated ANJ), vol. 1578–1594, leaf 220; ANJ, vol. 1594–1600, leaves 56, 115–115v; Bermúdez Gorrochotegui, "Jalapa," vol. 1, pp. 80–101.

25. François Chevalier, *Land and Society in Colonial Mexico,* 77; Fernando Sandoval, *La industria del azúcar en Nueva España,* 126–217; Bermúdez Gorrochotegui, "Jalapa," vol. I, 136.

26. Bravo de Lagunas, *Relación de Xalapa,* 15, 42, 44, 55, 59, 69–70; Vicente Nieto, *Padrón de Xalapa,* 18–19; Bermúdez Gorrochotegui, "Jalapa," vol. I, map, 210–211.

27. Sandoval, *Industria del azúcar,* 23–24; Ward Barrett, *The Sugar Hacienda of the Marquesas del Valle,* 11; Bernardo García Martínez, *El Marquesado del Valle,* 45–46.

28. Zorita, *Lords,* 267–268; Palmer, *Slaves of the White God,* 3; Gibson, *Aztecs,* 221; Barrett, *Sugar Hacienda,* 86.

29. William Taylor, *Drinking, Homicide, and Rebellion in Colonial Mexican Villages,* 20, 27.

30. Van Young, *Hacienda and Market,* 344–345.

31. APJ, Caja 1, Libros 1–4, passim; Gibson, *Aztecs,* 58–59, 98; Taylor, *Landlord and Peasant in Colonial Oaxaca,* 36; Chevalier, *Land and Society,* 36–37.

32. Gerhard, *Historical Geography,* 374–375. Bernardo García Martínez documents a ninth *encomienda* involving Indians from Jalancingo, Atzalan, and Altotonga in 1599 and 1602. See Bernardo García Martínez, *Los pueblos de la sierra,* 254–255, n. 98.

33. Jonathan Israel, *Race, Class, and Politics in Colonial Mexico, 1610–1670,* 186.

34. AGN, Mercedes, vol. 3, leaves 228v–229; ibid., vol. 2, leaves 177v–178; ibid., vol. 13, leaf 59v; "Almolonga," bound volume, leaves 139–140; Sandoval, *Industria del azúcar,* 49, 126–127; Bermúdez Gorrochotegui, "Jalapa," vol. I, 76–77, 143.

35. John Te Paske, et al., *La real hacienda de Nueva España: La Real Caja de México, 1576–1816,* 9.

36. Hamnett, *Politics and Trade,* 19–25. Charles Gibson, working on the Valley of Mexico, discovered a somewhat different Spanish method for integrating Indians into the colonial economy. There, natives more commonly paid taxes and tithe in goods rather than in specie. See Gibson, *Aztecs,* 221–225; Israel, *Race,* 4–6, 49, 186–187. Gibson and Israel's findings proved much more analogous to the pre-Colombian tribute system than tax payment procedures in central Veracruz, Oaxaca, and Puebla. These differences imply a lack of conformity in Spanish methods to work Indians into the colonial economy. They also suggest that despite regional variation in strategy an overall economic goal emerged during the first century of contact, and that goal aimed at integrating peoples into the Atlantic Basin economic system that operated throughout the colonial period.

37. Bravo de Lagunas, *Relación de Xalapa,* 9–19; Nieto, *Padrón de Xalapa,* 15–16; González de Cossio, *Xalapa,* 49–50; Humboldt, *Ensayo político,* 175–176, 181.

38. Bermúdez Gorrochotegui, "Jalapa," vol. I, 150–157; Nieto, *Padrón de Xalapa,* 16; Rivera, Jalapa, vol. I, 72.

39. For a good overview on why European peasant labor proved a non-viable source of workers for colonial Spanish and Portuguese America, see

Herbert Klein, *African Slavery in Latin America and the Caribbean*, 22–27.

40. Ruth Pike, "Sevillian Society in the Sixteenth Century: Slaves and Freedmen," *Hispanic American Historical Review*, 53, no. 3 (August 1967): 345, 353; Lesley B. Rout, *The African Experience in Spanish America*, 15; *Documentos inéditos relativos a Hernán Cortés y su familia*, 254–266; Philip D. Curtin, *The Atlantic Slave Trade*, 17–21; José Antonio Saco, *Historia de la raza africana en el Nuevo Mundo y en especial en los países Americo-Hispanos*, vol. 1, 22–25, 141–143, 158–159; Rout, *African Experience*, 22–25; Herbert Klein, *Slavery in the Americas*, 89.

41. Aguirre Beltrán, *Población negra*, 15–28; Curtin, *Atlantic Slave Trade*, 15, 25; Daniel P. Mannix, *Black Cargoes*, 3–5; Saco, *Historia de la raza africana*, vol. 1, 146–147; Ibid., vol. 4, 285; Robert West, *Colonial Placer Mining in Columbia*, 32; Frederick Bowser, *The African Slave in Colonial Peru*, 26–27, 36–37.

42. Aguirre Beltrán, *Población negra*, 15–29; Gonzalo Aguirre Beltrán, "The Slave Trade in Mexico," *HAHR*, 24 (August 1944) 413; Oriol Pi-Sunyer, "Historical Background to the Negro in Mexico," *The Journal of Negro History*, 42 (October 1957): 239–240; Joaquin Roncal, "The Negro Race in Mexico," *HAHR*, 24 (August 1944): 530–532; Sandoval, *Industria del azúcar*, 36–37, 45, 57, 62, 82–88; Adriana Naveda Chávez-Hita, "Esclavitud en la jurisdicción de la villa de Córdoba en el siglo XVIII," (master's thesis, Universidad Veracruzana, 1977), ii–iii, 25–27; *Gazeta de México* 25 (September 5, 1762) Hemeroteca Nacional, Mexico City; Brading, *Miners and Merchants*, 249; David Brading, "Grupos étnicos: Clases y estructura ocupacional en Guanajuato," *Historia mexicana* 21, no. 3 (January–March 1972), 464, 471, 477; Richard Garner, "Zacatecas, 1750–1821" (Ph.D. dissertation, University of Michigan, 1970), 68, 76; Vincent Mayer, "The Black Slave on New Spain's Northern Frontier: San José de Parral, 1632–1676," (Ph.D. dissertation, University of Utah, 1975), 6, 70–73; Charles H. Harris, *A Mexican Family Empire*, 14, 63, 212.

43. Peggy Liss, *Mexico Under Spain*, 137–139; Palmer, *Slaves of the White God*, 73–74; Taylor, *Landlord and Peasant*, 21, 144; Gibson, *Aztecs*, 243; Chance, *Race and Class*; Frederick P. Bowser, "The Free Person of Color in Mexico City and Lima: Manumission and Opportunity, 1580–1650" in *Race and Slavery in the Western Hemisphere*, edited by Stanley Engerman and Eugene Genovese, 334, 341–343, 348.

44. "Papeles del Conde del Valle de Orizaba," vol. 4a, leaves 11–29, Edmundo O'Gorman Collection, NLBC-UTx. (hereinafter abbreviated EOC); AGN, General de Parte, vol. 5, *expediente* 270, unnumbered leaves; "Almolonga," bound volume, leaves 189–193; ANJ, vol. 1578–1594, leaves 55, 60, 72, 90, 117, 149; Bravo de Lagunas, *Relación de Xalapa*, 9–20.

2. The Hows, Whens, Whos, and Whys of the Afro-Veracruz Slave Trade

1. Bakewell, *Silver Mining*, 225.

2. David Northrup, *Trade Without Rulers*, 3–7, 13. Northrup found this trend within the Gulf of Guinea Basin.

3. Ibid., 11–12, 18–22, 26–27; Joseph Miller, "The Slave Trade in Congo and Angola," in *The African Diaspora*, edited by Martin Kilson and Robert Rotberg, 75–77, 84; Mannix, *Black Cargoes*, 9–12; Northrup, *Trade Without Rulers*, 28–29.

4. Northrup, *Trade Without Rulers*, 65–84.

5. Miller, "Slave Trade," 75–76.

6. Northrup, *Trade Without Rulers*, 86–87; Aguirre Beltrán, *Población negra*, 126.

7. Curtin, *Atlantic Slave*, 101; Aguirre Beltrán, *Población negra*, 101, 107, 116, 126.

8. See, for example, Thomas Skidmore and Peter Smith, *Modern Latin America*, 58.

9. Christopher Fyfe, "The Dynamics of African Dispersal: The Transatlantic Slave Trade," in Kilson and Rotberg, *African Diaspora*, 69, 74.

10. Miller, "Slave Trade," 82–92; Fyfe, "African Dispersal," 69–70.

11. Marion Dusser de Barenne Kilson, "West African Society and the Atlantic Slave Trade, 1441–1865," in *Key Issues in the Afro-American Experience*, edited by Nathan Huggins et al., vol. 1, 41–43; David Brion Davis, *Slavery and Human Progress*, 57–58.

12. Pike, "Sevillian Society," 345.

13. Miller, "Slave Trade," 81–82.

14. Palmer, *Slaves of the White God*, 187; Aguirre Beltrán, *Población negra*, 15; Bowser, *African Slave in Colonial Peru*, 3–4; James Lockhart, *Spanish Peru*, 171; Mario Góngora, *Studies in the Colonial History of Spanish America*, translated by Richard Southern, 31.

15. See Appendix 1, Table A.1.

16. Palmer, *Slaves of the White God*, 28.

17. Miller, "Slave Trade," 83–84; Fyfe, "African Dispersal," 60, 65; Curtin, *Atlantic Slave Trade*, 108–112; Mannix, *Black Cargoes*, 10–13; Donald Wiedner, *Africa South of the Sahara*, 50–51.

18. Palmer, *Slaves of the White God*, 12–13.

19. Aguirre Beltrán, "Slave Trade," 415–427; Aguirre Beltrán, *Población negra*, 16.

20. Palmer, *Slaves of the White God*, 14–16. Palmer could not estimate the Mexican percentage of the market in later years because the slave registries he used stopped making reference to final destinations of cargoes in 1623. He does, however, imply from his general discussion of the post-1623 Atlantic trade that imports to Mexico may have dropped after 1622. An examination of new material presented by other authors supports this conclusion.

21. See Appendix 1, Table A.2.

22. See Appendix 1, Table A.2.

23. See Appendix 1, Table A.3.

24. Gilberto Bermúdez Gorrochotegui compiled slave sales for these years from the district's notarial records and illustrated them in a bar graph.

25. Bermúdez Gorrochotegui does not clearly differentiate sales by time in the 1578–1600 cohort. He does, however, hint at the distribution of the trade. At one point he says that 177 of the 208 sales he records took place be-

tween 1590 and 1600 (Bermúdez Gorrochotegui, "Jalapa," vol. 1, p. 170). In a later table he identifies the African origins of 171 of the 208 slaves he found, representing 85 percent of his total sample (Ibid., 175). By multiplying the 177 African sales he identifies by this percentage, I arrived at an estimate of 151 *bozales* traded in the district during the decade of the 1590s. To this 151 I added the 142 Africans I found recorded in the notarial archives between 1601 and 1610. The combined total was 292. I rounded this off to 300 cases because, combined, Bermúdez and I found 87 cases of slaves sold whose origin was not listed. If one assumes that 85 of these 87 individuals were Africans, another 70 to 75 cases would be added to the totals for *bozales* traded during this twenty-year time span. In order to be conservative, I selected a range half this great and added 35 cases to the 292 total Bermúdez Gorrochotegui and I actually found, yielding a total of 327 cases, which I rounded to 325.

26. Bermúdez Gorrochotegui, "Jalapa," vol. 1, 168–170.

27. Appendix 2, Table A.4, and "Jalapan and Mexican Withdrawal from the Atlantic Slave Trade," 324–326.

28. Bakewell, *Silver Mining*, 128, 226–230.

29. ANJ, vol. 1600–1608, leaves 471–473v; ANJ, vol. 1632–1645, leaves 433–434v; ANJ, vol. 1651–1663, leaves 79–84; "Almolonga," bound volume, leaves 77v, 107v–110, 272.

30. ANJ, vol. 1600–1608, leaves 71–72v, 256v–257v; ANJ, vol. 1609–1617, leaves 39v–41, 93v–95.

31. More will be said about intradistrict migration patterns in Chapters 3 and 7.

32. Scholars that explain Latin American development within varying contexts of the region's subordination to sixteenth-century European capitalism include Immanuel Wallerstein, *The Modern World System: Capitalist Agriculture and the Origins of the European World Economy in the Sixteenth Century;* Frank, *Capitalism and Underdevelopment;* Stanley and Barbara Stein, *The Colonial Heritage of Latin America.*

3. Regional Production, Market, and Capital Development

1. Wallerstein, *Modern World System II*, 6–7, 9.

2. Before describing Mexican economic conditions, I must point out the existence of a good deal of chronological overlap. Thus, the periodization that follows represents a very loose one.

3. For a good critical discussion of the application of Wallerstein's model in a Latin American context, see Steve Stern, "Feudalism, Capitalism, and the World System in the Perspective of Latin America and the Caribbean," *American Historical Review* 93, no. 4 (October 1988), especially 829–830, 840.

4. Stuart Schwartz describes the unique labor demands of sugar culture within the Brazilian context. Eventual reliance on African slavery as part of a variegated labor force proved almost universal to mainland Meso-American and South American sugar culture. Some variation on this mix did, however, occur in response to different local conditions. For example, because of the

different demographic and cultural characteristics of Mexican and Brazilian natives, Indian slavery endured much longer in Brazil and existed alongside African slavery. See Stuart Schwartz, *Sugar Plantations in the Formation of Brazilian Society*, 34–41.

5. Bravo de Lagunas, *Relación de Xalapa*, 9–19.

6. Francisco Javier Clavijero, *Historia an antigua de México*, 312.

7. González de Cossio, *Xalapa*, 312–316.

8. ANJ, vol. 1606, leaves 41–43; González de Cossio, *Xalapa*, 316–318.

9. Pedro Carrasco, "The Political Economy of the Aztec and Inca States," in *The Inca and Aztec States, 1400–1800*, edited by George Collier et al., 23, 25.

10. Francisco López de Gómera, *Cortés, The Life of the Conqueror*, translated and edited by Lesley Byrd Simpson, 58; Brading, *Miners and Merchants*, 2; Martin, *Colonial Morelos*, 23.

11. Gibson, *Aztecs*, 272; Taylor, *Landlord and Peasant*, 4–5. Other studies that concur with these findings include Gerhard, *Historical Geography*, 374–375; James Lang, *Conquest and Commerce*, 15–16; and Richard Salvucci, *Textiles and Capitalism in Mexico*, 104. John Chance describes Spanish economic reliance on natives in Oaxaca as "parasitic." Chance, *Race and Class*, 63–64.

12. Liss, *Mexico under Spain*, 36–43, 52, 58–59; Gibson, *Aztecs*, 61; Lang, *Conquest and Commerce*, 10–13.

13. E. J. Hamilton, *American Treasure and the Price of Revolution in Spain, 1501–1650*, 34–35.

14. Liss, *Mexico under Spain*, 54, 61; Nieto, *Padrón de Xalapa*, 16.

15. Lang, *Conquest and Commerce*, 13–14; Gibson, *Aztecs*, 62–63. Peter Gerhard includes a section on *encomiendas* for each district he examines. His data shows the encomienda declining during these years. He also demonstrates that the period of greatest decline ran from about 1540 to 1610. See Gerhard, *Historical Geography*.

16. Liss, *Mexico under Spain*, 4–7, 19–23; Lang, *Conquest and Commerce*, 16–17.

17. Israel, *Race*, 49–50; Liss, *Mexico under Spain*, 36–37.

18. Gibson, *Aztecs*, 289–290; Szewczyk, "New Elements in the Society of Tlaxcala," in *Provinces of Early Mexico*, edited by Ida Altman and James Lockhart, 143–145; Martin, *Colonial Morelos*, 20–23, 29–38. See Chapter 1. There were exceptions to this pattern. In Yucatán, commercial estates made their appearance in the second half of the sixteenth century, but these were much smaller in scale than they were in central Mexico (see Fariss, *Maya Society*, 34–36). Marta Espejo-Ponce Hunt illustrates this development indirectly through her account of the encomienda within the region, a labor system that was closely linked to the rise of the large estate (see Marta Espejo-Ponce Hunt, "The Processes of the Development of Yucatán, 1600-1700," in Altman and Lockhart, *Provinces of Mexico*, 34–35). The large estate in the north varied primarily in timing. It emerged a bit later in this area than it did in the heartland of the viceroyalty. This was also the case in such northern subregions as Querétaro and San Luis Potosí (see John Tutino, "Life and Labor on the North Mexican Haciendas: The Querétaro–San Luis

Potosí Region: 1775–1810," in *El trabajo y los trabajadores en la historia de México*, edited by Elsa Frost et al., 339–341; Chevalier, *Land and Society*, 165–184; Harris, *Mexican Family Empire*, 3–27). Oaxaca proved an exception to this rule (see Taylor, *Landlord and Peasant*, 163).

Spanish control of urban industries existed from the outset (see Gibson, *Aztecs*, 243–246; Salvucci, *Textiles and Capitalism*, 29–30). But from 1550 onward these industries grew along with the cities themselves. Although its percentage of viceregal production did not expand and may have actually diminished, urban industrial output did increase in absolute terms especially in Mexico City, Puebla, Querétaro and Tlaxcala (see Samuel Kagen, "The Labor of Prisoners in the Obrajes of Coyoacán, 1660–1673," in *El trabajo y los trabajadores en la historia de México*, edited by Elsa Frost et al., 201, 210; John Super, "The Agricultural Near North: Querétaro in the Seventeenth Century," in Altman and Lockhart, *Provinces of Mexico*, 238–239). Iberian-enhanced dedication to mining after 1550 proved one of the most obvious economic adjustments of all. Indian placer methods never produced enough precious metals to satisfy Iberian demands. As Peter Bakewell concludes, native population decline did not retard growth of this critical industry. European demand for bullion would have dictated Spanish control of the production of precious metals even without the Indian demographic crisis. Old World technology, the importation of African slave labor, and the discovery of even richer veins of silver contributed most heavily to the boom in mining after 1550 (see Bakewell, *Silver Mining*, 7–9). Between 1550 and 1570 the value of silver, arriving primarily from Mexico and secondarily from Peru, rose from 7 to 23 million pesos annually (see Lang, *Conquest and Commerce*, 48). Silver encouraged other commerce, and the level of Mexico's involvement in the Iberian mercantile system rose (see Lang, *Conquest and Commerce*, 47–49)

19. See Appendix 2, Table A.4.

20. Bravo de Lagunas, *Relación de Xalapa*, 18–19.

21. Daniel Fusfield, *The Age of the Economist*, 11–12.

22. Robert Heilbroner, *The Economic Transformation of America*, 24–27.

23. Chevalier, *Land and Society*, 77–78.

24. Four prominent members of this school of thought include Woodrow Borah, *New Spain's Century of Depression*, Ibero-Americana no. 45, especially 19–28; Chevalier, *Land and Society*, 309–311; Hugette and Pierre Chaunu, *Seville et l'Atlantique, 1594–1650*, vol. 8, 1534–1535; and Wallerstein, *Modern World System II*, 149–150.

25. Bakewell, *Silver Mining*, 226–235.

26. Aristides Medina Rubio, *La iglesia y la producción agrícola en Puebla, 1540–1795*, 180–189.

27. Jean-Pierre Berthe, "Xochimancas: Les travaux et les jours dans une hacienda sucrière de Nouvelle-Espagne au XVIIe," *Jahrbach für Geschichte von Staat, Wirtshaft and Gesellschaft Latteinamerikas* 3 (1966): 102.

28. ANJ, vol. 1617–1631, leaves 34–34v, 65–65v, 81–82v; ANJ, vol. 1609–1717, leaves 56–56v, 116v-117, 170–171, roll 2, CCSU Veracruz Microfilm Collection; ANJ, vol. 1617–1631, leaves 81v-82.

29. An arroba is equivalent to about twenty-five pounds.

30. ANJ, vol. 1647, leaves 231–233v; ANJ, vol. 1648, leaves 202–202v; ANJ, vol. 1651–1653, leaf 65.

31. Santísima Trinidad in 1606 and Concepción in 1619: ANJ, vol. 1600–1608, leaf 426; ANJ, vol. 1617–1631, leaves 41v–43.

32. Sandoval, *Industria del azúcar*, 88.

33. Barrett, *Sugar Hacienda*, 103–105; Herman Konrad, *A Jesuit Hacienda in Colonial Mexico: Santa Lucia, 1576–1767*, 69–70, 76–95; Jan Bazant, *Cinco haciendas mexicanas: tres si siglos de vida rural en San Luis Potosí*, 14–16, 80–81.

34. David Brading and Cheryl Martin working on the Bajío and Morelos regions respectively also found that large estates had more economic difficulty than smaller ones during the middle third of the seventeenth century (see Brading, *Haciendas and Ranchos*, 171–172; Martin, *Colonial Morelos*, 77, 92–93.)

35. ANJ, vol. 1600–1608, leaves 381–387; Ibid., vol. 1609–1617, leaves 10v–11; Ibid., vol. 1617–1632, leaves 440–441; Ibid., vol. 1648, leaves 250–251; Ibid., vol. 1651–1653, leaves 74–74v, 79v–82; Ibid., vol. 1663–1667, leaves 9–9v, 20–20v, 357–364v; Ibid., vol. 1632–1645, leaves 241–249, 260–260v, 320–324, 520v–528; Ibid., vol. 1645–1651, leaves 250–251v, 302.

36. Histories of commercial estates in the Valley of Mexico and San Luis Potosí indicate that Jalapa's experience did not represent a peculiar local variant of the Mexican norm. Herman Konrad did not find the Jesuit estate of Santa Lucia floundering after 1630. In his words, "By the middle of the seventeenth century, Santa Lucia stood as an outstanding hacienda in its own right, probably one of the largest and economically dynamic in the central plateau of New Spain." From 1647 through the end of the century the estate expanded (see Konrad, *Jesuit Hacienda*, 66–68, 69, 75–84.) Jan Bazant's investigations of estates in San Luis Potosí indicated more evidence of economic growth than decline. See Bazant, *Cinco haciendas mexicanas*, 21–24, 73–80.

37. Taylor, *Drinking, Homicide, and Rebellion*, 20. Brian Hamnett judges that the Spanish policy to redirect the main current of Mexican economic development back toward the Atlantic and Spain actually had its roots in the last quarter of the seventeenth century during the reign of Philip V. See Hamnett, *Política y comercio*, 49.

38. Carrera Stampa, "Las ferias Novohispanas," 320–323.

39. Rivera, Historia de Xalapa, vol. 1, 119–122; ANJ, vol. 1772, leaves 86–87, 90–91, 281–283; Carrera Stampa, "Las ferias Novohispanas," 320, 327; Brading, *Miners and Merchants*, 122.

40. Rivera, *Historia de Xalapa*, vol. 1, 120–122; Humboldt, *Ensayo político*, 497.

41. Carrera Stampa, "Las ferias Novohispanas," 321–323; Nieto, *Padrón de Xalapa*, 15–17; González de Cossio, *Xalapa*, 67–69.

42. Nieto, *Padrón de Xalapa*, 16; González de Cossio, *Xalapa*, 79–80; Carrera Stampa, "Las ferias Novohispanas, 320–322; Brading, *Miners and Merchants*, 114–115.

43. See Appendix 2, Table A.8.

44. Joseph Antonio Villa-Señor y Sánchez, *Theatro americano,* vol. 1, 283; ANJ, vol. 1736, leaves 5v–6, 30–31v, 97v–98, 104v–105, 163–163v; ANJ, vol. 1737, leaves 9–10; ANJ, vol. 1738, leaves 18–19; APJ, Entierros, Caja 3, Libro 9, leaf 53v.

45. ANJ, vol. 1773, leaves 227v–232, 305–314.

46. *Gazeta de México,* 18 August 1788, p. 140, Hemeroteca Nacional, Mexico City; Archivo del Ayuntamiento de Jalapa (hereinafter abbreviated AAJ), Libro 30, leaves 128–133v.

47. Nieto, *Padrón de Xalapa,* 23; AAJ, Libro 1, leaves 1–3.

48. Franklin Knight, *Slave Society in Cuba During the Nineteenth Century,* 12; Schwartz, *Sugar Plantations,* 164; John Fagg, *Cuba, Haiti, and the Dominican Republic,* 120–125.

49. Relan Ely, *La economía cubana entre los Isabeles, 1492–1832,* 52–55; Humboldt, *Political Essay,* vol. 3, 1–4.

50. Humboldt, *Political Essay,* vol. 3, 2–3.

51. Sandoval, *Industria del azúcar,* 161–164.

52. For statistical data on aguardiente imports 1812–1919, see Miguel Lerdo de Tejada, *Apuntes históricos de la ciudad de Vera-Cruz,* vol. 3, 369, 373, 378, 383, 388, 397, 407, 418, 428, 441, 454, 463, 472, 483, 492, 512.

53. AAJ, Libro 23, leaves 122–126, 131–132; Ibid., Libro 22, leaves 42–43; Ibid., Libro 21, leaves 340–341,

54. APJ, Entierros, Caja 5, Libro 18, leaves 9, 11v, 12, 12v, 15v, 19v, 20, 23v, 24, 28, 29, 29v, 30, 30v, 36v, 38, 44v, 62, 100.

55. AAJ, Libro 21, leaves 46–52v, 340–341v, 364; Ludivina Gutiérrez, *Monumentos coloniales de Xalapa,* 51–52.

56. AAJ, Libro 21, leaves 339–364; Ibid., Libro 20, leaves 9v–10; Ibid., Libro 23, leaves 29–30, 131–132, 305v–312, 328–336, 340–341v.

57. See Appendix 2, Table A.9.

58. AAJ, Libro 23, *passim.*

59. See Appendix 2, Table A.10.

60. Lerdo de Tejada, *Vera-Cruz,* vol. 3, 368–369.

61. AAJ, Libro 32, leaf 609; Ibid., Libro 33, leaf 581; Ibid., Libro 34, leaf 485.

62. John Coatsworth, "The Limits of Colonial Absolutism: The State in Eighteenth Century Mexico," in *Essays in the Political, Economic, and Social History of Latin America,* edited by Karen Spaulding, 31, 33–34, 37–38.

63. John Kicza, *Colonial Entrepreneurs: Families and Business in Bourbon Mexico City,* 45–48, 61.

4. Afro-Veracruzanos and Changing Colonial Labor Patterns

1. Gerhard, *Historical Geography,* 375

2. Klein, *African Slavery,* 60, 66.

3. Schwartz, *Sugar Plantations,* 152.

4. Schwartz describes Bahian integration of slavery into sugar culture (see Ibid., 152–158). Klein offers a less detailed but similar line of reasoning

for sugar culture and slavery in all of Latin America and the Caribbean. Klein, *African Slavery*, 61.

5. Palmer, *Slaves of the White God*, 65.

6. Cheryl Martin found this the case until sometime between 1625 and 1676 in Morelos. See Martin, *Colonial Morelos*, 54, 57, 70.

7. Sandoval, *Industria del azúcar*, 26; Barrett, *Sugar Hacienda*, 78. Barrett does not give this date. He merely says that Cortés first imported large numbers of Africans for this estate in 1544.

8. Sandoval, *Industria del azúcar*, 31; Cardoso, *Negro Slavery*, 25.

9. Sandoval, *Industria del azúcar*, 32; Cardoso, *Negro Slavery*, 24.

10. R. L. Brady, "The Emergence of a Negro Class in Mexico, 1524–1640," (Ph.D. dissertation, State University of Iowa, 1965), 62; Sandoval, *Industria del azúcar*, 24–25.

11. Mining was a second rural-based industry that went beyond the personal tribute economy prior to 1550. Blacks also worked in large numbers in mining. The first Spanish-controlled mines were discovered in 1531. These were the result of silver strikes in Pachuca, Sultepec, Tlalpujahua, and Taxco—all in or near the Valley of Mexico. As in urban *obrajes* African slaves worked alongside native laborers in this developing colonial industry. Much of the importance of mining at this stage of economic growth lay, however, in the precedents that it set. Spaniards simply did not have the technology to refine large amounts of Mexican silver. Most native lodes came from arid and semiarid regions. These ores were typically of medium to poor quality. They did not profitably yield large amounts of silver until the introduction of a German amalgamation process that used mercury rather than scarce water to separate silver from other substances. A decade or so later silver finds in northern New Spain became even more important to the growth of this sector of the emerging economy. Neither of these happenings took place until the beginning of the next stage of economic development around midcentury (see Brading, *Miners and Merchants*, 10–11). However, when mining did become important in Mexico, black labor was already a part of the industry.

12. Rout, *African Experience*, 79; Palmer, *Slaves of the White God*, 69–70; Aguirre Beltrán, *Población negra*, 180–183.

13. Lang, *Conquest and Commerce*, 17–18; Gibson, *Aztecs*, 24, 220; Chance, *Race and Class*, 63–64; Brading, *Miners and Merchants*, 2.

14. Gibson, *Aztecs*, 357–358; Salvucci, *Textiles and Capitalism*, 40.

15. This also proved true in other early industries including mining with strong ties to the Spanish economy during this early period.

16. Ward Barrett broke down the slave population on 1549 Tlaltenango. Males enjoyed a 34:19 favorable sex ratio over females, and two-thirds of the slave community was over twenty-one. See Barrett, *Sugar Hacienda*, 81.

17. *Documentos inéditos relativos a Hernán Cortés y su familia*, 242, 254–255, 263–266, 277–278. There were 125 slaves in this sample.

18. "Conde de Orizaba," EOG, vol. 4a, leaves 19–29, NLBC-UTx.

19. Klein, *American Slavery*, 60–61.

20. ANJ, vol. 1600–1608, leaf 389v.

21. Carroll, "Mexican Society in Transition," 156–157.

22. "Almolonga," bound volume, leaf 3, NLBC-UTx.

23. Sandoval, *Industria del azúcar,* 47–50.

24. ANJ, vol. 1632–1645, leaves 569–572.

25. ibid., vol. 1651–1663, leaves 127–127v.

26. Ibid., vol. 1632–1645, leaves 535–538v.

27. ibid., vol. 1645–1651, leaves 176–178.

28. Ibid., vol. 1645–1651, leaf 313v; Ibid., vol. 1651–1663, leaves 125v–129.

29. Ibid., vol. 1645–1651, leaves 227–227v.

30. ibid., vol. 1632–1645, leaves 274v–280.

31. "Almolonga," bound volume, leaves 22–23, NLBC-UTx.

32. See Appendix 2, Tables A.6 and A.7.

33. "Almolonga," bound volume, leaves 73v, 107v–110, 140v–143, NLBC-UTx.

34. "Almolonga," bound volume, leaves 77v, 272, NLBC-UTx.

35. See Appendix 2, Table A.7.

36. Reflection is the appropriate word because the statistics that follow in Table A.8 do not directly show a profile of the entire population living on the Santísima Trinidad. They come from registries of the parish of San Gerónimo de Coatepec that served the Trinidad's spiritual needs. In other words, I am not examining the estate population in their homes but, rather, a percentage of them in an outside setting. Consequently, this sample might slightly underrepresent slaves, *castas,* and Indians because these groups probably received the sacraments less often than Spaniards and Indians did. The changes illustrated appear great enough, however, to indicate real shifts. Thus the quality of the data may cast the degree of change in doubt but not the fact that some change did take place in the directions indicated.

37. See Appendix 2, Table A.8.

38. "Almolonga," bound volume, leaves 73, 107–110, NLBC-UTx.

39. AGN, Media Annata, vol. 60, *expediente* 2, leaves 17v–19v, 21–24, 83–83v.

40. Ibid., *expediente* 6, leaves 22–23

41. Ibid., *expediente* 6, leaves 78–79. John Tutino documents this type of Indian village–estate labor arrangement in central Mexico, the eastern Bajío, and San Luis Potosí during the late colonial period (see Tutino, "Life and Labor," 365. Eric Van Young comes close to describing this pattern for eighteenth-century rural Guadalajara. He notes that estate owners and managers often recruited temporary seasonal workers from surrounding Indian villages. He is unable, however, to provide information on the nature of this recruitment, as both this Veracruz and Tutino's cases do. See Van Young, *Hacienda and Market,* 262–264.

42. This conception of the Porfirian hacienda is currently being challenged by such scholars as Enrique Florescano and Friedrich Katz. See Enrique Florescano, *Estructuras y problemas agrarias de México,* 160–162; Friedrich Katz, "Labor Conditions on Haciendas in Porfirian Mexico: Some Trends and Tendencies," *HAHR,* 54 (February 1974): 1–47. John Tutino's,

Cheryl Martin's, and Eric Van Young's works on late colonial hacienda society add further to knowledge about the relationships between large Spanish agricultural units and neighboring Indian Villages. See Tutino, "Life and Labor," 233–237; Martin, *Colonial Morelos*, 146–147; Van Young, *Hacienda and Market*, 259–261.

43. "Conde de Orizaba," EOG, vol. 4a, leaves 11–29; AGN, Media Annata, vol. 60, *expediente* 2, leaves 21–24; AGN, Media Annata, vol. 107, *expediente* 1, leaves 21–24v.

44. AGN, Media Annata, vol. 107, *expediente* 2, leaves 21–24; AGN, Padrónes, vol. 19, leaves 241v–425.

45. AGN, Media Annata, vol. 60, *expediente* 2, leaves 21, 26; Ibid., *expediente* 3, leaf 46v.

46. AGN, Media Annata, vol. 107, *expediente* 1, leaves 21–23v, 40, 73v.

47. See Appendix 2, Table A.9.

48. Joseph Miller, *Way of Death: Merchant Capitalism and the Angolan Slave Trade, 1730–1830*, 492.

49. Klein, *African Slavery*, 83–84.

50. "Conde de Orizaba," EOG, vol. 4a, leaves 11–29, NLBC-UTx.

51. For an explanation of the computations that yielded rates of change see Carroll, "Mexican Society in Transition," 72–74.

52. Ibid., 173–174.

53. Figure 4; ANJ, vol. 1814–1815, *passim*.

54. AGN, Media Annata, vol. 60, *expediente* 2, leaves 35–62v, 64v–67; Ibid., vol. 107, *expediente* 1, leaves 78–79.

55. Adriana Naveda Chávez-Hita's study on Córdoba documents the essentially same patterns only those she documents occurred two generations later. See Naveda Chávez-Hita, *Esclavos negros*, 96–97.

56. AGN, Media Annata, vol. 60, *expediente* 2, leaves 35–67, 83–83v; Ibid., vol. 107, *expediente* 1, leaves 78–79.

57. Chapter 6 deals with these topics.

5. Slaves and Social Change, 1570–1720

1. For a discussion of social conditions on Iberia in the early colonial period see Schwartz, *Sugar Plantations*, 246–249.

2. Bermúdez Gorrochotegui, "Jalapa, " vol. 1, 160–164.

3. Chapter 2, Table 3.

4. Liss, *Mexico under Spain*, 3–4; Aguirre Beltrán, *Cuijla*, 10–11.

5. Herbert Spencer developed this nineteenth-century philosophy.

6. "Almolonga," bound volume, leaves 73v, 107v–110, 140v–153, NLBC-UTx.

7. AGN, Media Annata, vol. 60, *expediente* 7, leaves 1–3, 62–62v, 82–83v; Ibid., *expediente* 1, leaves 25v, 72–86, 103; ANJ, vol. 1723, leaf 154v.

8. APJ, Entierros, Caja 1, Libro 1, leaves 1, 2–3v.

9. See Appendix 3, Table A.18.

10. Aguirre Beltrán, *Medicina y magia*, 14, 275, *passim*; Luz-María Martínez Montiel, "Integration Patterns and the Assimilation Process of Negro Slaves in Mexico," in *Comparative Perspectives on Slavery in New*

World Plantation Societies, edited by Vera Rubin and Arthur Tuden, 447–448; Mendoza Collection, Biblioteca Nacional, Mexico City. These authors state that despite Spanish and Indian opposition Africans brought considerable cultural influence to America. This is valid up to a point. Creole culture did benefit from some enduring African influences, but the African affects proved far lighter than those of Iberian and native-American cultures.

11. Alejandro Portes and Robert Bach, *Latin Journey*, 20–26, 347.

12. See Appendix 3, Table A.13. In Córdoba, however, *bozales* outnumbered creoles through 1710. See Naveda Chávez-Hita, *Esclavos negros*, 28–30. In Morelos, *bozales* dominated the slave population through the 1680s. See Martin *Colonial Morelos*, Tables 6.4 and 6.5, 120–129. Barrett observes that *bozal* representation declined after 1623. See Barrett, *Sugar Hacienda*, 78.

13. *Colecciones de documentos inéditos relativo, al descubrimiento, conquista y organización de las antiguas posesiones españolas de ultramar*, vol. 10, no. 111, p. 274.

14. Frederick P. Bowser, "Colonial Spanish America," in *Neither Slave Nor Free*, edited by David Cohen and Jack P. Greene, 57–58; Magnus Mörner, "Historical Research on Race Relations in Latin America During the National Period," in *Race and Class in Latin America*, edited by Magnus Morner, 200.

15. APJ, Bautizos, Caja 7, Libro 23, leaf 127v; Ibid., Caja 7, Libro 25, leaves 20, 94v; Ibid., Caja 8, Libro 28, leaf 43; AAJ, Libro 8, unnumbered leaves appended to the back of this volume; AAJ, Libro 19, leaves 3v–4; ANJ, vol. 1772, leaves 90–91; ANJ, vol. 1774, leaf 90v; ANJ, vol. 1789–1790, leaves 178, 204, 282–283; Archivo Notarial de Orizaba (hereinafter abbreviated ANO), Legajo 1792, *expediente* 16, Biblioteca Central, Universidad Veracruzana, Jalapa, Veracruz.

16. APJ, Entierros, Caja 2, Libro 7, leaves 4v, 48, 147; API, Bautizos, Caja 7, Libro 23, leaf 79; APJ, Bautizos, Libro 25, leaves 24–24v; APJ, Bautizos, Libro 27, leaf 19v; AGN, Padrones, vol. 20, leaf 333v; "Resumen general de las personas que habitan en la Calle Segunda de la Montrilla, y siguientes," n.d., Map Collection, NLBC-UTx; "División del curato de Jalapa," *expediente* 960, leaves 78, 151, 328; ANJ, vol. 1736, leaves 16v–17v; ANJ, Vol. 1737, leaves 34–35; ANJ, vol. 1737–1741, leaves 18–19; Ernesto de Vignaux, *Viaje a México*, 106; Aguirre Beltrán, *Población negra*, 175–179; Mörner, *Race Mixture*, 58–59.

17. APJ, *passim*; "División del curato de Xalapa," *expediente* 960, leaves 247, 264.

18. See Appendix 3, Table A.14.

19. See Appendix 3, Tables A.16 and A.17.

20. Ibid.

21. Information presented in Chapter 7 suggests that the patterns represent illusory trends, and that might be the case, as well as that, in rural areas, blacks, like *pardos*, retained stronger social ties with Indians. Chapter 7 also indicates that mulattoes, like mestizos, favored closer bonds with whites. Also see Appendix 3, Table A.17.

22. Appendix 3, Table A.17.

23. This also held true for mulattoes. Nonetheless, mulattoes formed stronger bonds with whites than with Indians.

24. Lockhart, *Spanish Peru*, 171–172.

25. See Appendix 3, Table A.15.

26. See Appendix 2, Table A.6.

27. González de Cossio, *Xalapa*, 56–57; Manuel B. Trens, *Historia de Veracruz*, vol. 2, 311–312.

28. Aguirre Beltrán, *Población negra*, 232.

29. Ibid.; Palmer, *Slaves of the White God*, 60, 62; Aguirre Beltrán, *Medicina y magia*, 66–67, 131.

30. Patrick Carroll, "Mandinga: The Evolution of a Mexican Runaway Slave Community, 1735–1827," *Comparative Studies in Society and History*, 19, no. 4 (October 1977): 493–505.

6. Two Routes to Freedom: Córdoba and Jalapa

1. "Dictamen de la Comisión de esclavos," *Documentos para la historia de México*, no. 313, leaves 3–5, Lafragua Collection, Biblioteca Nacional, Mexico City.

2. In order of places listed, see the following citations: AGN, Tributos, vol. 53, *último expediente*, unnumbered leaves; Aguirre Beltrán, *Población negra*, 227; Gerhard, *Historical Geography*, 151, 323; AGN, Padrones, vol. 21, leaves 53–53v; AGN, Historia, vol. 72, unnumbered leaves; AGN, Tributos, vol. 43, *último expediente*, unnumbered leaves; Villa-Señor y Sánchez, *Theatro americano*, vol. 1, 313; Aguirre Beltrán, *Población negra*, 226; Gerhard, *Historical Geography*, 317; Villa-Señor y Sánchez, *Theatro americano*, vol. 1, 268, 271–277, 284–285, 310, 313, 317–319, 371–378; Jesús Silva Herzog, *Relaciónes estadísticas de Nueva España de principios del siglo XIX*, in *Archivo histórico de Hacienda*, vi, viii, x, 31; José Melgarejo Vivanco, "Carta etnográfica de Veracruz," in *La población de Veracruz*, edited by Felipe Montemayor, 24–25.

3. Naveda Chávez-Hita, *Esclavos negros*, 9–10, 155–156; Carroll, "Mandinga," 503; Enrique Herrera Moreno, *El Cantón de Córdoba*, Fondo de Origen, Caja 8b, Biblioteca Nacional, Mexico City, 265, 295–296.

4. AGN, Tierras, vol. 3543, *expediente* 1, leaf 81.

5. See Table 6 and Appendix 2, Table A.10.

6. See Appendix 2, Table A.10.

7. Knight, *Slave Society in Cuba*, 189–190; Klein, *African Slavery*, 189–190.

8. Adriana Naveda Chávez-Hita, "Esclavitud en la jurisdicción de la villa de Córdoba en el siglo XVIII" (master's thesis, Universidad Veracruzana, 1977), 9–10.

9. "Padrón de los individuos que componen las haciendas y los ranchos de la jurisdicción de Córdoba," vol. 16, unnumbered leaves, Archivo Municipal de Córdoba (hereinafter abbreviated AMC) and rolls 5 and 13, TAMUCC Veracruz Microfilm Collection; Naveda Chávez-Hita, *Esclavos negros*, 92–94.

10. Humboldt, *Ensayo político,* 296–297. (Humboldt gives 1764 as the date for the establishment of Córdoba's royal tobacco monopoly; Brading, *Miners and Merchants,* 27, 29; Naveda Chávez-Hita, *Esclavos negros,* 93–94.

11. AGN, Tierras, vol. 3543, *expediente* 1, leaves 23–23v, 76v–82v; William B. Taylor, "The Foundation of Nuestra Señora de Guadalupe de Amapa," *The Americas* 26, no. 4 (April 1970): 442; Naveda Chávez-Hita, *Esclavos negros,* 132–147; Carroll, "Mandinga," 494.

12. Herrera Moreno, *Cantón de Córdoba,* 125; AGN, Tierras, vol. 3543 *expediente* 1, leaves 76v–82v.

13. Octaviano R. Corro, *Los cimarrones en Veracruz y la fundación de Amapa,* 23.

14. AGN, Tierras, vol. 3543 *expediente* 1, leaves 82–82v.

15. John Tutino, *From Insurrection to Revolution in Mexico,* 134, 137.

16. Hugh Hammill, *The Hidalgo Revolt,* 171–172; Timothy Anna, *The Fall of the Royal Government in Mexico City,* 64–65; Colin MacLachlan and Jaime Rodríguez, *The Forging of the Cosmic Race,* 313; Naveda Chávez-Hita, *Esclavos negros,* 153–154; José Domingo de Isassi, *Memorias de lo acontedido en Córdoba en tiempo de la revolución, para la historia de la independencia megicana, 1827,* 11; Luis Chávez Orozco and Enrique Florescano, *Agricultura e industria textil en Veracruz,* 59.

17. MacLachlan and Rodríguez, *Forging of the Cosmic Race,* 325–327.

18. Naveda Chávez-Hita, *Esclavos negros,* 154–155

19. Herrera Moreno, *Cantón de Córdoba,* 170; Isassi, *Memorias,* 17, 25–26; Naveda Chávez-Hita, *Esclavos negros,* 154–155; Herrera Moreno, *Cantón de Córdoba,* 172, 180–181.

20. Naveda Chávez-Hita, *Esclavos negros,* 154–155.

21. Eugene Harrell, "Vicente Guerrero and the Birth of Modern Mexico" (Ph.D. dissertation, Tulane University, 1976), 2.

22. Bravo de Lagunas, *Relación de Xalapa,* 10–11.

23. Angel Rosenblat, *Población indígena de América,* 110; Woodrow Borah and Sherburne Cook, *Aboriginal Population of Central Mexico on the Eve of the Spanish Conquest,* 4.

24. Philip Curtin, "Epidemiology and the Slave Trade," *Political Science Quarterly* 33 (June 1968): 190–209.

25. APJ, Entierros, Caja 5, Libro 16, leaves 40–63; Ibid., Caja 7, Libro 33, leaves 66v–72v; AAJ, Libro 21, leaves 183–183v.

26. AAJ, Libro 21, leaves 183–183v.

27. Within this context, "class" is meant to mean economic rank. For the effect of disease on other population centers, see Sherburne Cook and Woodrow Borah, *Essays in Population History: Mexico and the Caribbean,* vol. 1, 106; Sherburne Cook, "The Incidence of Disease Among the Aztecs and Related Tribes," *HAHR,* 26 (August 1946): 200; Donald Cooper, *Epidemic Disease in Mexico City, 1761–1813.*

28. APJ, Entierros, Caja 5, Libro 16, leaves 40–63v; Ibid., Caja 2, Libro 6, leaves 58–69v; Ibid., Caja 2, Libro 7, leaves 125–155v; Ibid., Caja 3, Libro 9, leaves 48–142v; Ibid., Caja 5, Libro 16, leaves 40–63v; Ibid., Caja 7, Libro 33, leaves 66v–72v.

29. Humboldt's words are quoted in González de Cossio, *Xalapa,* 68, and in Rivera, *Historia de Xalapa,* vol. 1, 122. His observation is corroborated by Gerhard, *Historical Geography,* 376, and in Tables 6 and A.11.

30. See Appendix 2, Table A.11 and the accompanying text.

31. Carrera Stampa, "Las ferias Novohispañas," 321; ANJ, vol. 1773, leaves 10v–12.

32. APJ, Entierros, Caja 4, Libro 13, leaves 1–48v.

33. See Appendix 2, Table A.12. For an explanation of the calculations involved in arriving at population figures, see Carroll, "Mexican Society in Transition," 316.

34. "La división del Curato de Jalapa, 1773," uncatalogued manuscript in W. B. Stevens Collection, Wallet 27, *expediente* 960, NLBC-UTx., leaves 34–35, 43–44, 124–125, 264, 266, 312, 328–334, 353; Gutiérrez, *Monumentos colonials de Xalapa,* 113.

35. See Table 7.

36. Archivo Parroquial de Xilotepec, Matrimonios, Libro 9, leaf 15.

37. Nieto, *Padrón de Jalapa,* 16.

38. AGN, Historia, vol. 522, leaf 239; Ibid., Padrones, vol. 20, leaves 302, 321v–325v.

39. AAJ, Libro 21, leaves 36–43; Ibid., Libro 24, leaves 128–132v; Ibid., Libro 36, leaves 252–254

40. ANJ, vol. 1769–1770, leaves 392–393v.

41. Humboldt, *Ensayo político,* vol. 1, 404.

42. "Dictamen de la Comisión de esclavos," leaves 3–7, 41, Lafragua Collection, Biblioteca Nacional; Manuel Ruíz Mendez, "La emancipación de los esclavos en Yucatán," *Revista de la Universidad de Yucatán,* 12, (January–February 1970): 35.

43. Arthur Noll, *From Empire to Republic,* 109.

44. Juan Wenceslao Barquera, Documentos relativos a 1774–1827, Genaro García Collection, Legajo 10, NLBC-UTx.

45. G. G. Lyon, *Journal of a Residence and Tour in the Republic of Mexico in the Year 1826,* vol. 2, 225.

7. Free Afro-Veracruzanos and the Late Colonial Socioeconomic Order

1. Robert McCaa, Stuart Schwartz, and Arturo Grubessich also take the position that tests of correlation between marriage patterns, occupational rank, and race "confirm the caste-like basis of colonial Oaxaca's social ideology." They conclude that "race remained a strong principle of social stratification even in the relatively commercial and proto-industrial economy of colonial Oaxaca." See their "Race and Class in Colonial Latin America: A Critique," *Comparative Studies in Society and History,* 21, no. 3 (July 1979): 433. David Brading also defends the caste-system interpretation of late colonial social stratification. See his "Grupos étnicos," 479–480.

2. Lyle McAlister, "Social Structure and Social Change in New Spain," *HAHR* 43, no. 3 (1963): 349–370 especially 363.

3. Magnus Mörner, "Economic Factors and Stratification in Colonial Spanish America With Special Regard to Elites," *HAHR* 63, no. 2 (May 1983): 367–368. Mörner judges that the medieval Castilian caste system eroded and was replaced in the late colonial period by a more open regimen that stressed economic class as the predominant determinant of social rank. He argues that this change came as a result of Bourbon emphasis on "commercial capitalism," which I call resurgent mercantilism in Chapter 3. John Chance and William Taylor, in "Estate and Class in a Colonial City: Oaxaca in 1792," *Comparative Studies in Society and History* 19, no. 4 (October 1977): 485, are careful not to exclude race as an important determinant of social rank, but they argue that class had probably overtaken it in significance as a criteria for socioeconomic status. Rodney Anderson, Patricia Seed, and Philip Rust also support this interpretation. See Anderson's "Race and Social Stratification: A Comparison of Working-Class Spaniards, Indians, and Castas in Guadalajara, Mexico, in 1821," *HAHR* 68, no. 2 (May 1988): 239–241; and Seed and Rust's, "Estate and Class in Colonial Oaxaca Revisited," *Comparative Studies in Society and History* 25, no. 4 (October 1983): 707.

4. Mörner, "Economic Factors and Stratification," 339–340, 347; Ruggiero Romano, "American Feudalism," *HAHR* 64, no. 1 (February 1984): 121–134.

5. Anderson, "Race and Social Stratification," see especially 239–241; also see Chance and Taylor, "Estate and Class in a Colonial City," 485–486.

6. Census compilers also assigned racial labels.

7. "El tributo real de los niños expósitos," in AGN, Varios, vol. 1, leaves 82–85.

8. ANJ, vol. 1736, leaves 6v–7, 263–264v; Ibid., vol. 1737–1741, leaves 34v–36; Ibid., vol. 1750, leaves 276–277; Ibid., vol. 1770, leaves 27–28v; Ibid., vol. 1771–1772, leaves 248–248v; Ibid., vol. 1796–1797, leaf 103v.

9. APJ, Entierros, Caja 1, Libro 1, leaf 245.

10. Certain writers judge that the term *pardo* was merely a euphemism for the terms mulatto and *negro*. See Aguirre Beltrán, *Población negra*, 173; Pedro Alonso O'Crouley, *A Description of the Kingdom of New Spain*, edited and translated by Sean Galbin, 21.

11. APJ, Bautizos, Caja 1, Libro 1, leaf 23.

12. Ibid., Entierros, Caja 1, Libro 1, leaf 16v.

13. Ibid., Entierros, Caja 2, Libro 7, leaf 62v.

14. Ibid., Bautizos, Caja 2, Libro 7, leaf 59.

15. Ibid., Bautizos, Caja 1, Libro 1, leaf 19; Ibid., Bautizos, Caja 7, Libro 6, leaf 16v; Ibid., Entierros, Caja 2, Libro 7, leaves 4v, 16, 18v; Ibid., Matrimonios, Legajo 5, 1790–1797; Ibid., Matrimonios, Legajo 6, 1800–1809; Ibid., Matrimonios, Legajo 7, 1810–1819; Nieto, *Padrón de Xalapa*, 146.

16. I would like to state two qualifications to this figure of urban spatial distribution. First, as already mentioned, census data for Córdoba is extremely limited. As a result, I could not estimate overall residential patterns for this important local setting. Secondly, this figure reflects general racial concentrations. It represents collective rather than individual patterns. Rodney Anderson has rightly observed that all sectors of most early nineteenth-century Mexican cities had representatives of all racial groups (see his "Race

and Social Stratification," 228). However, I do not agree with Anderson's conclusion that little correlation existed between race and residential distribution. Certain racial groups, even as the largest minority, did display strong association with certain urban zones.

17. Afro-*castas* in the district of Jalapa provide a mild exception to this trend. There, many members of this group did inhabit *pueblos*, but the greatest single cohort in their sample fell into the *rancho* population.

18. See Figure 5 and Table A.21 in Appendix 3.

19. "Padrón de los individuos," vol. 16, AMC unnumbered leaves, and rolls 5 and 13, TAMUCC Veracruz Microfilm Collection.

20. This represents only a tentative conclusion based upon qualitative rather than quantitative evidence. In fact, rural differences may have proved more illusory than real since the data provides no basis of residential differentiation there. The possibility exists that in *pueblos* and on *ranchos* and estates race did govern patterns of residential distribution in some way. See Appendix 3, 179, 183, and AGN, Padrones, vol. 19, leaves 1–240v.

21. The bifurcated nature of economic life in colonial Veracruz presents one difficulty. A peasant Indian agricultural economy existed but was lightly integrated with a Hispanic commercial agricultural economy in the hinterlands of Veracruz. For lack of sufficient data, I limit my analysis to those persons involved in the Hispanic-dominated economic activity. Since members of all races (including Indians) participated in this branch of the regional economy at a level comparable to their respective representation in the overall population, the exclusion of the Indian economy does not compromise the ability to measure the impact of race on occupational rank.

A second methodological consideration involved construction of an occupational hierarchy that reflected the reality of the setting. For colonial Veracruz, that presented a formidable task. Inconsistencies in the records make rank very difficult to assess. Skilled artisans present a case in point. Actually, two very different groups comprised this standard occupational category—masters and journeymen. The former enjoyed relatively high rank, the latter did not. Compilers seldom distinguished between these two groups. They simply lumped both groups together into a single category. I followed their lead. Recognizing the ambiguity in the evidence, I adopted a rough, three-tiered ranking system, sacrificing precision for reliability.

22. This category included persons with diversified economic activities involving some combination of international or interregional commerce, estate agriculture, and urban real-estate investment (persons who owned at least 3,000 pesos worth). Professionals included lawyers and bureaucrats. This category included notaries, royal and/or local civil officials such as town council members, military officers, clerics, and the like.

23. Since the sample contained so few free *negro* cases, I cannot describe their occupational status. They represented such a small percentage of the population within the overall region that absence of information on them does not seriously impede an overall inquiry into the significance of race in assigning occupational rank.

24. See Appendix 3, Table A.19.

25. "Padrón de los individuos," vol. 16, AMC, unnumbered leaves, and

rolls 5 and 13, TAMUCC Veracruz Microfilm Collection; AGN, Tributos, vol. 43, *último expediente,* unnumbered leaves.

26. Chance and Taylor, "Estate and Class in a Colonial City," 473–477; Anderson, "Race and Social Stratification," 234–237, 240–241.

27. See Appendix 3, Table A.19.

28. This appears somewhat surprising given the stronger Indian presence in the countryside. The percentage differences seem moderately high, and I cannot explain them. See Table 8 and Appendix 3, Tables A.20 and A.21, and Carroll, "Mexican Society in Transition," 275, 290.

29. See Appendix 3, Tables A.20 and A.21.

30. See Appendix 3, Tables A.14 and A.20.

31. Actually, multiple African ethnic groups made the middle-Atlantic passage to Veracruz. Chapter 2 identifies them.

32. Ibid.; Appendix 3, Tables A.14 and A.20.

33. See Appendix 3, Table A.20 The sample for *negros* proved too small to draw conclusions on the correlation between race and marriage.

34. See Appendix 3, Tables A.14 and A.20.

35. As already noted, urban data for Córdoba is too limited for most types of analysis.

36. Ibid.; Appendix 3, Tables A.14, A.20 and A.24.

37. See note 35; Table 9 and Appendix 3, Tables A.15, A.20 and A.24.

38. See Appendix 3, Table A.20.

39. See note 35; Appendix 3, Tables A.14 and A.20.

40. Table 9 and Appendix 3, Table A.20.

41. Three obstacles stand in the way of an understanding of race relations in New Spain. First, three centuries of miscegenation increased the complexity of racial classification. Catalogers drew up complicated racial charts aimed at depicting the physical prototypes of the many hybrid groups that evolved. By the eighteenth century, some, such as those of Vicente Riva Palacio, Pedro Alonso O'Crouley, and an anonymous compiler in the National Museum of Mexico, contained listings for the products of as many as sixteen "racial" combinations (see Aguirre Beltrán, *Población negra,* 175– 177; O'Crouley, *Kingdom of New Spain,* 19; Mörner, *Race Mixture,* 58–59). This problem is, however, somewhat of a moot question. Commonly used racial indicators were too imprecise to discern such fine physical distinctions.

A second interpretive problem involves regional variation in colonial racial nomenclature. For example, three district capitals enumerated in the Revillagigedo military census of 1793, had different racial divisions. Tlapa compilers lumped all residents of African descent into the single category of *mulato.* The census taker for Orizaba divided these groups into *negros* and *pardos.* Compilers for Jalapa used four classifications, blacks, *pardos, mulatos,* and *morenos* (ebony-colored persons) (see AGN, Padrones, vols. 19–21, *passim*). Pedro O'Crouley did not list blacks as a separate group. He merely counted them as *castas.* He used only three terms—Spaniard, Indian, and *casta.* This was the same man who had drawn up a chart that included separate categories for fifteen racial mixtures (see O'Crouley, *Kingdom of New Spain,* 17). In 1820, Don Fernando Navarro y Noriega again used the same three basic categories employed by O'Crouley in the 1770s (see Fernando Navarro y Noriega, *Memoria sobre la población de Nueva España*, 15).

Simón Tadeo Ortíz de Ayala, writing soon after independence, reflects a third problem in evaluating the colonial meaning and application of race. This involved rounding off the products of miscegenation. Tadeo Ortíz placed whites and Indians into two separate groups but then discarded the customary colonial term of *casta* to describe persons of mixed racial ancestry and substituted the term mestizo that had previously been ascribed only to persons of mixed white-Indian origin (see Simón Tadeo Ortíz de Ayala, *Resumen de la estadística del Imperio Mexicano, 1822*, edited by Tarsicio García Díaz, 18–19).

42. Lockhart, *Spanish Peru*, 25, 115.

43. Nieto, *Padrón de Xalapa*, 280.

44. APJ, Matrimonios, Legajo 3, Libro 1790–1791, unnumbered leaves; AGN, Padrones, vol. 20, leaf 231v.

45. APJ, Matrimonios, Legajo 3, unnumbered leaves; Nieto, *Padrón de Xalapa*, 258.

46. Archivo Notorial de Orizaba (hereinafter abbreviated ANO), 1792, *expediente* 16, unnumbered leaves.

47. AGN, Padrones, vol. 20, leaf 299v; Papers of the Carraza y Pardo family, document 53, in an untitled bound volume of the miscellaneous documents located in the family library on the sugar plantation of Concepción, Jalapa; ANJ, vol. 1771–1772, leaves 86–87, 281–283; ANJ, vol. 1789–1790, leaves 204–204v; ANJ, Matrimonios, Legajo 1792–1794, unnumbered loose *expedientes*.

48. ANJ, vol. 1772, leaves 90–91; Ibid., vol. 1774, leaf 90v; Ibid., vol. 1789–1790, leaves 178, 204, 282–283; APJ, Bautizos, Caja 7, Libro 23, leaf 127v; APJ, Bautizos, Caja 7, Libro 25, leaf 20v; APJ, Bautizos, Caja 8, Libro 28, leaf 43; "División del Curato de Jalapa," *expediente* 960, leaves 151–152, 178, 180, 240, NLBC-UTx.

49. ANJ, vol. 1737–1741, leaf 574; Ibid., vol. 1754–1757, leaves 44v, 383–387; Ibid., vol. 1820–1821, leaf 305.

50. APJ, Caja 8, Libro 28, leaf 43.

51. AAJ, Libro 8, eighty unnumbered leaves attached to the back of this volume; APJ, Matrimonios, Legajo 6, 1800–1809, unnumbered loose *expedientes*.

52. Anderson, "Race and Social Stratification," 231, 241; Chance and Taylor, "Estate and Class," 485–486.

8. Adjustment, Independence, Politics, and Race

1. Carlos María Bustamante, *Cuadro histórico de la revolución mexicana*, vol. 5, 336–337; Rivera, *Jalapa*, vol. 2, 141–142.

2. John Lynch, *The Spanish-American Revolutions, 1808–1826*, 320, 329–334. Brian Hamnett states that the revolutionary struggle with Spain, "produced an explosion of . . . racial hatreds and fears. . . . Central to any explanation of its occurrence is an understanding of the provocative power of

social and racial disdain." See Brian Hamnett, *Roots of Insurgency: Mexican Regions, 1750–1824*, 12.

3. William F. Sprague, *Vicente Guerrero, Mexican Liberator*, 41; Rivera, *Jalapa*, vol. 2, 144.

4. Harrell, "Vicente Guerrero," 2–6.

5. Lynch, *Spanish-American Revolutions*, 328–334

6. [José María Luis Mora], "Examen Crítico de la administración establecida en consequencia del Plan de Jalapa," *El Indicador*, no. 2 (16 October 1833), 23, 25, 27; Michael Costeloe, *Primera república federal de México, 1824–1835*, 59–60; Hamnett, *Roots of Insurgency*, 12–13, 211–214.

7. Ward, *Mexico*, vol. 2, 238–239; Charles Macune, "A Test of Federalism: Political, Economic, and Ecclesiastical Relations Between the State of Mexico and the Mexican Nation, 1823–1835" (Ph.D. dissertation, University of Texas at Austin, August, 1970), 308; Costeloe, *Primera república federal*, 56–60.

8. Costeloe, *Primera república federal*, 49–60; José María Bocanegra, *Memorias para la historia de México independiente, 1822–1846*, vol. 1, 390–396; Harrell, "Vicente Guerrero," 111; Macune, "A Test of Federalism," 308.

9. Harrell, "Vicente Guerrero," 130–132; Rivera, *Jalapa*, vol. 2, 423–424; González de Cossío, *Xalapa*, 169–172; Macune, "A Test of Federalism," 312.

10. Lucas Alamán, *Historia de Méjico*, vol. 5, 825; Sprague, *Guerrero*, 66; Costeloe, *Primera república federal*, 71–81; Harrell, "Vicente Guerrero," 133–134. Macune claims that the *yorkinos* also captured a majority in the Senate, "A Test of Federalism," 311.

11. Harrell, "Vicente Guerrero," 137–139; Macune, "A Test of Federalism," 320.

12. The first *escocés*-backed plot purportedly involved a Spanish cleric named Joaquín Arenas. He approached General Ignacio Mora, military Commandant of the Federal District, and invited him to join in a conspiracy aimed at reuniting Mexico with Spain. It centered in the states of Puebla and Veracruz. If successful, Arenas planned to imprison two of the three most famous insurgents-turned-politicians of the Hidalgo-Morelos years, President Guadalupe Victoria and Vicente Guerrero. Mora informed President Victoria of the conspiracy. In the ensuing weeks Vice President Nicolás Bravo and the Scottish rite (in which Bravo was the Grand Master) came under strong suspicion for complicity. Authorities, the press, and *yorkinos* subjected the vice president and his party to vehement public attack. Guerrero led this opposition. See Harrell, "Vicente Guerrero, " 145–148; Costeloe, *Primera república federal*, 91–95; Alamán, *Historia de Méjico*, vol. 5, 826–828; Sprague, *Guerrero*, 66–67.

A second *escocés*-backed uprising occurred on December 23, 1827. A lieutenant colonel stationed in Otumba led it. His name was José Manuel Montaño. He called for an end to Masonic politics by outlawing secret societies and the recall of Joel Poinsett who many suspected had helped instigate the *yorkino* attack on *escocés* politicians during the 1826 campaign. This time Nicolás Bravo did not remain in the wings. He fled the capital and joined the rebels. The Veracruz legislature, one of but two not controlled by *yorkinos,* endorsed the Montaño Plan. In this time of crisis President Victoria turned to the ablest *yorkino* military figure at hand, Vicente Guerrero. He placed the Mexico state militia at Guerrero's disposal and told him to put down the revolt. By January 6, 1828, it was all over. Guerrero had done his job well and gone from early patriot fighter to politician to military hero in the public's eye. See Costeloe, *Primera república federal,* 69–71; Harrell, "Vicente Guerrero," 318.

13. Costeloe, *Primera república federal,* 71–72; Sprague, *Guerrero,* 152; Macune, "A Test of Federalism," 320; Charles Hale, *Mexican Liberalism in the Age of Mora, 1821–1853,* 104.

14. Macune, "A Test of Federalism," 322–323.

15. Nettie Lee Benson, "Texas as Viewed From Mexico, 1820–1834," *Southwestern Historical Quarterly,* Special Issue (1987): 262.

16. Ibid.

17. Sprague, *Guerrero,* 91–96; Benson, "Texas as Viewed From Mexico," 270.

18. Alamán, *Historia de Méjico,* 847–849; Bocanegra, *Memorias,* vol. 2, 56–61; Costeloe, *Primera república federal,* 241–245; Sprague, *Guerrero,* 91–96.

19. Macune, "A Test of Federalism," 331–337.

20. Carlos María Bustamante, *O matan a los ingleses, o el gobierno los sostiene!,* vol. 257, *expediente* 99, unnumbered leaves, Lafragua Collection, Biblioteca Nacional, Mexico City.

21. Macune, "A Test of Federalism," 309.

22. AGN, Gobernación, Legajo 72, one of several unnumbered *expedientes* and broadsides dealing principally with Guerrero's disputed presidential race of 1828.

23. Sprague, *Guerrero,* 53, 80, 87, 94, 96; Ivan Gomezcesar, "El partido del progreso," in *El pensamiento político de México,* Alonso Aguilar M. et al., eds., 152–155; [José María Luis Mora], "Malo periculosam libertatem," *El Indicador,* no. 3 (1833): 17; [Mora], "Examen crítico," 32; Alamán, *Historia de Méjico,* vol. 5, 851; Costeloe, *Primera república federal,* 73–75.

24. Alamán, *Historia de Méjico,* vol. 5, 832–834, 838–845; [Mora], "Malo periculosam libertatem," 9; Costeloe, *Primera república federal,* 77–89; Harrell, "Vicente Guerrero," 106, 108, 119, 122, 134; Macune, "A Test of Federalism," 312.

25. Hamnett, *Roots of Insurgency,* 45.

26. Ibid., 12–13.

27. The first movement involved the Arenas plot. See Harrell, "Vicente Guerrero," 145–148; Costeloe, *Primera república federal,* 91–95; Alamán, *Historia de Méjico,* vol. 5, 826–828; Sprague, *Guerrero,* 66–67. Antonio López de Santa Anna's Plan de Jalapa issued on September 11, 1828, represented the second Jalapa-based movement. It claimed that Manuel Gómez Pedraza had won the presidential election of 1828 by fraud and called for the installation of the runner-up candidate as president—Vicente Guerrero. Finally, the second Plan de Jalapa issued on December 4, 1829, called for the ouster of Guerrero on the grounds that he refused to surrender special executive powers, granted during the Spanish invasion of Mexico, after the crisis

had passed. See Benson, "Texas as Viewed From Mexico," 262; Sprague, *Guerrero*, 91–96.

28. Alamán, *Historia de Méjico*, vol. 5, 825, 835–836, 840–841, 847; [Mora], "Examen Crítico," 5, 9; [Mora], "Malo periculosam libertatem," 49, 51; Costeloe, *Primera república federal*, 66–67, 81, 93–94, 105; González de Cossio, *Xalapa*, 172; Rivera, *Jalapa*, vol. 2, 436–438; Sprague, *Guerrero*, 66–69.

29. Rivera, *Jalapa*, vol. 2, 439; Costeloe, *Primera república federal*, 109.

30. Archivo de Valentín Gómez Farías, of Miguel Angel de Hesa (a descendent), Hacienda de San Bruno, Jalapa, Veracruz.

31. Rivera, *Jalapa*, vol. 2, 433–436 438; Sprague, *Guerrero*, 66–69.

32. AAJ, Libro 1, leaves 1–80.

33. Ibid.; Roger Cunniff, "Mexican Municipal Electoral Reform, 1810–1822," in *Mexico and the Spanish Cortes, 1810–1822*, edited by Nettie Lee Benson, 67–68.

34. AAJ, Libro 19, leaves 23–23v.

35. Cunniff, "Mexican Municipal Electoral Reform," 68.

36. AGN, Padrones, vol. 20, leaf 306; APJ, Bautizos, Caja 9, Libro 31, leaf 35v.

37. The 1828 drop in Afro-Jalapan political participation may or may not have been significant. Election returns themselves did not racially identify the individuals involved. In order to determine Afro-Jalapans, I found it necessary to try and record-link each individual listed in the election results with biographical data compiled from census, parochial, notarial, and other town council documents dated before August, 1822, when a law went into effect prohibiting racial identifications in public documents. Since source materials proved richest for the period 1790–1810, the further these elections chronologically extended from this period, the more difficult identification of Afro-Jalapan participants through record-linking became.

38. AAJ, Libro 31, leaf 13v.

39. Ibid., leaf 14v.

40. AAJ, Libro 31, leaf 14.

41. AGN, Padrones, vol. 20, leaf 309; ANJ, vol. 1822–1823, leaves 189–191.

42. APJ, Bautizos, Caja 7, Libro 25, leaf 43; ANJ, vol. 1822–1823, leaves 189–191; AAJ, Libro 31, leaf 14v.

43. Carroll, "Mexican Society in Transition," Table 9, 105.

44. Sprague, *Guerrero*, 66–69; Costeloe, *Primera república federal*, 74–102.

45. AAJ, Libro 31, leaf 27v.

46. Ibid., Libros 1–31, *passim*.

47. Ibid., Libro 31, leaves, 14, 16, 19v, 20v, 24v, 26v, 27v, 33v, 36v, 46v, 57v, 60.

48. AGN, Padrones, vol. 20, leaf 312.

49. AAJ, Libro 31, leaves 20, 20v, 26, 26v, 28v, 31v, 33v, 36v, 41v, 46, 46v, 51, 52v, 57v, 58.

50. Ibid., Libro 31, leaves 52–53v; APJ, Matrimonios, Legajo 8, 1800–1809, unnumbered loose *expedientes*.

51. AAJ, Libro 31, leaf 60; APJ, Bautizos, Caja 8, Libro 27, leaf 53v.
52. AAJ, Libro 31, leaves 19v, 46; AGN, Padrones, vol. 20, leaf 335; APJ, Bautizos, Caja 7, Libro 23, leaf 165v; APJ, Entierros, Caja 3, Libro 9, leaf 128.
53. Bustamante, *Cuadro histórico*, vol. 5, 319–323, 327, 329–334.

Conclusions

1. Alfred Crosby, *Columbian Exchange*, 37–39.
2. Borah, *Century of Depression*, 19–28; Chevalier, *Land and Society*, 309–311; Chaunu, *Seville et l'Atlantique*, vol. 8, 1534–1535; Wallerstein, *Modern World System II*, 149–150.
3. Bakewell, *Silver Mining*, 226–235.
4. Richard Salvucci observed similar patterns of economic change in the Mexican textile industry. (See Salvucci, *Textiles and Capitalism*, 157–158.)
5. Martin, *Colonial Morelos*, 117; Tutino, *Insurrection to Revolution*, 46–97.
6. Naveda Chávez-Hita, *Esclavos negros*, 154–155; Herrera Moreno, *Cantón de Córdoba*, 170; Isassi, *Memorias*, 17, 25–26.
7. Hamill, *Hidalgo Revolt*, 171–172; Anna, *Fall of the Royal Government*, 64–65; Harrell, "Vicente Guerrero," 2–5.
8. Nettie Lee Benson, ed., *Mexico and the Spanish Cortes, 1810-1822*, 3–5.
9. Lynch, *Spain under the Hapsburgs*, vol 2, 12–13; Anna, *Fall of the Royal Government*, 64–65.
10. Lynch, *Spanish-American Revolutions*, 327–334.
11. John Tutino and Cheryl Martin, however, attribute economic stagnation in the Chalco and Morelos regions during the half century after independence to physical destruction wrought by the struggle for freedom from Spain. Tutino recognizes that damage was lighter in many other areas including Veracruz. See John Tutino, "Hacienda and Social Relations in Mexico: The Chalco Region in the Era of Independence," *HAHR* 55, no. 3 (August 1975): 528; Martin, *Colonial Morelos*, 194. I generally agree with Tutino's observation about the unevenness of the war's effects. Based on the contrasting experiences of Córdoba and Jalapa, I would go a step further and argue that this unevenness commonly existed at the intraregional level.
12. Guadalupe Victoria served out his elected term from 1824 to 1828, and José Joaquín de Herrera held office from 1848 to 1852.
13. I have over-extended myself in the second section of this conclusion, reaching far beyond the evidence at my disposal. I did not do this because I was sure of what I was saying. On the contrary, I did so because I was unsure of conclusions, however plausible, drawn from a limited regional perspective and pushed well beyond the chronological boundaries of their primary documentation. Therefore, I offer these comments as speculations for testing rather than accepting.

My first set of conclusions dealing with the Afro-Veracruzano experience, however, appear less presumptuous to me. This largely forgotten group that gave so much in so many ways to the emergence of colonial and early national Veracruz deserves more attention than it has received from scholars.

I add this limited monograph to the writings of a handful of authors who have pioneered this field of inquiry, and upon whose findings I have so heavily relied.

Appendix 1. Materials Relating to the Afro-Mexican and Afro-Veracruz Slave Trade

1. Aguirre Beltrán, *Población negra*, 240.
2. Ibid., 242; Palmer, *Slaves of the White God*, 23; Curtin, *Atlantic Slave Trade*, 112–113.
3. Palmer, *Slaves of the White God*, 28.
4. Aguirre Beltrán, *Población negra*, 48.
5. Bowser, *African Slave in Colonial Peru*, 33–34.
6. Palmer, *Slaves of the White God*, 35. Palmer does not, however, make the argument that this policy was an attempt to curb Portuguese profits and fraud.
7. Bowser, *African Slave in Colonial Peru*, 35–36.
8. Palmer, *Slaves of the White God*, 14–15.
9. Aguirre Beltrán, *Población negra*, 47–48.
10. Chaunu, *Séville et l'Atlantique*, vol. 6, 402–403.
11. Curtin, *Atlantic Slave Trade*, 103–108.

Appendix 2. Materials Relating to Demographic and Economic Change

1. Cook and Borah, *Essays in Population History*, vol. 1, 107.
2. Günter Volmer, "La evolución cuantitativa de la población indígena en la región de Pueblo (1570–1810)," *Historia Mexicana* 23 (July–September 1973): 48.
3. Brading and Wu, "Population Growth and Crisis," *Journal of Latin American Studies* 5 (1973), 17.

Appendix 3. Materials Relating to Afro-Veracruzanos and Socioeconomic Change

1. Rodney Anderson, "Race and Social Stratification," 213–216, 232–233.

Sources Cited

Archival Material

Archivo del Ayuntamiento de Jalapa, Libros 1, 8, 19, 20, 21, 22, 23, 30, 32, 33, 34. Jalapa, Veracruz.

Archivo Carraza y Pardo. Ingenio de la Concha, Jalapa, Veracruz.

Archivo General de la Nación. General de Parte, Gobernación, Historia, Hospital de jesús, Mexico City. Media Annata, Mercedes, Padrones, Tierras, Tributos, and Varios.

Archivo General de las Indias. Seville, Spain.

Archivo Notorial de Jalapa, Biblioteca Central, Universidad Veracruzana, Jalapa, Veracruz. Also in CCSU Veracruz Microfilm Collection (1570–1830). rolls 16–52.

Archivo Notorial de Orizaba. Biblioteca Central, Universidad Veracruzana, Jalapa, Veracruz.

Archivo Parroquial de Coatepec. Coatepec, Veracruz.

Archivo Parroquial de Córdoba. Córdoba, Veracruz.

Archivo Parroquial de Naulinco. Naulinco, Veracruz.

Archivo Parroquial de Xilotepec. Xilotepec, Veracruz.

Archivo de Valentín Gómez Farías. Hacienda de San Bruno, Jalapa, Veracruz.

Bustamante, Carlos María. *O matan a los ingleses, o el gobierno los sostiene!* Lafragua Collection. Biblioteca Nacional, Mexico City.

"Dictamen de la Comisión de esclavos." Documentos para la historia de México, Lafragua Collection. Biblioteca Nacional, Mexico City.

"La división del Curato de Jalapa,1773." Uncatalogued. W B. Stevens Collection, Nettie Lee Benson Latin American Collection, University of Texas at Austin.

Gazeta de México 25. Hemeroteca Nacional, Mexico City.

Herrera Moreno, Enrique. *El Cantón de Córdoba.* Córdoba, 1892. Fondo de Origen, Caja 8b. Biblioteca Nacional, Mexico City.

"Ingenio de Almolonga y Rancho de Santa Cruz." Uncatalogued, one bound volume and sixteen folders. Nettie Lee Benson Latin American Collection, University of Texas at Austin.

Mendoza Collection. Biblioteca Nacional, Mexico City.

Notario Eclesiástico de la Parroquia del Sagrado Corazón. Jalapa, Veracruz.

"Padrón de los individuos que componen las haciendas y los ranchos de la jurisdicción de Córdoba." Vol. 16, Archivo Municipal de Córdoba. Also in the CCSU Veracruz Microfilm Collection, rolls 5, 13.

"Papeles del Conde del Valle de Orizaba." Vol. 4a, Edmundo O'Gorman Collection. Nettie Lee Benson Latin American Collection, University of Texas at Austin.

Papers of the Carraza y Pardo Family. Miscellaneous documents, untitled bound volume, Document 53. Family Library, Nuestra Señora de la Concepción Plantation, Jalapa, Veracruz.

"Resumen general de las personas que habitan en la Calle Segunda de la Montrilla, y siguientes." Map Collection, Nettie Lee Benson Latin American Collection. University of Texas at Austin.

Wenceslao Barquera, Juan. Documentos relativos a 1774–1827. Genaro García Collection, Legajo 10. Nettie Lee Benson Latin American Collection, University of Texas at Austin.

Books and Articles

Acosta de Saignes, Miguel. *Vida de los esclavos negros en Venezuela.* Caracas: Ediciones Hesperides, 1967.

Aguirre Beltrán, Gonzalo. *Cuijla, esbozo etnográfico de un pueblo negro.* Mexico City: Fondo de Cultura Económica, 1958.

———. *Población negra de México.* Second edition. Mexico City: Fondo de Cultura Económica, 1972.

———. *Medicina y magia.* Mexico City: Instituto Indigenista, 1963.

———. "The Slave Trade in Mexico." *Hispanic American Historical Review* 24 (August 1944).

Alamán, Lucas. *Historia de Méjico.* 5 vols. Mexico City: Imprenta de J. M. Lara, 1849–1851.

Alberro, Solange. "Herejes, brujas y beatas: Mujeres ante el Tribunal del Santo Oficio de la Inquisición en la Nueva España." In *Presencia y transparencia: La mujer en la historia de México,* ed. Carmen Ramos Escandón, 79–94. Mexico City: El Colegio de México, 1987.

Anderson, Rodney. "Race and Social Stratification: A Comparison of Working-Class Spaniards, Indians, and Castas in Guadalajara, Mexico, in 1821." *Hispanic American Historical Review* 68, no. 2 (1988).

Anna, Timothy. *The Fall of the Royal Government in Mexico City.* Lincoln: University of Nebraska Press, 1978.

Bakewell, Peter. *Silver Mining and Society in Colonial Mexico: Zacatecas, 1546–1700.* Cambridge: Cambridge University Press, 1971.

Barrett, Ward. *The Sugar Hacienda of the Marqueses del Valle.* Minneapolis: University of Minnesota Press, 1970.

Bazant, Jan. *Cinco haciendas mexicanas: Tres siglos de vida rural en San Luis Potosí*. Mexico City: El Colegio de México, 1975.

Benson, Nettie Lee. "Texas as Viewed From Mexico, 1820–1834." *Southwestern Historical Quarterly*. Special Issue. 1987.

———, ed. *Mexico and the Spanish Cortes, 1810–1822*. Austin: University of Texas Press, 1966.

Bermúdez Gorrochotegui, Gilberto. *Historia de Xalapa, siglo XVII*. Xalapa, Veracruz: Universidad Veracruzana, 1995.

Berthe, Jean-Pierre. "Xochimancas: Les travaux et les jours dans une hacienda sucrière de Nouvelle-Espagne au XVIIe." *Jahrbach für Geschichte von Staat, Wirtshaft and Gesellschaft Latteinamerikas* 3 (1966).

Bocanegra, José María. *Memorias para la historia de México independiente, 1822–1846*. 2 vols. Mexico City: Imprenta del Gobierno Federal en el ex-Arzobispado, 1892.

Boletín de Geografía de Veracruz. Jalapa, Veracruz, 1831.

Borah, Woodrow. *El juzgado general de indios en la Nueva España*. Translation by Juan Utrilla. Mexico City: Fondo de Cultura Económica, 1985.

———. *New Spain's Century of Depression*. Ibero-Americana, no. 45. Berkeley: University of California Press, 1951.

Borah, Woodrow, and Sherburne Cook. *Aboriginal Population of Central Mexico on the Eve of the Spanish Conquest*. Berkeley: University of California Press, 1963.

Bowser, Frederick. *The African Slave in Colonial Peru*. Stanford: Stanford University Press, 1974.

———. "Colonial Spanish America." In *Neither Slave Nor Free*, ed. David Cohen and Jack P. Greene. Baltimore: Johns Hopkins University Press, 1972.

———. "The Free Person of Color in Mexico City and Lima: Manumission and Opportunity, 1580–1650." In *Race and Slavery in the Western Hemisphere*, ed. Stanley Engerman and Eugene Genovese. Princeton: Princeton University Press, 1975.

Boxer, Charles. *The Golden Age of Brazil*. Berkeley: University of California Press, 1964.

Brading, David. "Grupos étnicos: Clases y estructura ocupacional en Guanajuato." *Historia Mexicana* 21, no. 3 (January–March 1972).

———. *Haciendas and Ranchos in the Mexican Bajío, León, 1700–1860*. Cambridge: Cambridge University Press, 1978.

———. *Miners and Merchants in Bourbon Mexico, 1763–1810*. Cambridge: Cambridge University Press, 1971.

Brading, D. A., and Cecilia Wu. "Population Growth and Crisis: León, 1720–1860." *Journal of Latin American Studies* 5 (1973).

Bravo de Lagunas, Constantino. *Relación de Xalapa, 1580*. Mexico City: Editorial Citlaltepetl, 1969.

Bray, Warwick. *Everyday Life of the Aztecs*. New York: Putnam, 1968.

Bustamante, Carlos María. *Cuadro histórico de la revolución mexicana*. 5 vols. Mexico City: Instituto Cultural Helénico and Fondo de Cultura Económica, 1980.

Cardoso, Gerald. *Negro Slavery in the Sugar Plantations of Veracruz and Pernambuco, 1550–1680.* Washington, D.C.: University Press of America, 1983.

Carrasco, Pedro. "The Political Economy of the Aztec and Inca States." In *The Inca and Aztec States, 1400–1800,* ed. George Collier et al. New York: Academic Press, 1982.

Carrera Stampa, Manuel. "Las ferias Novohispañas." *Historia Mexicana* 2, (January–March 1953).

Carroll, Patrick J. "Los mexicanos negros, el mestizaje y los fundamentos olvidados de la 'Raza Cósmica': Una perspectiva regional." *Historia Mexicana* 44, no. 3 (January–March 1995): 403–438.

———. "Mandinga: The Evolution of a Mexican Runaway Slave Community, 1735–1827." *Comparative Studies in Society and History* 19, no. 4 (October 1977).

Castillo Palma, Norma Angélica. "Matrimonios mixtos y cruce de la barrera de color como vías del mestizaje de la población negra y mulata (1674–1796)." Paper presented at the X Reunion of North American Scholars of Mexico, Fort Worth (1999).

Castillo Palma, Norma Angélica, y Francisco González Hermosillo Adams. "Raza y status, mestizos, mulatos, criollos, españoles e indios y sus definiciones en testamentos coloniales." *Signos* 5, no. 2 (1991): 17–45.

Chambers, J. D. *Population, Economy, and Society in Pre-Industrial England.* London: Oxford University Press, 1972.

Chance, John. *Race and Class in Colonial Oaxaca.* Stanford: Stanford University Press, 1978.

Chance, John, and William Taylor. "Estate and Class in a Colonial City: Oaxaca in 1792." *Comparative Studies in Society and History* 19, no. 4 (October 1977).

Chaunu, Hugette and Pierre. *Seville et l'Atlantique, 1594–1650.* 8 vols. Paris: Institut des Hautes Etudes de l'Amérique Latine, 1955–1960.

Chávez Orozco, Luis, and Enrique Florescano. *Agricultura a industria textil en Veracruz.* Jalapa: Universidad Veracruzana, 1965.

Chevalier, François. *Land and Society in Colonial Mexico.* Translated by Alvin Eustis. Edited by Lesley Byrd Simpson. Berkeley: University of California Press, 1970.

Clavijero, Francisco Javier. *Historia antigua de México.* 3d ed. Mexico City: Editorial Porrua, 1971.

Coatsworth, John. "The Limits of Colonial Absolutism: The State in Eighteenth Century Mexico." In *Essays in the Political, Economic, and Social History of Latin America,* ed. Karen Spaulding. Wilmington: University of Delaware Press, 1983.

Coe, Michael. *Mexico.* 2d ed. New York: Praeger, 1977.

Colecciones de documentos inéditos relativo al descubrimiento, conquista, y organización. de las antiguas posesiones españolas de ultramar. 2d series, vol. 10, no. 111. Madrid: Est. Tip. Sucesores de Rivadeneyra, 1897.

Contreras Arias, Alfonso. *Mapa de las provincias climatológicas de la Re-*

pública Mexicana. Mexico City: Secretaría de Agricultura y Fomento, 1942.

Cook, Sherburne. "The Incidence of Disease among the Aztecs and Related Tribes." *Hispanic American Historical Review* 26 (August 1946).

Cook, Sherburne F., and Woodrow Borah. *Essays in Population History: Mexico and the Caribbean.* 3 vols. Berkeley: University of California Press, 1971, 1974, 1979.

Cooper, Donald. *Epidemic Disease in Mexico City, 1761–1813.* Austin: University of Texas Press, 1965.

Cope, R. Douglas. *The Limits of Racial Domination: Plebeian Society in Colonial Mexico City, 1660–1720.* Madison: University of Wisconsin Press, 1994.

Corro, Octaviano R. *Los cimarrones en Veracruz y la fundación de Amapa.* Jalapa: Imprenta Comercial, Veracruz, 1951.

Cortés de Jacome, María Elena. "La memoria familiar de los negros y mulatos, siglos XVI–XVII." In *La memoria y el olvido.* Segundo Simposio de Historia de las Mentalidades, 125–133. Mexico City: INAH, 1985.

Cortez, Hernando. *Five Letters, 1519–1526.* Translated by F. Bayard Morris. New York: W. W. Norton, 1962.

Costeloe, Michael. *Primera república federal de México, 1824–1835.* Translated by Manuel Fernandes Gasalla. Mexico City: Fondo de Cultura Económica, 1975.

Crosby, Alfred. *Columbian Exchange.* Westport, Conn.: Greenwood Publishing, 1972.

Cunniff, Roger. "Mexican Municipal Electoral Reform, 1810–1822." In *Mexico and the Spanish Cortes, 1810–1822,* ed. Nettie Lee Benson. Austin: University of Texas Press, 1966.

Curtin, Philip. *The Atlantic Slave Trade.* Madison: University of Wisconsin Press, 1969.

———. "Epidemiology and the Slave Trade." *Political Science Quarterly* 33 (June 1968).

Davidson, David. "Negro Slave Control and Resistance in Colonial Mexico, 1519–1650." *Hispanic American Historical Review* 46, no. 3 (August 1966).

Davies, Nigel. *The Toltecs.* Norman: University of Oklahoma Press, 1977.

Davis, David Brion. *Slavery and Human Progress.* New York: Oxford University Press, 1984.

Deans-Smith, Susan. *Bureaucrats, Planters, and Workers: The Making of the Tobacco Monopoly in Bourbon Mexico.* Austin: University of Texas Press, 1992.

de la Serna H., Juan Manuel. "Disolución de la esclavitud en los obrajes de Querétaro a finales del siglo dieciocho." Paper presented at the X Reunion of North American Scholars of Mexico, Fort Worth (1999).

Díaz del Castillo, Bernal. *The True History of the Conquest of Mexico.* Translated by Maurice Keating. New York: Robert M. McBride, 1927.

Dinnerstein, Leonard, et al. *Natives and Strangers.* New York: Oxford University Press, 1979.

Documentos inéditos relativos a Hernán Cortés y su familia. Mexico City: Talleres Gráficos de la Nación, 1983.

Dusser de Barenne Kilson, Marion. "West African Society and the Atlantic Slave Trade, 1441–1865." In *Key Issues in the Afro-American Experience,* ed. Nathan Huggins et al. 2 vols. New York: Harcourt Brace Jovanovich, 1971.

Ely, Relan. *La economía cubana entre los Isabeles, 1492–1832.* 3d ed. Bogota: Aedita Editores, 1962.

Espejo-Ponce Hunt, Marta. "The Processes of the Development of Yucatán, 1600–1700." In *Provinces of Mexico,* ed. Ida Altman and James Lockhart. Los Angeles: UCLA Press, 1976.

Fagg, John. *Cuba, Haiti, and the Dominican Republic.* Englewood Cliffs, N.J.: Prentice-Hall, 1965.

Fariss, Nancy. *Maya Society under Colonial Rule.* Princeton: Princeton University Press, 1984.

Fernández Repetto, Francisco, and Genny Negroe Sierra. *Una población perdida en la memoria: Los negros de Yucatán.* Mérida: Universidad Autónoma de Yucatán, 1995.

Florescano, Enrique. *Estructuras y problemas agrarias de México.* Mexico City: Secretaría de Educación Pública, 1971.

Frank, André Gunder. *Capitalism and Underdevelopment in Latin America: Historical Studies of Brazil and Chile.* New York: Monthly Review Press, 1969.

Fusfield, Daniel. *The Age of the Economist.* 4th ed. Glenview, Ill.: Scott Foresman and Co., 1982.

Fyfe, Christopher. "The Dynamics of African Dispersal: The Transatlantic Slave Trade." In *The African Diaspora,* ed. Martin Kilson and Robert Rotberg. Cambridge, Mass.: Harvard University Press, 1976.

García Martínez, Bernardo. *El Marquesado del Valle.* Mexico City: El Colegio de México, 1969.

———. *Los pueblos de la sierra.* Mexico City: El Colegio de México, 1987.

———, ed. Historia general de México. 2 vols. Mexico City: El Colegio de México, 1976.

Gerhard, Peter. *A Guide to the Historical Geography of New Spain.* Cambridge: Cambridge University Press, 1972.

Gibson, Charles. *The Aztecs under Spanish Rule.* Stanford: Stanford University Press, 1964.

Gomezcesar, Ivan. "El partido del progresso." In *El pensamiento político de México,* ed. Alonso Aguilar M. et al. 2 vols. Mexico City: Editorial Nuestro, 1986–1987.

Góngora, Mario. *Studies in the Colonial History of Spanish America.* Translated by Richard Southern. Cambridge: Cambridge University Press, 1975.

González de Cossio, Francisco. *Xalapa.* Mexico City: Talleres Gráficos de la Nación, 1957

Gutiérrez, Ludivina. *Monumentos coloniales de Xalapa,* Mexico City: Editorial Citlaltepetl, 1970.

Hale, Charles. *Mexican Liberalism in the Age of Mora, 1821–1853*. New Haven: Yale University Press, 1968.

Hamill, Hugh. *The Hidalgo Revolt*. Gainesville: University of Florida Press, 1966.

Hamilton, E. J. *American Treasure and the Price of Revolution in Spain, 1501–1650*. Cambridge, Mass.: Harvard University Press, 1934.

Hamnett, Brian. *Politics and Trade in Southern Mexico, 1750–1821*. Cambridge: Cambridge University Press, 1971.

———. *Política y comercio en el sur de México, 1750–1821*. Mexico City: Instituto Mexicano de Comercio Exterior, 1976.

———. *Roots of Insurgency: Mexican Regions, 1750–1824*. New York: Cambridge University Press, 1986.

Haring, C. H. *The Spanish Empire in America*. New York: Oxford University Press, 1963.

Harris, Charles H. *A Mexican Family Empire: The Latifundio of the Sánchez Navarros*. Austin: University of Texas Press, 1975.

Harris, Marvin. *Patterns of Race in the Americas*. New York: Walker and Co., 1967.

Heilbroner, Robert, and Aaron Singer. *The Economic Transformation of America*. 2d ed. New York: Harcourt Brace Jovanovich, 1984.

Helfritz, Hans. *Mexican Cities of the Gods*. New York: Praeger, 1968.

Helps, Arthur. *The Spanish Conquest in America*. 4 vols. London: J. W. Parker and Son, 1855–1861.

Herrera Casasús, María Luisa. *Presencia y esclavitud del negro en la Huasteca*. Mexico City: Miguel Angel Porrúa, 1989.

Humboldt, Alejandro de. *Ensayo político sobre el reino de la Nueva España*. Edited by Juan A. Ortega y Medina. Mexico City: Editorial Porrua, 1966. [*See also* von Humboldt, Alexander]

Isassi, José Domingo de. *Memorias de to acontedido en Córdoba en tiempo de la revolución, para la historia de la independencia megicana, 1827*. Mexico City: Editorial Citlaltepetl, 1960.

Israel, Jonathan. *Race, Class, and Politics in Colonial Mexico, 1610–1670*. London: Oxford University Press, 1975.

Jornal económico y mercantil de Veracruz 1 (10 April 1806).

Kagen, Samuel. "The Labor of Prisoners in the Obrajes of Coyoacán, 1660–1673." In *El trabajo y los trabajadores en la historia de México*, ed. Elsa Frost et al. Mexico City: El Colegio de México, 1979.

Katz, Friedrich. "Labor Conditions on Haciendas in Porfirian Mexico: Some Trends and Tendencies." *Hispanic American Historical Review* 54 (February 1974).

Kellog, Susan. "African Women in Central Mexico, 1648–1707: Their Testaments and Their Lives." Paper delivered at the X Reunion of North American Historians of Mexico, Fort Worth (1999).

———. "Gendered Images of Ethno-Race in Colonial Mexican Texts." *Journal of Women's History* (in press).

Kicza, John. *Colonial Entrepreneurs: Families and Business in Bourbon Mexico City*. Albuquerque: University of New Mexico Press, 1983.

Kilson, Martin. "Political Change in the Negro Ghetto, 1900–1940s." In *Key Issues in the Afro-American Experience*, ed. Nathan Huggins et al. 2 vols. New York: Harcourt Brace Jovanovich, 1971.

Klein, Herbert. *African Slavery in Latin America and the Caribbean*. New York: Oxford University Press, 1986.

———. *Slavery in the Americas*. Chicago: Quadrangle Books, 1967.

Knight, Franklin. *Slave Society in Cuba During the Nineteenth Century*. Madison: University of Wisconsin Press, 1970.

Konetzke, Richard. *América Latina: La época colonial*. Mexico City: Siglo Veintiuno, 1971.

Konrad, Herman. *A Jesuit Hacienda in Colonial Mexico: Santa Lucia, 1576–1767*. Stanford: Stanford University Press, 1980.

Kubler, George. *The Art and Architecture of Ancient America*. 2d ed. Baltimore: Penguin, 1975.

Lang, James. *Conquest and Commerce*. New York: Academic Press, 1975.

Lerdo de Tejada, Miguel. *Apuntes históricos de la ciudad de Vera-Cruz*. 3 vols. Mexico City: Imprenta de Vicente García Torres, 1958.

Liss, Peggy. *Mexico under Spain*. Chicago: University of Chicago Press, 1975.

Lobato, José. *Consideraciones generales sobre la geografía, meteorología, y climatología de la zona intertropical de la República Mexicana*. Mexico City: Imprenta de J. M. A. Ortiz, 1874.

Lockhart, James. "The Social History of Colonial Spanish America: Evolution and Potential." *Latin American Research Review* 7, no. 1 (Spring 1972).

———. *Spanish Peru*. Madison: University of Wisconsin Press, 1968.

López de Gómera, Francisco. *Cortez, The Life of the Conqueror*. Translated and edited by Lesley Byrd Simpson. Berkeley: University of California Press, 1966.

Lynch, John. *Spain under the Hapsburgs*. 2 vols. New York: Oxford University Press, 1964.

———. *The Spanish-American Revolutions, 1808–1826*. New York: Norton and Co., 1973.

Lyon, G. G. *Journal of a Residence and Tour in the Republic of Mexico in the Year 1826*. 2 vols. Port Washington, N.Y.: Kennikat Press, 1971.

McAlister, Lyle. "Social Structure and Social Change in New Spain." *Hispanic American Historical Review* 43, no. 3 (1963).

McCaa, Robert, et al. "Race and Class in Colonial Latin America: A Critique." *Comparative Studies in Society and History* 21, no. 3 (1979).

MacLachlan, Colin, and Jaime Rodríguez. *The Forging of the Cosmic Race*. Berkeley: University of California Press, 1980.

Mannix, Daniel. *Black Cargoes*. New York: Viking Press, 1962.

Martin, Cheryl. *Rural Society in Colonial Morelos*. Albuquerque: University of New Mexico Press, 1985.

Martínez Montiel, Luz María. "Integration Patterns and the Assimilation Process of Negro Slaves in Mexico." In *Comparative Perspectives on Slavery in New World Plantation Societies*, ed. Vera Rubin and Arthur Tuden. New York: New York Academy of Sciences, 1977.

Medina Rubio, Aristides. *La iglesia y la producción agrícola en Puebla, 1540–1795.* Mexico City: Centro de Estudios Históricos, Colegio de México, 1983.

Melgarejo Vivanco, José. "Carta etnográfica de Veracruz." In *La población de Veracruz,* ed. Felipe Montemayor. Jalapa: Talleres del Gobierno de Veracruz, 1950–1956.

———. "Historia Antigua de Coatepec." In *Coatepec,* comp. Leonardo Pasquel. Mexico City: Editorial Citlaltepetl, 1960.

Mellafe, Rolando. *La introducción de la esclavitud negra en Chile.* Santiago: Universidad de Chile, 1959.

Miller, Joseph. "The Slave Trade in the Congo and Angola." In *The African Diaspora,* ed. Martin Kilson and Robert Rotberg. Cambridge, Mass.: Harvard University Press, 1976.

———. *Way of Death: Merchant Capitalism and the Angolan Slave Trade, 1730–1830.* Madison: University of Wisconsin Press, 1988.

Montemayor, Felipe. *La población de Veracruz.* Jalapa: Gobierno de Veracruz, 1956.

[Mora, José María Luis]. "Examen crítico de la administración establicida en consequencia del Plan de Jalapa." *El Indicador,* no. 2 (16 October 1833).

Mörner, Magnus. "Economic Factors and Stratification in Colonial Spanish America with Special Regard to Elites." *Hispanic American Historical Review* 63, no. 2 (1983).

———. "Historical Research on Race Relations in Latin America during the National Period." In *Race and Class in Latin America,* ed. Magnus Mörner. New York: Columbia University Press, 1970.

———. *Race Mixture in the History of Latin America.* Boston: Little, Brown, 1967.

Motolinía, Toribio de. *Memoriales.* Mexico City: Universidad Nacional Autónoma de México, 1971.

Navarro y Noriega, Fernando. *Memoria sobre la población de Nueva España.* Mexico City: En la Oficina de Juan Batista de Arispe, 1820.

Naveda Chávez-Hita, Adriana. *Esclavos negros en las haciendas azucareras de Córdoba, Veracruz, 1690–1830.* Jalapa: Universidad Veracruzana, 1987.

———. "Trabajadores esclavos en las haciendas azucareras de Córdoba, Veracruz, 1714–1763." In *El Trabajo y los trabajadores en la historia de México,* comp. Elsa Frost et al. Mexico City: El Colegio de México, 1979.

Negroe Sierra, Genny. "Procedencia y situación social de la población negra de Yucatán." *Boletín de la Escuela de Ciencias Antropología de la Universidad de Yucatán,* nos. 106–107 (1991): 3–20.

Nelli, Humbert. *Italians in Chicago.* New York: Oxford University Press, 1970.

Nieto, Vicente. *Padrón de Xalapa.* Mexico City: Editorial Citlaltepetl, 1971.

Noll, Arthur. From *Empire to Republic.* Chicago: A. C. McClurg and Co., 1903.

Northrup, David. *Trade without Rulers.* Oxford: Clarendon Press, 1978.

O'Crouley, Pedro Alonso. *A Description of the Kingdom of New Spain.* Translated and edited by Sean Galbin. San Francisco: J. Howell, 1972.

Olson, James S. *The Ethnic Dimension in U.S. History.* New York: St. Martin's Press, 1979.

Ortíz de Ayala, Simón Tadeo. *Resumen de la estadística del Imperio Mexicano, 1822.* Edited by Tarcisio Garcia Diaz. Mexico City: Biblioteca Nacional de México, 1918.

Padden, R. C. *The Hummingbird and the Hawk.* Columbus: Ohio State University Press, 1967.

Palerm, Angel. *Agricultura y sociedad en Meso-America.* Mexico City: Secretaría de Educación Pública, 1972.

Palmer, Colin. *Slaves of the White God: Blacks in Mexico, 1570–1650.* Cambridge, Mass.: Harvard University Press, 1976.

Paso y Troncoso, Francisco del, ed. *Papeles de Nueva España.* 9 vols. Madrid: Sucs. de Rivadeneyra, 1905–1948.

Pasquel, Leonardo. *Biografía integral de la Ciudad de Veracruz.* Mexico City: Editorial Citlaltepetl, 1969.

Peterson, Frederick. *Ancient Mexico.* New York: Capricorn Books, 1959.

Pi-Sunyer, Oriol. "Historical Background to the Negro in Mexico." *The Journal of Negro History:* 42 (October 1957)

Pike, Ruth. "Sevillian Society in the Sixteenth Century: Slaves and Freedmen." *Hispanic American Historical Review* 53, no. 3 (August 1967).

Pitt-Rivers, Julian. "Race in Latin America: The Concept of *Raza.*" In *Race, Ethnicity, and Social Change,* ed. John Stone. North Scituate, Mass.: Duxbury Press, 1977.

Portes, Alejandro, and Robert Bach. *Latin Tourney.* Berkeley: University of California Press, 1985.

Ramos Escandón, Carmen, ed. *Presencia y transparencia: La mujer en la historia de México.* Mexico City: Colegio de México, 1987.

Redondo, Brígedo. *Negritud en Campeche.* Campeche: Ediciones de Congreso del Estado, 1994.

La República Mexicana, Veracruz. Mexico City, 1914.

Restall, Matthew. "Alterity and Ambiguity: Spanish and Maya Perceptions of Africans in Colonial Yucatán." Paper delivered at the X Reunion of North American Scholars of Mexico, Fort Worth (1999).

———. *Maya Conquistador.* Boston: Beacon Press, 1998.

Ricard, Robert. *The Spiritual Conquest of Mexico.* Translated by Lesley Byrd Simpson. Berkeley: University of California Press, 1966.

Rivera, Manuel. *Historia antigua y moderna de Jalapa.* 5 vols. Mexico City: Imprenta de I. Cumplido, 1869.

Romano, Ruggiero. "American Feudalism." *Hispanic American Historical Review* 64, no. 1 (February 1984).

Roncal, Joaquín. "The Negro Race in Mexico." *Hispanic American Historical Review* 24 (August 1944).

Rosenblat, Angel. *Población indígena de América.* Buenos Aires: Institución Cultural Española, 1945.

Rout, Lesley B. *The African Experience in Spanish America.* London: Cambridge University Press, 1976.

Ruíz Mendez, Manuel. "La emancipación de los esclavos en Yucatán." *Revista de la Universidad de Yucatán* 12 (January–February 1970).

Russell-Wood, A. J. R. *Fidalgos and Philanthropists*. Berkeley: University of California Press, 1968.

Saco, José Antonio. *Historia de la raza africana en el Nuevo Mundo y en especial en los países Americo-Hispanos*. 4 vols. Havana: Colección Libros Cubanos, 1938.

Salvucci, Richard. *Textiles and Capitalism in Mexico*. Princeton: Princeton University Press, 1987.

Sánchez-Albornoz, Nicolás. *Population of Latin America: A History*. Translated by W. A. R. Richardson. Berkeley: University of California Press, 1974.

Sandoval, Fernando. *La industria del azúcar en Nueva España*. Mexico City: Instituto de Historia, 1951.

Saunders, William T. "The Anthropogeography of Central Veracruz." In *Huastecos, Totonocos y sus vecinos*, ed. Ignacio Bernal and Eusebio Davalos Hurtado. Mexico City: Sociedad Mexicana de Antropología, 1953.

Schwartz, Stuart. *Sugar Plantations in the Formation of Brazilian Society*. London: Cambridge University Press, 1985.

Secretaría de Economía. *Compendia estadístico del estado de Veracruz*. Mexico City: Talleres Gráficos de la Nación, 1950.

Seed, Patricia, and Philip Rust. "Estate and Class in Colonial Oaxaca Revisited." *Comparative Studies in Society and History* 25, no. 4 (October 1983).

Serna, Juan Manuel de la. "Disolución de la esclavitud en los obrajes de Querétaro a finales del siglo dieciocho." Paper presented at the X Reunion of North American Scholars of Mexico. Fort Worth, 1999.

Silva Herzog, Jesús, comp. *Relaciones estadísticas de Nueva España de principios del siglo XIX*. In *Archivo histórico de Hacienda*, vol. 3. Mexico City: Secretaría de Hacienda y Crédito Público, 1944

Simpson, Lesley Byrd. *Many Mexicos*. 4th ed. Berkeley: University of California Press, 1967.

Skidmore, Thomas, and Peter Smith. *Modern Latin America*. New York: Oxford University Press, 1983.

Soustelle, Jacques. *The Daily Life of the Aztecs*. Translated by Patrick O'Brian. New York: MacMillan Press, 1962.

Spores, Ronald. *Mixtec Kings and Their People*. Norman: University of Oklahoma Press, 1967.

Sprague, William F. *Vicente Guerrero, Mexican Liberator*. Chicago: R. R. Donnelley and Sons, 1939.

Stein, Stanley, and Barbara. *The Colonial Heritage of Latin America*. New York: W. W Norton, 1970.

Stern, Steve. "Feudalism, Capitalism, and the World System in the Perspective of Latin America and the Caribbean." *American Historical Review* 93, no. 4 (October 1988).

———. *The Secret History of Mexico: Women, Men, and Power in Late Colonial Mexico*. Chapel Hill: University of North Carolina Press, 1985.

Super, John. "The Agricultural Near North: Querétaro in the Seventeenth Century." In *Provinces of Early Mexico*, ed. Ida Altman and James Lockhart. Los Angeles: UCLA Press, 1976.

Szewczyk, David. "New Elements in the Society of Tlaxcala, 1519–1618." In *Provinces of Early Mexico*, ed. Ida Altman and James Lockhart. Los Angeles: UCLA Press, 1976.

Taylor, William. *Drinking, Homicide, and Rebellion in Colonial Mexican Villages*. Stanford: Stanford University Press, 1979.

———. "The Foundation of Nuestra Señora de Guadalupe de Amapa." *The Americas* 26, no. 4 (April 1970).

———. *Landlord and Peasant in Colonial Oaxaca*. Stanford: Stanford University Press, 1972.

Te Paske, John, et al. *La real hacienda de Nueva España: La Real Caja de México, 1576–1816*. Mexico City: Instituto Nacional de Antropología e Historia, 1976.

Trens, Manuel B. *Historia de Veracruz*. 2 vols. Jalapa: Gráficos del Gobierno de Veracruz, 1947.

Tutino, John. *From Insurrection to Revolution in Mexico*. Princeton: Princeton University Press, 1986.

———. "Hacienda and Social Relations in Mexico: The Chalco Region in the Era of Independence." *Hispanic American Historical Review* 55, no. 3 (1975).

———. "Life and Labor on the North Mexican Haciendas: The Querétaro–San Luis Potosí Region: 1775–1810." In *El trabajo y los trabajadores en la historia de México*, comp. Elsa Frost et al. Mexico City: El Colegio de México, 1979.

Van Young, Eric. *Hacienda and Market in Eighteenth-Century Mexico: The Rural Economy of the Guadalajara Region, 1675–1820*. Berkeley: University of California Press, 1981.

Vigneaux, Ernesto de. *Viaje a México*. Guadalajara: Banco Industrial de Jalisco, 1950.

Villa-Señor y Sánchez, Joseph Antonio. *Theatro americano*. 2 vols. Mexico City: Imprenta de la Viuda de Don Joseph Bernardo de Hogel, 1746, 1748.

Viqueira Albán, Juan Pedro. *Propriety and Permissiveness in Bourbon Mexico*. Translated by Sonya Lipsett-Rivera and Sergio Rivera Ayala. Wilmington: SR Books, 1999.

Volmer, Günther. "La evolución cuantitativa de la población indígena en la región de Puebla (1570–1810)." *Historia Mexicana* 23 (July–September 1973).

von Humboldt, Alexander. *Political Essay on the Kingdom of New Spain*. Translated by John Black. 4 vols. New York: I. Riley, 1811. [*See also* Humboldt, Alejandro de]

von Mentz, Brígida. *Trabajo, sujeción y libertad en el centro de la Nueva España: Esclavos, aprendices, campesinos y operarios manufactureros, siglos XVI–XVIII*. Mexico City: CIESAS, 1999.

Wallerstein, Immanuel. *The Modern World System: Capitalist Agriculture and the Origins of the European World Economy in the Sixteenth Century*. 2 vols. New York: Academic Press, 1974, 1980.

Ward, Henry. *Mexico*. 2 vols. London: H. G. Ward, 1829.

West, Robert. *Colonial Placer Mining in Columbia*. Baton Rouge: Louisiana State University Press, 1952.

Wiedner, Donald L. *A History of Africa South of the Sahara.* New York: Random House, 1962.
Winfield Capitaine, Fernando. *Los Cimarrones de Mazateopan.* Xalapa, Veracruz: Gobierno del Estado de Veracruz, 1992.
———, comp. *Esclavos en el Archivo Notorial de Xalapa, 1668–1699.* Jalapa: Universidad Veracruzana, 1984.
Wolf, Eric. *Sons of the Shaking Earth.* Chicago: University of Chicago Press, 1959.
Wrigley, E. A. *Population and History.* New York: McGraw-Hill, 1969.
Zorita, Alonzo de. *The Lords of New Spain.* Translated by Benjamin Keen. London: Phoenix House, 1963.

Dissertations and Theses

Bennett, Herman. "Lovers, Family and Friends: The Formation of Afro-Mexico, 1580–1810." Ph.D. dissertation, Duke University, 1997. Ann Arbor: U.M.I.
Bermúdez Gorrochotegui, Gilberto. "Jalapa en el siglo XVI." 2 vols. Master's thesis, Universidad Veracruzana, Jalapa, Veracruz, 1977.
Brady, R. L. "The Emergence of a Negro Class in Mexico, 1524–1640." Ph.D. dissertation, State University of Iowa, 1965.
Carroll, Patrick. "Mexican Society in Transition: The Blacks in Veracruz, 1750–1830." Ph.D. dissertation, University of Texas at Austin, 1975.
Garner, Richard. "Zacatecas, 1750–1821." Ph.D. dissertation, University of Michigan, 1970.
Harrell, Eugene. "Vicente Guerrero and the Birth of Modern Mexico." Ph.D. dissertation, Tulane University, 1976.
Macune, Charles. "A Test of Federalism: Political, Economic, and Ecclesiastical Relations between the State of Mexico and the Mexican Nation, 1823–1835." Ph.D. dissertation, University of Texas at Austin, 1970.
Mayer, Vincent. "The Black Slave on New Spain's Northern Frontier: San José de Parral, 1632–1676." Ph.D. dissertation, University of Utah, 1975.
Naveda Chávez-Hita, Adriana. "Esclavitud en Córdoba: Composición y distribución racial, 1788." Manuscript submitted to the Gonzalo Aguirre Beltrán competition for studies on Afro-Mexicans. August 1987.
———. "Esclavitud en la jurisdicción de la villa de Córdoba en el siglo XVIII." Master's thesis, Universidad Veracruzana, 1977.
———. "Hacendados, tabaqueros y libertos en el desarrollo de la Villa de Córdoba, 1750–1810." Doctoral thesis, Universidad Veracruzana (in progress).
Vinson, Ben, III. "Bearing Arms for His Majesty: The Free Colored Militia in Colonial Mexico." Ph.D. dissertation, Columbia University, 1998.

Index

CPSIA information can be obtained at www.ICGtesting.com
Printed in the USA
LVOW06s0625210714

395162LV00001B/65/P